CfE NATIONAL 5

ENGLISH
COURSE BOOK

Dr Christopher Nichol
Contributing editor Andrew Leask

First published in 2018 by:
Bright Red Publishing Ltd
1 Torphichen Street
Edinburgh
EH3 8HX

A CIP record for this book is available from the British Library

ISBN 978-1-849483-05-6

With thanks to: PDQ Digital Media Solutions Ltd (layout), Jill Broom (editorial)

Cover design and series book design by Caleb Rutherford – e i d e t i c

Acknowledgements

Permission has been sought from all relevant copyright holders and Bright Red Publishing are grateful for the use of the following:

Extract from Rosemary Goring, 'Why I rarely remember the ending of books', from *The Herald*, 27 February 2016. Reproduced by permission of Newsquest Media Group Ltd. (p 12); Extract from Johan Hari, 'The Dark Side of Dubai', from *The Independent*, 6th April 2009. Reproduced by permission of Independent Digital News & Media Ltd (p 13); Extract from Beppe Severgnini, *La Bella Figura: An Insider's Guide to the Italian Mind* © 2006 Beppe Severgnini. Reproduced by permission of Hodder and Stoughton Limited (p 14); Extract from Paddy Woodworth, 'Paradise Found', from *The Irish Times*, 1 September 2012. Reproduced by permission of Paddy Woodworth (p 22); Extract from Elizabeth Gilbert, *Eat, Pray, Love* (Bloomsbury, 2006) (p 24); Image © Yo Pizza (CC BY 2.0)[1] (p 29); Extract from Jonathan Thompson, 'A Cookery Class at Alain Ducasse's House in Provence', *The Guardian*, 17th May 2013. Copyright Guardian News & Media Ltd 2018 (p 34 & 36); Extract from Jonathan Thompson, 'Cycling Scotland's new Hebridean Trail', from *The Guardian*, 31st August 2012. Copyright Guardian News & Media Ltd 2018 (p 36); Extract from Chloe Veltman 'The Passion of the Morrissey', from *The Believer*, July–August 2012 Music Issue. Reproduced by permission of Chloe Veltman (p 36); Image © David Ball – www.davidball.net (CC BY-SA 3.0)[2] (p 43); Extract from D.K. Broster, *The Flight of the Heron* (Heinemann, 1947) (p 44); Extract from Giles Coren 'Shouldn't we tax fatties?' in the *Daily Mail* 27 May 2006. Reproduced by permission of Associated Newspapers Ltd (p 45–46); Extract from Nish Kumar, 'Schoolmates used to ask me about Indian trains. I can now confirm British ones are worse', in *The Guardian* 14 August 2016. Copyright Guardian News & Media Ltd 2018 (p 47–8); Extract from W. H. Auden, *Another Time* published by Random House. Copyright © 1940 W. H. Auden, renewed by the Estate of W. H. Auden. (p 57); Extract from James Reeves, *The Wandering Moon* (Heinemann, 1950) (p 60); Extract from Gwendolyn Brookes 'Cynthia in the Snow', from *Bronzeville Boys and Girls* (HarperCollins, 1956) (p 60); Extract from W. H. Auden, *Another Time* published by Random House. Copyright © 1940 W. H. Auden, renewed by the Estate of W. H. Auden. (p 60); Extract from Robert Frost, 'Birches' from *The Poetry of Robert Frost* (Henry Holt, 1969) (p 60); Extract from Scottish Review of Books, 'The SRB Interview: Rona Munro', 11 November 2014. Reproduced by permission of Scottish Review of Books (p 62–3); Image © Albert Bridge (CC BY-SA 2.0)[3] (p 63); Image © Waiting for the Word (CC BY 2.0)[1] (p 63); Extract from Rona Munro, *Bold Girls* copyright © 1991 Rona Munro. Excerpted with permission of Nick Hern Books Ltd: www.nickhernbooks.co.uk (p 64–74); Extract from Douglas Gifford, 'Making Them Bold and Breaking the Mould'. Copyright © Douglas Gifford 1996 (p 66); A still from a video production of 'All the Glisters'. Reproduced by permission of Claire Lamond (www.clairelamond.com) (p 77); Extract from Anne Donovan, 'All that Glisters' from *Hieroglyphics And Other Stories* (Canongate, 2004). Copyright © Anne Donovan 2001 (p 77, 78 & 83); Extract from Anne Donovan, 'Away in a Manger' from *Hieroglyphics And Other Stories* (Canongate, 2004). Copyright © Anne Donovan 2001 (p 81, 83 & 85); Extract from Anne Donovan, 'Hieroglyphics' from *Hieroglyphics And Other Stories* (Canongate, 2004). Copyright © Anne Donovan 2001 (p 82, 83 & 84); Extract from Anne Donovan, 'Dear Santa' from *Hieroglyphics And Other Stories* (Canongate, 2004). Copyright © Anne Donovan 2001. (p 83); Extract from 'Edwin Morgan, 'Siesta of a Hungarian Snake' from *Collected Poems* (Carcanet Press, 1990). Copyright © 1990 Edwin Morgan (p 87); Extract from Edwin Morgan, 'Good Friday' from *Collected Poems* (Carcanet Press, 1990). Copyright © 1990 Edwin Morgan (p 89 & 98); Extract from Edwin Morgan, 'In the Snack-bar' from *Collected Poems* (Carcanet Press, 1990). Copyright © 1990 Edwin Morgan (p 89, 90 & 98); Extract from Edwin Morgan, 'Trio' from *Collected Poems* (Carcanet Press, 1990). Copyright © 1990 Edwin Morgan (p 91, 92 & 98); Extract from Edwin Morgan, 'Winter' from *Collected Poems* (Carcanet Press, 1990). Copyright © 1990 Edwin Morgan (p 92, 93, 98 & 99); Edwin Morgan, 'Glasgow Sonnet No 1' from *Collected Poems* (Carcanet Press, 1990). Copyright © 1990 Edwin Morgan (p 94, 95, 98 & 100); Extract from Edwin Morgan, 'Glasgow 5 March 1971' from *Collected Poems* (Carcanet Press, 1990). Copyright © 1990 Edwin Morgan (p 96, 97 & 98); Image © Chicago: National Prtg. & Engr. Co. (CC BY-SA 3.0)[2] (p 102); Image © Ibusca/iStock.com (p 109); Extract from Anne Donovan, *Buddha Da* (Canongate, 2003). Copyright © Anne Donovan 2002. (p 161); Extract from Alastair Reid 'Scotland' from *Inside Out – Selected Poetry and Translations* (Polygon, 2008). Reproduced with permission of Birlinn Ltd through PLSclear (p 161); Extract from Angela McSeveney 'Changing a Downie Cover' from *Coming Out With It* (Polygon, 2001). Reproduced with permission of Birlinn Ltd through PLSclear (p 162); Extract from John Steinbeck, *Of Mice and Men* (Covici Friede, 1937). Copyright © 1937 and renewed 1965 by John Steinbeck (p 175); Image licensed by ingram image (p 177); Extract from Michael Chabon, *Wonder Boys* (Harper Perennial, 2006) Copyright © Michael Chabon 1995 (p 178); Extract from Iain Crichton Smith, 'Napoleon and I' from *Selected Stories* (Carcanet 1990). Copyright © 1990 The Estate of Iain Crichton Smith (p 180); Extract from Ina Caro Norton, *Paris to the Past* (WW Norton & Co, 2011) (p 184); Extract from Leslie Thomas, *This Time Next Week* (Constable, 1991) (p 186); Extract from Haig Gordon, *Tales of the Kirkcudbright Artists* (Galloway Publishing, 2006) (p 200); Image © Caleb Rutherford eidetic (p 224); Image © Pressmaster/Shutterstock.com (p 230); Image © Sergii Figurnyi/Shutterstock.com (p 230); Image © Robert Kneschke/Shutterstock.com (p 230); Image © AlexandreNunes/Shutterstock.com (p 230); Extract from Elena Orde, 'Vegan diets for children aren't abusive – raising a child to eat meat is actually more extreme' from *The Independent* 26 July 2016. Reproduced by permission of Independent Digital News & Media Ltd (p 217–218).

Printed and bound by Replika Press Pvt. Ltd.

CONTENTS

YOUR PASSPORT TO NATIONAL 5 SUCCESS - WELCOME ABOARD!

The fact that you're reading this in class or at home suggests you are serious about achieving the highest grade possible in National 5 English. Be assured, we're on your wavelength entirely.

This coursebook has been carefully structured to cover all aspects of the knowledge and practice you'll need come exam time. In very straightforward language, we'll talk you through the complete course – from taking your first tentative steps in National 5 work, to tackling exam-type practice tests with real confidence.

PRACTICE TESTS

Our carefully prepared tests for 'Reading for Understanding, Analysis and Evaluation', and for 'Critical Reading' of Scottish texts, mirror the format and wording of the actual exams. But, long before we get to tests, you'll be given step-by-step advice on how to tackle individual question types.

CLASSROOM CHALLENGES

Almost every page has at least one 'Classroom challenge' which, in very practical terms, invites you to check how sure you are about the section's information before you move on.

HOMEWORK HELPERS

And, just to make sure your knowledge is fully secure, you'll find further exercises you can do at home to ensure your new information is as firmly embedded as you think it is.

The practice you'll get in 'Classroom challenges' and 'Homework helpers' is specially shaped to sharpen your familiarity with the wording and approaches you can expect in exam questions. And, even more importantly, with how to best answer them!

HOW DOES THAT WORK?

These are sections you will find invaluable. They take you through worked examples to ensure you reach full understanding of the new information and knowledge necessary for exam success.

CREATING AND REFINING YOUR PORTFOLIO

Advancing further in the course, we need to examine the conventions of the various genres in which you'll be asked to write. What are sensible guidelines for each genre? How do you go about applying them to your own ideas? How can you avoid common pitfalls?

We'll be offering tips and strategies throughout to help you with all aspects of the writing process. Here, you'll also find 'Classroom challenges' and 'Homework helpers' to ensure what you learn becomes a natural part of your own writing skills.

USING THIS COURSEBOOK

Happily, there are many ways to use this guide. The best place to start is probably the 'Contents' page where you'll see that we've broken down all aspects of the course into easily digestible sections. Some of you may wish to begin at the beginning and work your way through; others may wish to dip into the sections where you feel your skills need some strengthening.

We know that, however you choose to use it, this coursebook will help you increase your potential for exam success **and** boost your self-confidence.

So, let's get down to it. Good luck!

ONLINE

For additional help on preparing for your exam, head to www.brightredbooks.net

OVERVIEW

WHAT'S INVOLVED IN THIS PAPER?

This paper accounts for 30 of the 70 marks in the final examination. The questions will be based on a quality non-fiction text of roughly 1000 words. Your final score will be determined by:

- how well you **understand** what is going on in this text,
- your ability to **analyse** how the writers make their effects, and
- your ability to **evaluate** how well you feel these effects are made.

This chapter will help you to become familiar and comfortable with these words in bold, so that you can respond to them in the way examiners expect.

What's coming up?

- How to prepare for the paper
- Where to find useful practice texts
- The skills being tested

How to prepare for the paper

'Reading for Understanding, Analysis and Evaluation' (RUAE) is a paper unlike most you will encounter in other subjects. You could be asked to answer questions on a topic you're completely unfamiliar with. The secret of success here is to have a vocabulary which will equip you to deal effectively with the challenges of new information and ideas. The text on which you'll be asked to answer questions will be selected by the examiners from a non-fiction text of distinction. Quality journalism, biography and travel writing are the kinds of text you can expect to encounter.

DON'T FORGET

Don't wait for the exam to encounter texts of this kind. Make it a regular practice to read quality newspapers or magazines. (Written by expert writers, these articles can also provide models for your own writing.)

Where to find useful practice texts

Wide reading of all kinds is the key to an adequate vocabulary. Regular reading of quality newspapers such as *The Guardian, The Scotsman, The Herald, The Observer* and *The Independent* is a helpful way to develop the required vocabulary. In particular, look for the 'Opinion' or 'Comment' sections where distinguished writers put forward their views on the world around them. Look not just at the vocabulary but at the ways they organise their ideas. Skim read the opening lines of each paragraph first to get an overall idea of where the piece is going. It could be just such a piece that will come up in the exam.

ONLINE

Quality papers can now be found online. Many will offer free opinion pieces for your practice reading. *The Scotsman, The Herald, The Guardian* and *The Independent* are good places to start.

Classroom challenge

Look at these article headings. Which ones sound most relevant when you're checking out which articles to read to practise for the 'Reading for Understanding, Analysis and Evaluation' paper? Which ones sound like news stories; which sound like 'opinion' or 'comment' pieces? Explain the reasons behind your choices.

a Thousands in late-night queuing for Harrods sale.

b PILOT CAPTURED AFTER WARPLANE SHOT DOWN.

c NO, INDIE MUSIC IS NOT FOR ME.

d Island-hopping and its hazards

e Judge rejects witness statement of faithless husband.

f Why, oh why these endless sales?

TEACHING NOTES

You can download additional notes for this challenge at www.brightredpublishing.co.uk/Shop/national-5-english-course-book

The skills being tested

The skills tested fall into three distinct categories:

Understanding skills	This is the most straightforward skill. You will be asked to demonstrate your grasp of **what** the piece is all about and your understanding of certain items of vocabulary; you may also be asked **why** certain comments are made. The skill here is being able to paraphrase ideas and expressions into your own words. You also need to be able to summarise key information from an indicated stretch of text, using bullet points if you wish. There will also be questions testing your ability to infer what the writer is hinting at but not saying outright – in other words, 'reading between the lines'. When you are tested on your understanding, you'll be required to express answers in your own words.
Analysis skills	Here, you need to look at **how** a writer created a certain effect, by identifying how certain techniques and words or phrases are used to create that effect. You will need to quote certain terms from the text, identify the technique at work and suggest what its effect on the reader is. The skill here is knowing the relevant techniques and being able to comment on them.
Evaluation skills	Here, you need to **say how well, in your opinion,** something has been said. As with analysis, you'll need to back up your comments with items of evidence from the text: a particularly successful simile, a striking contrast in **word choice** or some other such item.

What you need to know

These three categories of skill become much more manageable if you think of them simply under the following two headings. Look out for certain keywords indicating to which category the question belongs. We'll start to look at these keywords in the next chapter.

QUESTIONS BROADLY ABOUT UNDERSTANDING	QUESTIONS BROADLY ABOUT ANALYSIS
• Questions which test factual information, i.e. **understanding** • Questions which ask you to find key points, i.e. **summarising** • Questions which ask you to work out what the writer is suggesting without saying directly, i.e. **inferring**	• Questions which test your knowledge of language features and how they work on the reader, i.e. **analysing** • Questions which ask you to say how well, in your opinion, certain identified features work, i.e. **evaluating**

DON'T FORGET

Questions broadly about understanding put the emphasis on using your own words. Questions broadly about analysis will need quoted items from the text as evidence for your answer.

What you now know

- ✔ The text on which the 'Reading for Understanding, Analysis and Evaluation' exam paper will be based is taken from quality non-fiction texts.
- ✔ You can prepare for this paper by familiarising yourself with the language of opinion and comment sections of quality newspapers, journals and magazines.
- ✔ There are three categories of skills which you can expect to be tested on, but they can be broadly considered under two headings: questions testing understanding and questions testing analysis.
- ✔ During the course, you will need to acquire the knowledge, and develop the skills, to demonstrate convincingly your mastery of the different challenges of each of the various question categories.

UNDERSTANDING

What's coming up?

- How to recognise questions testing understanding
- How to explain in your own words
- How to summarise
- How to understand inference-making
- Practice with questions testing understanding

RECOGNISING 'UNDERSTANDING' QUESTIONS

The clues

The wording of questions testing understanding may take a variety of forms, but here are some possible formats:

Explain in your own words what *the writer feels about ...*

Explain what *is meant by the expression ...*

As far as possible in your own words, ***summarise*** *...*

Explain in your own words why *this advice might be seen as ...*

Why *does the writer say ...?*

Questions of this kind are testing:

- your basic understanding of the text, and
- your ability to express this understanding **in your own words**.

Classroom challenge

Which of these questions is testing understanding? Why have you rejected the other questions? What do your rejected questions seem to be asking you to do?

a) Show fully how the writer's word choice or sentence structure in lines 15–19 helps convey his ideas effectively.

b) Explain what the attitude of the judge is to this type of driving.

c) Explain in your own words what the writer means when he calls continuous assessment a 'valid alternative'.

d) Explain in your own words two aspects of 'pleasure' or 'happiness' as defined in the past, and two as defined today.

e) Pick an expression from the final paragraph (lines 88–94), and show how it helps to contribute an effective ending to the passage.

f) Show fully how the writer conveys his friend's apparent attitude, and his actual attitude to his decision.

TEACHING NOTES

You can download Teaching Notes for this challenge at www.brightredpublishing.co.uk/Shop/national-5-english-course-book

EXPLAINING IN YOUR OWN WORDS

What do I change?

As we've already said, you're being tested on your understanding of the factual content of certain passages, but you're also being tested on your ability to express this information in your own words, without 'lifting' words or expressions from the passage. However, the examiners are reasonable people: there are certain items you're allowed to retain in answering these types of questions, and certain items you need to change. So, what are they?

ITEMS TO KEEP	ITEMS TO CHANGE
Proper nouns Common nouns with no obvious alternatives: 'crocodile', 'brakes', 'mortgage', etc.	Verbs, adverbs, adjectives and writing techniques such as similes, metaphors, etc. will all need to be rephrased in your own words.

DON'T FORGET

'Explain', 'summarise', 'what' and 'why' are usually good clues to spotting an understanding question; one that you'll need to answer in your own words as far as possible.

Tracking down the answer

In 'understanding' questions, a good tip is to adopt a two-stage approach:

- Stage 1: Highlight or underline the words or phrases where you think the answer lies.
- Stage 2: Work on putting these words or phrases in a new way, perhaps reshaping the elements to present the information in your personal 'take' on the selected words.

DON'T FORGET

To explain in your own words, you need a good vocabulary. This is where regular and wide reading of quality newspapers and literature will help you. A good vocabulary is built up over time. You can't acquire one the night before the exam!

Beware 'word-for-word' substitutions

DON'T FORGET

At all costs, avoid repeating any word, or part of the word, in the expression you are being asked to explain. Be sure to cover all the words in an expression, not just the most obvious one.

The words or expressions chosen for comment will require some careful thinking to ensure you have covered ALL elements in them. Avoid struggling for word-for-word substitutions. If you can manage this, well done. But most of us may have difficulty coming up with precise 'translations'. A better idea is to try to explain, or gloss, the idea rather than try to find exact substitutes for individual words.

POSSIBLE QUESTION	POSSIBLE ANSWER EXPLAINING THE UNDERLYING IDEA
Explain in your own words what the writer means when he describes the waiter as 'grudgingly polite'.	The waiter was showing good manners/being courteous but he didn't seem to be doing this very willingly/enthusiastically.

Classroom challenge

Join with a partner to inspect these practice phrases for getting into the habit of putting items into your own words. Choose three each to answer and be sure to account for the content of *both* words. A dictionary at your elbow might be a good idea here. Then swap results. Has your partner answered in a way that deserves 2 marks in your opinion?

'grubby charm' (for example, of a hotel)
'entrenched poverty' (for example, of a country)
'garishly attractive' (for example, of a dress)
'erratically brilliant' (for example, of a pupil)
'mute hatred' (for example, towards an enemy)
'controversial success' (for example, of a film)

TEACHING NOTES

You can download Teaching Notes for this challenge at www.brightredpublishing.co.uk/Shop/national-5-english-course-book

Homework helper

Try your understanding skills here, where the writer talks of the pleasure of discovering 'grown-up' fiction for the first time.

(1) To a young reader there was something exhilarating in the discovery that fiction did not always come gift-wrapped, and that the concept of a neatly tied up conclusion was not merely artificial but unrealistic. (2) Up to that age – we must have been 12 or 13 – books considered suitable for our enjoyment had always combined quietly improving subtexts, overlaid with adventure and a comforting end, where all fears were conquered, and evil-doers safely despatched.

Rosemary Goring, 'Why I rarely remember the ending of books', *The Herald*, 27th February 2016

a) Look at sentence (1) and then explain in your own words what the writer means when she says the first stories she had read had come 'gift-wrapped'. 2

b) Look at sentence (2) and then give **two** reasons, using your own words as far as possible, why these early texts might have been chosen for young children. 2

ONLINE

Why not try reading the full article online? It would be good preparation practice for the paper.

TEACHING NOTES

You can download Teaching Notes for this challenge at www.brightredpublishing.co.uk/Shop/national-5-english-course-book

SUMMARISING

Here, again, you're being asked for information from the text. This time, you need to pick out certain **key ideas** from an indicated passage (for example, 'lines 22–37') and explain what they are in your own words as far as possible. The number of key ideas required may be suggested by the number of marks on offer.

'Lifting' words and expressions is to be avoided. (Once again, you'll find that a broad vocabulary will stand you in good stead.)

It's really important to eliminate any details, no matter how interesting, which obscure the main points being sought. Usually, you can present these in bullet-point form or in very brief sentences. And, of course, in your own words as far as possible.

DON'T FORGET

When reading a passage for key points, underline what you **think** are key points. Then, go back and read the question again. Maybe some weren't as important as you thought?

So what do I leave out?

- Writing techniques such as similes, metaphors, etc.
- Examples
- Lists
- Comparisons
- Descriptions

Classroom challenge

For practice, read how a writer describes how, from desert beginnings, Dubai was transformed into the state we know today.

Thirty years ago, almost all of contemporary Dubai was desert, inhabited only by cactuses and tumbleweed and scorpions. But downtown there are traces of the town that once was, buried amidst the metal and glass. In the dusty fort of the Dubai Museum, one version of this story is told. In the mid-18th century, a small village was built here, in the lower Persian Gulf, where people would dive for pearls off the coast. It soon began to accumulate a cosmopolitan population washing up from Persia, the Indian subcontinent, and other Arab countries, all hoping to make their fortune. They named it after a local locust, the daba, who consumed everything before it. The town was soon seized by the gunships of the British Empire, who held it by the throat as late as 1971. As they scuttled away, Dubai decided to ally with the six surrounding states and make up the United Arab Emirates (UAE).

Johan Hari, 'The Dark Side of Dubai', *The Independent*, 6th April 2009

1. After you have read the passage, summarise, using your own words as far as possible, some of the changes that have occurred in Dubai since the beginning of the 18th century.

   You should make **four** key points in your answer. 4

Look carefully at the wording of that question again. We are to 'summarise' – that is to say, look for – key points about 'changes' that have happened 'since the beginning of the 18th century'. Make sure you do not include other interesting – but irrelevant – information. And, remember, you can do this in bullet points. This might give us:

- Around 1750, a minor pearl-diving settlement grew up there.
- Soon, money-hungry/money-seeking people from further east and neighbouring states settled.
- It next became a British colony until 1971.
- After independence, it amalgamated/joined with six other states to form the United Arab Emirates.

A good vocabulary will always help you to avoid lengthy, wordy explanations. And long explanations can sometimes lose focus on the precise nature of the task.

TEACHING NOTES

You can download Teaching Notes for this challenge at www.brightredpublishing.co.uk/Shop/national-5-english-course-book

DON'T FORGET

The wider your vocabulary, the easier you'll find summarising.

Homework helper

Now that you've looked at a worked model, here is a passage which you could attempt as homework. Read again about the elements in the original text which you need to eliminate before starting. (p.13)

The writer gives his personal views on what he saw were once the differences between British flight attendants and Italian ones when he travelled as a young man.

The Italian flight attendant sometimes takes her job title literally – the plane flies, she just attends. But she's always pleasant, elegant and ladylike, so much so that she can appear intimidating.

But then take a British flight attendant. You wouldn't mistake her for a model. She'll have very little make-up and no jewellery. Often, she is robustly built and until recently would be sporting one of these little round hats that you only see on British cabin staff and New Jersey ice-cream vendors. Her heels are low and her shoes 'sensible', as they say in Britain. Alitalia crews wear emerald green but British Airways has improbable combinations of red, white and blue or a mayonnaise-cum-apricot shade that nature felt no need to invent. The British woman is attentive, though. She comes back again and again, smiling all the time. She waits until your mouth is full, swoops on you from behind and beams, 'Is everything all right?'

Then something happens. Let's say you spill your coffee in your lap. At that point, the two personalities undergo an abrupt transformation that – you've guessed it – sums up the respective national characters.

The British attendant stiffens. You have deviated from the pattern. You have done something you shouldn't. All of a sudden, her inner nanny emerges. She doesn't say she's annoyed but she lets you know.

The attractive Italian also undergoes a change. In an emergency, her detachment disappears. At times of crisis, what emerges is her inner mum, sister, confidante, friend and lover. She takes off her jacket and actually helps you. Weak at, if not openly irritated by, routine administration, she comes into her own in exceptional circumstances that allow her to bring her personal skills to bear. Where did the ice goddess go? She melted. In her place is a smiling woman who is trying to be helpful.

Beppe Severgnini, *La Bella Figura: An Insider's Guide to the Italian Mind*, Hodder & Stoughton, London, 2007

a) The writer points out several differences between the personalities of Italian flight attendants and British ones in routine conditions. As far as possible in your own words, summarise what some of the main differences are. 5

AND/OR

b) The writer points out several differences between the reactions of Italian flight attendants and British ones at moments of crisis. As far as possible in your own words, summarise what some of the main differences are. 5

TEACHING NOTES

You can download Teaching Notes for this at www.brightredpublishing.co.uk/Shop/national-5-english-course-book

DON'T FORGET

Always read the wording of the summarising task carefully. Do not summarise points that are not being targeted in the wording of the question.

How does that work?

By now, you will have noticed that when summarising you are always working hard to find terms which express the same or a similar idea but which are not 'lifted' from the original text. In other words, a good grasp of **synonyms** is vital for success. And you acquire these from broad, general reading. But you can also acquire them from regular use of a **thesaurus**, either in published form or online.

Roget's Thesaurus is the popular print version; online versions include: www.collinsdictionary.com/englishthesaurus and www.thesaurus.com

Get into the habit of using one now if you don't already.

- Find the word alphabetically in a print version, or enter the keyword in the 'search' window of an online version.
- Study the synonyms on offer very carefully. Not all of them will work in the text/ **context** you are studying. Test out your new word in your sentence. Does it make sense here?
- Make sure you fully understand the meaning of the word you have selected. If in doubt, check it out in a dictionary.

INFERENCE-MAKING

What the writer is getting at but not quite saying

These are broader understanding questions which are asking you to look below the surface of the text. More accurately, you're being asked to 'read between the lines', and make some deductions of your own about:

- what the writer is hinting at, and
- what they are feeling.

Sometimes, the inferences you will be asked to pick up on are to do with information which may be surprising or strange, not quite in line with what is being said elsewhere. You're being given clues, but the writer's intention is not fully spelt out. You need to be sensitive to the 'vibes' coming off the text to understand the writer's full intentions. Picking up on these 'vibes' accurately will boost your mark.

How do I work this out?

(i) **From accumulated information**

Sometimes, there will be a build-up of factual information which may seem to contradict a statement that is being made. Let's look at a possible example of this where a travel journalist writes about a wonderful holiday he once had in Naples:

Should you get an opportunity to visit Naples, jump at it. Forget the piles of rubbish that periodically appear when the city authorities and their workforce fall out, don't be put off by anecdotes about pickpockets or the occasional presence of armed soldiers that are drafted in when security seems at risk.

Suppose our question was:

1. Explain fully using your own words why the advice to 'jump at' the opportunity to visit Naples might at first seem strange. 3

What might be the inference the writer is making here? At first reading, there seems to be a bit of a contradiction going on. He is saying 'go', but then he lists some information which may put you off going!

What's being left unsaid here, or being inferred, is this – for all its problems, Naples is a wonderful place to visit.

How does that work?

So, let's work out an answer for this question. We'll need to point to words or phrases that helped us understand this apparent contradiction of jumping at an opportunity to visit a place with so many negative points. These points will now need to be explained, or glossed, in our own words. In search of an answer, we could start by putting these words/phrases into our own words:

'forget the piles of rubbish'	ignore the garbage lying around
'don't be put off by anecdotes about pickpockets'	don't listen to what you're told about petty thieves
'armed soldiers'	army presence

Putting all this information together, we might get this possible answer for 3 marks:

It seems strange to be told to 'jump at' this chance since we will need to ignore garbage lying about, stories about petty thieving or seeing the army on the streets. The inference is that Naples is a great place to visit, despite its various troubles.

DON'T FORGET

Inference-making questions require just as much skill in using your own words as more straightforward understanding questions. Once again, a good grasp of synonyms is vital.

(i) **From explaining words/phrases**

Sometimes, you may be asked to look at certain words or phrases. You may be asked to explain in your own words what's meant by these words or phrases and what's surprising or contradictory about them in the context in which they are found. Let's take an example of this:

Bone-rattling skeletons leapt out at every bend, blood-curdling howls rang out periodically and a sticky red liquid dripped from the ceiling in places. For Joy, this was all delicious terror.

Suppose our question was:

Explain what is meant by the expression 'delicious terror', and explain what is surprising about this expression. 3

Again, at first glance there appears to be some sort of contradiction going on here. This is a truly scary place, so we understand the word 'terror' easily enough, but why is it 'delicious'? What does this infer, or leave unsaid, about Joy and her tastes? Quite simply, that she is one of these people who really enjoy being scared out of their minds.

How does that work?

As before, we need to find words or phrases, suggesting this time the source of terror:

'Skeletons ... leapt out'	They were attacked by skeletons.
'blood-curdling howls'	There were terrifying noises.
'sticky red liquid'	Blood-like fluid trickled down.

Piecing this together, we can start to write our answer, remembering that there are 3 marks at stake. So, three points to suggest terror:

We are surprised that Joy found the experience 'delicious' since they were attacked by skeletons, surrounded by terrifying noises and had blood-like fluid trickling onto them. The inference is that Joy really enjoyed being frightened.

DON'T FORGET

Always check out the marks on offer. A question offering 3 marks requires either more explanation or more examples than one giving only 2 marks.

TEACHING NOTES

You can download Teaching Notes for this challenge at www.brightredpublishing.co.uk/Shop/national-5-english-course-book

Classroom challenge

Now try out your skills with these.

(a) *David Bowie's 2013 single 'Where are we now?' was greeted in January with over-the-top praise by the British press, its lyrics hailed for their devilishly incisive wit and its video rated as a 'truly cool masterpiece'. So his more savvy fans started to prepare for the inevitable media backlash which would surely accompany the release of the album due for release later in the year.*

Explain fully using your own words why thoughtful fans might be expecting the album to be greeted by a 'inevitable media backlash'. 3

(b) *Looking around the crowded hall, Paul saw they were all there: Anne's mum and dad, her best buddy, Grace, even the representative from the RSPB, who was to present the award, was there, shifting uneasily in his place. It was nearly 11am. Where was she? All Paul could think of was Anne – and her conspicuous absence.*

Explain fully what is meant by the expression 'conspicuous absence', and explain what is surprising about this expression. 3

What you now know

- ✔ How the questions testing understanding may be worded
- ✔ How synonyms help in answering in your own words
- ✔ How to set about summarising key points
- ✔ How to recognise what a writer may be inferring
- ✔ The way to set about answering questions testing these skills

ANALYSIS

What's coming up?

- What is an analysis question?
- How analysis questions differ from understanding questions
- How to recognise questions testing analysis
- How to tackle questions testing word choice, sentence structure, **imagery** and **tone**
- Practice with questions testing analytical skills

ANALYSIS QUESTIONS

What is an analysis question?

Analysis questions are sometimes thought to be a little trickier to answer than those testing simply understanding. They are there to test your ability to analyse *how* writers make their effects on readers.

These questions require you to delve into the text and select examples of certain features. Sometimes, the question will specify which types of feature the examiners wish you to comment on (for example, word choice or sentence structure); sometimes, they'll ask you to select examples of your own. You then need to explain **in your own words** how the selected feature works on readers.

How do analysis questions differ from understanding questions?

In questions testing understanding, you should not 'lift' items from the text for your answer; in analysis questions, you are expected to do just that. But, your brief 'lift' must be accompanied by an explanation **in your own words** of how the word or phrase you've selected affects readers. Analysis questions require you to know and recognise several techniques commonly used by writers to influence readers.

How to recognise questions testing analysis

The wording of questions testing your analysis may take a variety of forms, but here are some possible formats:

Show fully how *examples of the writer's use of such features as ...*

With reference to three examples of ... ***show fully how*** *he makes clear ...*

Show fully how *the writer conveys ...*

Explain ***how*** *... giving two examples of the writer's word choice ...*

Analysis questions require you to:

- know a number of techniques commonly used by writers,
- find examples of these techniques at work in the passage, and
- be able to discuss their effects on readers.

DON'T FORGET

'Show fully how...' are the words to look out for if questions are requiring an analytical approach. Above all, look out for that 'how'. It is a sure-fire signal to go looking for certain items in the text – and then talk about their effect on readers.

DON'T FORGET

If you find yourself answering a 'Show fully how ...' question without short quoted examples from the text, stop! Something's wrong. Go back and find examples. Often, the question will stipulate how many are required. Or the marks will. Usually, it is one example for 2 marks (1 for item of evidence plus 1 for your comment on it). Or, if it's 4 marks on offer, you'll need 2 items of evidence plus 2 comments of your own. Always check the number of marks carefully.

Classroom challenge

Here are a mixture of questions: some testing understanding, some testing analysis. Work with a partner to determine which is which. Which words in the question helped you decide?

a) Look at lines 12–15. Explain what is meant by the expression 'deafening silence', and explain what is strange about this expression.

b) Look at lines 20–25. Show fully how the writer conveys her teacher's initial reaction, and then his later reaction to her essay.

c) Look at lines 3–15. With reference to three examples of word choice from these lines, show fully how he makes clear his disapproval of airlines.

d) Explain how the writer's word choice in lines 30–33 helps to show the positive effects of hard work.

e) Look at lines 59–62, and then explain as far as possible in your own words what differences the writer sees between living in Montrose and Glasgow.

f) Look at lines 20–35, and then summarise, using your own words as far as possible, some of the irritations she feels about Sunday newspapers. You should make five key points.

TEACHING NOTES

You can download Teaching Notes for this challenge at www.brightredpublishing.co.uk/Shop/national-5-english-course-book

How does that work?

How do I 'show fully how...'?

Your time is limited in the exam room and the examiners are well aware of this. So, in example (c) in the 'Classroom challenge', where the question asks for three examples of word choice, you can answer in note form. Your answer might look like this:

- *'gas-guzzling': seen as wasteful of fuel*
- *'unreliable': cannot be counted on to be on time.*
- *'glorified buses': sees them as just grander versions of urban transport*

As well as saving you time writing full sentences, this note-form approach makes your response much more clear to the marker.

Homework helper

Here's a short passage about an island that the writer visited. Using what you've learned about the wording of questions testing analysis, devise a question of your own, testing how the writer makes his reaction to the island clear. Look back at examples we've given to help you form your question. Make the question worth 4 marks. Hint: think word choice. If you're feeling ambitious, try answering your question, too!

It's still quite easy to walk alone on an idyllic beach in Phu Quoc, and imagine you are the only person on a pristine island. It's even easier to imagine you are alone if you walk 100 metres into one of the remaining patches of majestic jungle.

Paddy Woodworth, 'Paradise Found', *Irish Times,* 1st September 2012

TEACHING NOTES

You can download Teaching Notes for this at www.brightredpublishing.co.uk/Shop/national-5-english-course-book

TECHNIQUES OF ANALYSIS

Word choice

To answer a question focusing on word choice, you need to be on the lookout for words or short expressions which stand out, and which suggest some marked characteristic. These words or short expressions selected for the passage will usually be less than neutral in the associations they conjure up in our minds. In fact, they will exploit these associations.

Take the words 'slim' and 'scrawny'. Nobody minds being called 'slim': it suggests a trim figure, carrying just the right weight. But 'scrawny'? Does it not suggest a body that is unattractively thin? Yet both, technically, mean 'having little flesh on the body', a fairly neutral term, free of the above associations. To answer word-choice questions, we need to explore these associations in a little more depth. To do this, we need to look at what are called denotations and connotations.

Denotations and connotations

The **denotation** of a word is simply what the dictionary says about it. The **connotation** of a word is what we associate with it in our mind. Being prepared to talk about connotations is at the heart of a successful word-choice answer. So, let's look at these connotations, or associations, more closely.

Classroom challenge

Study these ten words, all suggesting thinness in some way. Work with a partner. List these adjectives in what you think is an order of attractiveness. Discuss the connotations you feel each one carries. Don't worry if you disagree; the important thing is to talk freely about the picture each adjective creates in your mind.

scrawny	lean	skinny	underweight	slight
slender	cadaverous	spare	svelte	slim

TEACHING NOTES

You can download Teaching Notes for this challenge at www.brightredpublishing.co.uk/Shop/national-5-english-course-book

How does that work?

Nouns, verbs and adverbs, like adjectives, all have their own connotations. Here is a short text describing the arrival in a classroom of a group of primary pupils. It will give you a chance to form answers to word-choice questions. Read the text and then answer the questions below, using the prompts if you need them. (Are there other examples of word choice you might wish to offer in an answer?)

They were late. As usual. Why was I not surprised? First in was Josh, who, unlike his friends who trailed in behind him, strode purposefully into the room as if he meant to work. But heaven knows how long he would keep that up. Melanie's entrance, five minutes later, was just the opposite. Clearly none too keen to meet up with me again after last Friday, she slouched in, the reluctant learner as always, her feet dragging with every step.

a) With reference to two examples of the writer's word choice, **show fully how** he makes clear Josh's attitude to coming to class. 2

b) **Show fully how** the writer suggests that this class is not popular with Melanie. 2

Possible answers:

(a) 'strode' suggests Josh walked in a determined way/confidently; 'purposefully' suggests he had a target/aim in mind as he moved.

(b) 'slouched' suggests Melanie sat in a droopy/slovenly/couldn't-care-less sort of way; 'reluctant' suggests she was not at all keen to learn anything.

TEACHING NOTES

You can download Teaching Notes for this at www.brightredpublishing.co.uk/Shop/national-5-english-course-book

DON'T FORGET

Word-choice questions can be answered very directly: select your word(s), place it/them in inverted commas and follow with a brief comment, using terms such as 'suggests'/'gives the impression that'/'makes me think of'. Then, in your own words, state the connotations you have with your selection.

Homework helper

The writer of the following extract describes how she initially misunderstood the history of Bali. Read the passage and, using the approach to answering word-choice questions we've been studying, answer the question below.

... It takes me only three afternoons of research in the local library to realize all my original ideas about a Balinese paradise were a bit misguided. I'd been telling people since I first visited Bali two years ago that this small island was the world's only true utopia, a place that has known only peace and harmony and balance for all time. A perfect Eden with no history of violence or bloodshed ever. I'm not sure where I got this grand idea, but I endorsed it with full confidence.

Elizabeth Gilbert, *Eat, Pray, Love*, Bloomsbury, London, 2006

(a) With reference to three examples of the writer's word choice, **show fully how** she makes clear she initially took a very positive view of the island. 6

TEACHING NOTES

You can download Teaching Notes for this at www.brightredpublishing.co.uk/Shop/national-5-english-course-book

Sentence structure

Good writers can do endlessly inventive things with sentence structures. However, the sentence structures on which you are likely to be asked questions tend to fall into certain recurring categories. As when answering word-choice questions, you need to be alert to the **effect** the choice of sentence structure is having on readers.

So, which types of sentence structure might you encounter? Here are some of the more common ones.

Sentence structures you should know about

Long sentences	Used to suggest the sheer length of something, for example, a route of a river or road, or the complexity of a process, or the boredom of something dragging on and on.
Short sentences	Used to intensify the impact/drama of what's being said. A brief piece of information in a short sentence of its own really stands out: 'And with that, she left.' Be very alert to the power of a short sentence after a particularly long one: the dramatic impact is intensified even more.
A list (neutral, with climax or anti-climax)	Used to underline/emphasise/highlight the **range** or sheer **number** of items, actions or people being described. Always check lists out for additional possibilities. It might build to a climax – 'She had played hostess to generals, princes, kings and even the mighty Napoleon himself' – a technique which adds to the impact of the final item. It might, however, end in an anti-climax – 'His case contained a pair of Gucci loafers, a Rolex watch, cologne by Chanel and a pair of dirty underpants' – a technique which is usually used for humorous effect. Of course, it might simply be a neutral list! But it's a sound idea to check any list for climax or anti-climax.
Sentences without verbs	These are known as minor sentences. Sometimes they create a chatty, informal effect – 'Great!' 'Another fine mess.' 'What next?' Or they can function like the short sentences described above: to add dramatic impact – 'A woman's glove. Slightly blood-stained.'

Inverted word order	Normal word order in English tends to follow this pattern: 'He was fierce in his claim to innocence.' But, to emphasise/underline/highlight a certain element in the sentence, we can invert the normal order, usually to place the important word(s) first. So, we get 'Fierce he was in his claim to innocence.' But the inversion can also be manipulated to place the important word to be emphasised at the end – 'In his claim to innocence he was fierce.' This technique often appears in songs: 'Here I stand' from *Let it go!* And let's not forget Yoda here either: 'Truly wonderful, the mind of a child is.' **Exam tip:** if you cannot see anything at all in a sentence to comment on, check out inversion. It's often one of the last things we think of. And it **could** just be the right answer!
Repetition	This may take the form of repeated words or phrases to underline/intensify the idea the writer is seeking to emphasise at a particular point – 'A good cyclist needs ... A good cyclist hopes that ... But a good cyclist knows, above all, that...' Note that these repetitions in the closing stages of a text might be building to a climax. It's worth mentioning in your answer if you detect this.
Balanced sentences	When writers wish to make us strongly aware of some contrast they want to make, they sometimes resort to balanced sentences. They are recognisable by the semi-colon (;) that acts as a pivot, or balancing point, in the middle of the sentence – 'Alive, she had been seen as a saint; dead, she was quickly demonised.'
Rhetorical question	These are questions expecting no direct answer, rather the reader's support for the writer's views – 'Who wants to see a child suffer in this way?' Here, the reader is expected to share the writer's horror at the ill treatment of children.
Parallel structures	These are patterns of either phrases or words which give a pleasing predictability and rhythm to the sentence. The effect is to add emphasis to what is being said – 'It is by logic we prove, but by intuition we discover' (da Vinci). The ants were everywhere: climbing over jam pots, swarming under the sink, scrambling into cupboards, diving into the bin.' The likeness of pattern here (verb + preposition) makes for a more memorable phrase and creates a greater impact than a less patterned structure would.

DON'T FORGET

You thoroughly need to know the many sentence types you may encounter. The chances are only one or two of them will form the basis of a question in the paper. But the problem is, you don't know which one!

DON'T FORGET

Sometimes, a question will ask you directly to look at sentence structure. Sometimes, you'll only be asked how 'the language used' contributes to an effect. This might be an opportunity to bring in what you know about sentence structure. Don't overlook sentence structure when the question just mentions 'language used'!

How does that work?

Let's look at how we might answer questions using sentence structure as the basis for our answer.

It might have been decades ago, but I remember the anguish of that first day as if it were yesterday. I remember the howling when my mum left me with Mrs Bell. I remember the strange looks the other kids gave me when I was at last coaxed into the classroom. Other people remember, too, and any time I meet up with them, they never let me forget this.

Long was the school day at that time. I remember it all: the seemingly vast building, the coal-fired stove, the 'large' pupils in primary 2, the honky-tonk tinkling of the piano, walking home in the winter dark. A time best forgotten.

(a) The writer develops the idea of his early school days being a miserable time for him. **Show how** his sentence structure in paragraph one helps to convey this idea effectively. 2

So, what do we notice? Perhaps the most noticeable feature is the fact that he says 'I remember' no less than three times. Looking at our sentence-structure grid, we see that this falls under the category of 'repetition'. After the 'I remember', he fills us in with all the things he recalls. This was 'decades ago' but he still remembers it all, suggesting how deeply he felt all these things.

We might write as our answer:

The writer uses repetition of the words 'I remember' (x 3) to convey the idea that his misery was such that he remembers all the details even today/details have never left him/are etched in his memory.

Homework helper

Using the 'early school-days' text overleaf, try these further practice questions on sentence structure.

a) **Show fully how** in paragraph two the writer uses sentence structure to emphasise the seemingly endless nature of the day. 2

b) In paragraph two, the writer makes clear the sharpness of his memory. **Show fully how** he uses sentence structure to convey this idea. 2

c) In the same paragraph, he indicates his deep unhappiness during this period. **Show fully how** he uses sentence structure to convey this feeling. 2

TEACHING NOTES You can download Teaching Notes for this at www.brightredpublishing.co.uk/Shop/national-5-english-course-book

So, we now know some of the ways writers can employ sentence structure to create certain effects on readers. But look at the passage below. The sentence structures employed are clearly working hard to create effects on the reader – but their effects seem to depend on some features we've not yet discussed. What new features are appearing in these sentences?

'It's just... well, I'd really like you to... to... well, think about it at least.'

'Nathan! Stop! Enough! It's always the same with you!' We had discussed the trip to Ireland many times – four times at least in the last six months – and every time Nathan had weaselled out of making any firm decision. First, there had been his chronic shortage of cash; then his famous 'grumbling appendix'; Jess's new litter of pups; a sudden desire to work for exams; the excuses just went on and on. Now it was all clear to me: Nathan had to be told that he and the trip were just not on. An idea started to take shape in my mind...

We see that the passage is rich in examples of sentences where various punctuation marks contribute significantly to the effect – exasperation chiefly – which the writer is creating as he relates the incident.

Clearly, a study of sentence structure – and the various effects it can have on readers – needs to be a study of punctuation and its functions, too. So, let's look at what punctuation can contribute before we do some work on it.

The role of punctuation

Punctuation performs three basic functions in a sentence:

- It marks out the limits of a sentence – full stop, question mark, exclamation mark.
- It shapes the sentence within these limits – comma, colon, semi-colon.
- It adds special effects to the sentence – inverted commas, **ellipsis**, dashes and brackets.

Within a sentence, these features can all influence the overall effect the writer is attempting to convey. Here are some punctuation marks which will be useful to know in discussing sentence structure.

Full stop	.	Its position indicates the completion of a sentence. The position of the full stop in a paragraph determines whether we are dealing with long or short sentences.
Comma	,	Usually used to separate brief items in a list – 'Apples, pears, bananas and a grapefruit.' Used before and after a phrase, commas are said to be used as **parenthesis** markers – 'Enter Arthur, a distant cousin, in love with Anne.' The phrase 'a distant cousin' is said to be **in parenthesis**. When answering questions, we say 'The phrase in parenthesis adds additional information about ...' See also, pairs of dashes and brackets below.
Semi-colon	;	Often used to separate larger items in a list – 'A beach house in Bermuda; a flat in Paris, on the Champs Elysee no less; a chalet in the Alps; a castle in Scotland with over 40 rooms: all these were owned by their aunt.' They also indicate a turning point in a balanced sentence – 'Sober, he was unpredictable; drunk, he was dangerous. To err is human; to forgive divine.'
Colon	:	A colon separates two statements when the second signals an explanation, illustration or expansion on what is to follow – 'It was now night: stars twinkled overhead and the moon was rising.' 'He now knew what he needed to do: accept their offer.' Or it may signal an upcoming quotation – 'Criticised for being harsh, Les replies: "Heart like a flint, that's me."' It may also introduce a list – 'Her garden was a picture: marigolds, lupins, roses, daisies and, in spring, masses of tulips.'
Dashes and brackets	– – ( )	Pairs of dashes, brackets or commas on either side of a phrase '– her mother's cousin –' are used to create what we call a phrase **in parenthesis**. When answering questions, we say 'The phrase in parenthesis adds additional information about ...'
	–	An individual dash can be used to add emphasis or importance to a word or phrase following it: 'And there it lay before them, glittering in the blue Aegean – Hydra.' An individual dash can sometimes also be used as a kind of informal colon, indicating a concluding list or explanation: 'He had taken great trouble over their evening meal – prawns, roast venison and a fine raspberry tart.'
Ellipsis	...	In mid-sentence, these three dots can be used to suggest an interruption, hesitation or indecision. Used at the end of the sentence, they can suggest anticipation or suspense: 'The door opened and a hand appeared ...'

Exclamation mark	!	Usually used to indicate strong emotion on the part of the writer – often surprise, excitement or anger: 'It was Bill!'
Question mark	?	To indicate a question which may be a structuring device for that section of the article, that is, the writer asks a question and then proceeds to answer it in the following paragraph. A series of questions may well be there to signal the writer's confusion or bewilderment: 'Who could she turn to? Was there anyone she could trust? What if they were all against her?' Sometimes, this can mark the end of a rhetorical question, which invites readers to share the writer's views: 'What kind of society turns its back on those in need?' You need to say precisely what the apparent aim of the writer is, for example: *'to win the reader's support for his views on what constitutes a just society.'*
Inverted commas	' '	In addition to their traditional use to shape direct speech, inverted commas can also be placed around an individual word or phrase, to suggest that the writer is casting doubt on the surface meaning of the word. 'I had little faith in the "help" being offered by the bank.' Here the writer is indicating that the 'help' is so-called help, rather than real assistance. They are also used to indicate the title of a book, film, play, etc.

DON'T FORGET

If a question asks you to consider 'sentence structure' or 'language', don't overlook items of punctuation. They could well help contribute to a successful answer.

Classroom challenge

Using the information in the punctuation grid, look at the 'Nathan' passage and answer these practice questions:

a) Look at lines 1–2 where the writer introduces the idea that Nathan is indecisive. **Show fully how** his use of sentence structure helps convey this idea effectively. 2

b) In lines 2–6 the writer makes clear his attitude to Nathan. **Show fully with reference to** sentence structure how he conveys this attitude. 4

c) In the second paragraph, the writer suggests that at least one of Nathan's excuses is not to be taken too seriously. **Show fully how** he conveys this idea. 2

d) Look at the final two lines, and then **explain how** two examples of the speaker's sentence structure reveal his character. 4

TEACHING NOTES

You can download Teaching Notes for this at www.brightredpublishing.co.uk/Shop/national-5-english-course-book

Homework helper

Now that you know more about how sentence structure and punctuation can be employed by writers to create particular effects on readers, try these practice exercises on your own. If you need to, look back at the sentence-structure and punctuation grids on pp. 24–25 and 27–28 to check out the various possibilities for your answers.

1. *The fitness culture is everywhere: London, Livingston, Krakow or Carnoustie, there's no escaping it. Think about how often we run into sweaty bodies in lycra – some decidedly unappealing in this most unforgiving of materials – when trying to negotiate our way home from work. Think of the number of times fit young men and women look out at us from media advertising, exhorting us to buy such and such a health-giving product. Think of the times we look sadly at our expanding waistlines and begin to wonder if perhaps it is not too late to do something about it. In a pessimistic mood, such reflections are depressing; in an optimistic mood, they're downright dangerous.*

a) The writer here develops the idea that the fitness culture is everywhere, making it difficult for us to avoid it. **Explain fully how** two examples of the writer's use of sentence structure help convey his ideas effectively. 4

b) Look at the final two lines. **Show fully how** the writer uses sentence structure to give emphasis to his attitude towards the fitness culture. 4

2. *Appearing in court to give evidence, Cluny seemed to Usher to be a very different man from the sad, down-trodden guy he'd seen two weeks before in his office: alert, youthful-looking, now enjoying himself mightily. From the dock, Anderson looked on sneeringly, as if Cluny's treachery was just another harsh lesson in the wicked ways of fate in his life. And life is what he got.*

a) **Show fully how** the writer uses sentence structure to emphasise how appearing in court had changed Cluny. 2

b) **How** does the writer use sentence structure to bring out the severity of the sentence? 2

3. *Would this chaos never end? In truth, Fiona had never cared for the Festival: traffic, never exactly free-flowing, came to an almost dead stop; tourists seemed to clog up all the pavements; her friends took off for all points of the compass; she could never get into her favourite restaurants; the infernal din of the Tattoo kept her awake for hours; there was always the feeling that she was about to have her pockets picked; and this morning there was a dead man in her front garden.*

'I'm not sure how to say this,' she explained to the police when her shock allowed her to get to the phone, 'but when I went out this morning, there was ... I found ... well, he was ... dead.'

a) In the first paragraph, the writer makes clear Fiona's disapproval of the Festival. **Show how** the writer uses sentence structure to convey this idea effectively. 4

b) **How** does the writer use sentence structure to convey the girl's state of mind in paragraph two? 2

TEACHING NOTES

You can download Teaching Notes for this at www.brightredpublishing.co.uk/Shop/national-5-english-course-book

Classroom challenge

A lot has been said here about sentence structure and punctuation. How much do you remember? Take this quiz to see. If an answer is 'false', give one which you think is true.

1. A short sentence after a long one reduces the powerful effect of the long one. True or false?
2. A colon is only ever used to introduce a list. True or false?
3. Inverted commas around a word or phrase suggest the writer does not take the word or phrase at face value. True or false?
4. Ellipsis at the end of a sentence suggests the writer does not know what to say next. True or false?
5. Chatty/informal tone can sometimes be created by using a short sentence. True or false?
6. A rhetorical question indicates the writer is lacking information. True or false?
7. A pair of dashes in the middle of a sentence is there to add vital information. True or false?
8. An exclamation mark is used to indicate strong emotion such as surprise, excitement or anger. True or false?
9. When writers use repetition of words or phrases over a series of questions, it's because they have run out of vocabulary. True or false?
10. A list is used to emphasise/highlight/underline the sheer number of items, actions, or people being described. True or false?

TEACHING NOTES

You can download Teaching Notes for this at www.brightredpublishing.co.uk/Shop/national-5-english-course-book

DON'T FORGET

Knowing the many effects writers can create with punctuation and sentence structure is a fairly straightforward way of picking up useful marks in an exam. It may take a bit of time committing them to memory, but working on these effects regularly will bring benefits come exam time.

Sentences which link

When you are asked to explain why a certain sentence forms a link between one section of a passage and another, you are being asked to do two things:

1. To understand how the sentence's structure connects earlier ideas to later ones.
2. To analyse which specific words or phrases make this connection.

You need to examine the structure of the sentence to understand and select the following:

- Which of the sentence's words or phrases look **back** to information you have already gathered in earlier sentences. Your selected words will also require a comment from you on exactly what they refer back to.
- Which parts look **forward** to information which is about to be discussed. Your selected words will require a comment from you on what the upcoming information is about.

So, let's try that out.

How does that work?

Suppose we had a paragraph which read:

(i) Growing up, Hansen enjoyed an idyllic childhood. (ii) Although the child of doting parents, he had never been overindulged or spoiled. (iii) In their home, high in the Swiss mountains, he was never happier than when skiing in winter with his many friends from the village or hanging out with his classmates from the local international school. (iv) In summer, the family decamped to Frejus where, under the hot Provençal sun, Hansen revelled in exploring his growing writing skills, even succeeding in having an early short story published in 'Midi Jeunesse'. (v) These happy days, however, came to an abrupt end with his entry into the family firm. (vi) Gone were the carefree pleasures of boyhood as he struggled with acquiring accounting skills, visiting clients with his father, interacting with an often-aggressive work force. (vii) Not for him was his father's dream of Hansen & Son.

Here is a possible 'link' question:

Explain why sentence (v) helps provide a link between ideas at this point in the passage. 2

So, we see that the earlier part of the passage talks of his happy childhood; the later part, of his unhappiness at work. Sentence (v) is our link sentence since it brings together reference to both. First, we look to see which words or phrases look back to happiness.

We select actual words. Then we need to make a brief comment on what these words refer to. This gives us:

'These happy days': these words look back to the pleasures of childhood.

But we can also see that some words look forward to the less happy future. A brief comment on them might be:

'his entry into the family firm': refers forward to the unhappiness of the world of work.

Classroom challenge

Now, let's try looking at the link sentence in another passage:

Compared to others around it, the state had only a dribble of oil. Poverty-stricken for decades, its roads were pitted, its schools primitive, its shops woefully old-fashioned. Stagnation was as firmly as entrenched as the malaria that often beset its inhabitants. With the advent of the new ruler, however, all this misery was turned on its head. Its tired capital was reinvented as a tourist centre, a financial service industry was imported virtually overnight from London, a new national university was launched in association with Princeton. In only twenty years, what had been the region's basket case had become a modern wonder of the world.

Explain why the sentence beginning 'With the advent of a new ruler …' provides a link between ideas in the passage. 2

TEACHING NOTES

You can download Teaching Notes for this challenge at www.brightredpublishing.co.uk/Shop/national-5-english-course-book

DON'T FORGET

In link questions, you can select **words which look back** and then comment on what it is they are looking back to. Or, you can select **words which look forward** and comment on what it is that they are looking forward to. So, a 'backward-looking' or a 'forward-looking' quotation plus comment will get you two marks.

Homework helper

Try reading this passage on your own and answering the link question below.

There was a time when the High Street in any town was a bustling hive of activity. Family-run shops, cafés, galleries, pubs, hairdressers – all played their part in giving a living heart to urban commerce. By the 1970s, however, out-of-town shopping malls had begun their relentless inroad into this established commercial model. Smaller businesses withered away, charity shops blossomed, trade quietly packed its tent and crept away. Shops stood empty, sometimes for years. The process was slow but unstoppable. By the turn of the century, the shopping mall was king. Yet this sad tale of commercial decay tells only half the story. For the human cost was even greater. With the departure of smaller businesses, the sense of community was lost. Customers might have greater choice in the megastores but gone were the days when you were greeted by name in the High Street butcher's; when the queue in the baker's led to many catch-up conversations; when, in short, commerce had a human face. Older people, often without cars and unable to make it so readily to out-of-town locations, suffered most, but the loss of community has affected everyone.

Explain why the sentence 'Yet this ... story' creates a link in the writer's ideas at this point in the passage. 2

TEACHING NOTES

You can download Teaching Notes for this challenge at www.brightredpublishing.co.uk/Shop/national-5-english-course-book

Imagery

When we speak about imagery, we are entering the world of 'figures of speech' or **figurative language.** This language is figurative because it creates figures, pictures or images in our mind. The opposite of figurative language is **literal** language; language that conveys meaning, not through images, but through dictionary definitions of words. Here are two sentences to explain the difference:

- **Literal language:** Our fields were in great need of water, and many communities went hungry.
- **Figurative language**: Our fields were crying out for water, and famine stalked the land.

The first example presents us with facts; the second sees the fields as thirsty people, and famine as some sort of ogre. This imagery has a powerful effect on our imaginations and writers frequently resort to imagery to make their topic come alive in vivid pictures. As the saying goes, a picture is worth a thousand words.

Always remember, it's not enough to spot and identify the imagery at work in your passage; you must say what the effect of this particular 'picture' is on the reader.

The figurative language family

In an analysis question in your exam ('Show fully how ...'), figurative language of imagery and sound techniques could provide a useful answer, particularly when you are invited to look at the passage's 'language'.

Here are some of the more common members of the figurative language family. They fall broadly into two categories: those which conjure up visual pictures, and those which create pictures in sound – aural pictures, so to speak.

VISUAL IMAGERY	SOUND TECHNIQUES
Simile: a comparison between two items using 'like' or 'as' – 'He's like a dog with a bone.' The effect of similes and metaphors is to add pictorial emphasis/impact to the written description.	**Alliteration:** the repetition of a particular consonant – or consonant sound – at the beginning of a group of words to create a certain sound effect – 'Cold clay clads his coffin.' Here the harsh sound of the letter 'c' matches the grimness of the description. 'Soft sighing of the southern seas.' Here the soft 's' mimics the gentleness of the water's sound.
Metaphor: also a comparison but this time the two items being compared are not 'like' each other, since one item becomes the other – 'You're an angel.'	**Assonance:** the repetition of a certain group of similar-sounding vowels in words close to each other, again used to create a certain aural effect – 'And murmuring of innumerable bees ...'
Personification: yet another way of making a comparison. Similes and metaphors can become examples of personification when an inanimate (without life) object is spoken of as if it were human and alive. For instance: 'The kettle whimpers on a crazy hob.'	**Onomatopoeia**: here the sound of the word mimics its meaning. 'Clink', 'fizz', 'rip', 'honk', 'boom', 'purr' suggest their meaning in their sound.
Hyperbole: an exaggerated image to create a certain effect (often humorous) or to emphasise something – 'The list goes on for miles.' 'He never fails to get lost.'	**Enjambment:** in poetry, this is the running on of one line into another or into several others, often to give either a conversational feel to the content or sometimes to suggest a speeding up for an effect of urgency. It can also make the reader wait for a key point to be made when the sentence finally stops. '... for my purpose holds To sail beyond the sunset, and the baths Of all the western stars, until I die.'

Classroom challenge

Before we start working on actual questions, let's check how many of these examples of figurative language you remember. Fill in the grid with the missing name of the example.

a) 'Like a school of fish in a fast-flowing stream'	
b) 'And moonbeams kiss the sea'	
c) 'Snap! Crackle! Pop!'	
d) 'Only the stuttering rifles' rapid rattle'	
e) 'I've seen more fat on a chip.'	
f) 'If I bleat when I speak it's because I just got fleeced.'	
g) 'Pressure is a privilege not a problem'	
h) 'The rain was coming down in stair-rods'	

TEACHING NOTES

You can download Teaching Notes for this at www.brightredpublishing.co.uk/Shop/national-5-english-course-book

DON'T FORGET

Even if the 'Show fully how ...' question does not mention the word 'imagery' or 'image', you may be able to use some example of figurative language as part of your answer if the question invites you to talk of 'language'.

DON'T FORGET

In a 'Show fully how...' question, remember always to include a short quoted item from the passage to illustrate your comment.

ONLINE

Before we start practising exam questions, why not ease yourself into the recognition process of figurative language with a game of Hangman? Try the activity found at http://www.brightredbooks.net. Work on your own or with a partner.

DON'T FORGET

It's not enough to identify an image or figurative device, you need to say what its effect on the reader is.

How does that work?

Travel writer Jonathan Thompson takes a cooking course in the South of France.

His team of five chefs move sleekly about the kitchen like a school of fish in a fast-flowing stream – albeit a stream with a cumbersome lump of rosbif* *carelessly dropped into it. Lines of herbs hang in handfuls from the homely ceiling like Christmas decorations, while old glass jars containing curious, exotic ingredients sit neatly on high shelves.*

*'rosbif' is French slang for a British person, from the French notion that everybody in Britain eats roast beef.

Jonathan Thompson, 'A Cookery Class at Alain Ducasse's House in Provence', *The Guardian*, 17th May 2013

Let's use this passage to see how you might answer a question which asked you:

Show fully how the writer's language demonstrates the efficiency of the kitchen staff. 4

Now, we know 'language' is a welcome word in a question because we can talk about all kinds of things – word choice, sentence structure, images, etc. (We could, of course, pick up 2 marks here for discussing 'move sleekly about' as a word-choice item.) But here we are working on imagery. So, for now, let's concentrate on the image possibilities.

After checking out our grid of visual and aural imagery, we see one obvious image: a simile:

'like a school of fish in a fast-flowing stream'

What picture springs to mind here? Write down any words what you associate with this image: 'darting about' – 'moving together'– 'moving at speed' – 'in perfect formation' – 'not bumping into each other'. Tidying up your thoughts, we might get:

> '... like a school of fish in a fast-flowing stream': the simile suggests/makes me think the chefs darted about/moved swiftly as a team, not bumping into each other at all. 2

OR

> '... like a school of fish in a fast-flowing stream': just as a school of fish darts about swiftly in perfect formation without bumping into each other, so, too, did the team of chefs move about in this simile. It suggested to me/made me think the chefs, like the fish, acted in swift unison/as if under some unseen control. 2

(With a full comment on the word choice of 'move sleekly', you would have your 4 marks.)

So, analysing imagery of whatever kind requires three steps:

1. **Locate** a device/image which you need to quote: for example, 'like a school of fish in a fast-flowing stream'.
2. **Identify** the device/image in question: simile, metaphor, alliteration, etc.
3. **Explain** what the effect of this device/image has on readers: For example, how does alliteration of a certain letter affect readers? Or, what does comparing a team of cooks with a school of fish have on readers? **'Just as** (a school of fish) ... **so, too,** (did the team of chefs) ...' is a handy formula for shaping up your comparison between the two items.

Homework helper

Try some practice questions on imagery. By now, you are skilful enough to answer questions which ask you about 'language', in terms of word choice and sentence structure, but let's practise answering these with reference to imagery.

1. *In the kitchen, lines of herbs hang in handfuls from the homely ceiling like Christmas decorations, while old glass jars containing curious, exotic ingredients sit neatly on high shelves. Outside, the sun-drizzled courtyard is heavy with lavender and, once my work in the kitchen is done, I can practise my French by the heated pool and enjoy the stunning views down the hillside. There's a deep sense of peace and tranquillity here; as if summer itself has somehow been captured in a glass jar, and the lid firmly sealed.*

Adapted from 'A Cookery Class at Alain Ducasse's House in Provence', the *Guardian*, 17th May 2013

a) With reference to two examples of the writer's language, show fully how he makes clear the 'peace and tranquillity' both indoors and out. 2

2. Jonathan Thompson takes off on a cycling holiday in the Outer Hebrides but runs into difficulties finding a taxi to get him from the airport to his hotel:

'Don't worry,' says the lady who makes the tea in the arrivals/departures/baggage lounge. 'The Post Office van will take you.' Half an hour later, I'm helping the local post lady, Morag, with her round – bouncing alongside her in the battered red van like a cross between Marty McFly and Jess the Cat. As we drive across the loch-dotted landscape, locals get into and out of the back of the van like human parcels, delivering themselves en route. They chat to each other in their first language, Gaelic, with a few English words – 'carpet'... 'loony'... '90-odd quid' – popping up within the lilting language like remote Atlantic islands.

Adapted from 'Cycling Scotland's new Hebridean Trail', *The Guardian*, 31st August 2012

a) Show fully how an example of the writer's imagery suggests he does not take his situation too seriously. 2

b) With reference to an example of the writer's imagery, show fully how comfort was not very important to the passengers. 2

c) Explain how an example of the writer's imagery demonstrates the random nature of English words in their conversation. 2

3. Chloe Veltman writes about the reaction of the audience to the stage performance of the British singer, Morrissey:

The gladioli are in flight. On the stage of the Henry Fonda Theatre in Hollywood, a slender man in heavy 1950s style eye-glasses, floral shirt, white jeans and pompadour hairdo is energetically hurling a bunch of gangly blooms into the audience whilst singing something about spending warm summer days indoors writing frightening verse to a buck-toothed girl in Luxembourg. In the auditorium, tough-looking twenty-somethings in cuffed jeans, baseball boots and voluminous quiffs, sing word-perfectly along, their eyes shining as they strain to catch the somersaulting stems, blushing bridesmaids outside a country church, you might say. Gradually, the adoration turns into unabashed devotion, as people try to clamber onto the stage. Those that make it past the heavy-set bouncers cling desperately onto their pop idol like lepers begging for a miracle.

Adapted from 'The Passion of the Morrissey', *The Believer*, July–August 2012 Music Issue

a) Show fully how the writer's language suggests the 'tough-looking twenty-somethings' are not as tough as they appear. 2

b) Explain how an example of the writer's language makes clear the strength of the fans' 'unabashed devotion'. 2

TEACHING NOTES

You can download Teaching Notes for this at www.brightredpublishing.co.uk/Shop/national-5-english-course-book

Tone

Our ears are quick to detect tone in conversation. We can hear quite well when people are being, say, chatty, or humorous, or persuasive, or emotive, or ironic, or matter-of-fact. Facial expressions and body language help spell this out, but trying to pin down the tone in a written piece of text can be trickier. One writer has called tone 'the unspoken attitude of the author to his subject and/or audience.' We need to look for clues or markers in the text which help us make out what this 'unspoken attitude' might be.

Identifying tone

A word of advice here: in an exam, it's usually not enough to say that a tone you have noted is 'positive' or 'negative', 'angry' or 'sarcastic' – unless you can back this up with evidence and a comment of your own to explain why you see it as such. The examiner is looking for something quite precise. Be alert, too, to the fact that a writer may change tone several times in a passage as their attitude changes.

Below, you'll find some of the more common types of tone which you may encounter in your reading. Beside them are some of the clues or markers for determining the character of the tone in question. Being able to recognise these markers is a necessary part of your exam preparation.

DON'T FORGET

Beware of confusing 'tone' and 'mood'. Mood is how the passage makes the reader feel, a product of the language and setting selected by the writer. 'Tone' is one way of expressing what the writer feels towards his subject.

TONE	MARKERS	INTENDED EFFECT
Chatty/ informal/ colloquial	• Short sentences • Abbreviations: 'can't', 'it'll', 'won't' • Free use of 1st/2nd person pronouns: 'I', 'you' • Chatty expressions: 'Come on', 'Right on!', 'No problem.' • Free use of exclamation and question marks • Sentences without a verb (minor sentences): 'No change there then.' • Slang expressions: 'Back in a jiffy', 'A smack on the gob' • Informal commands: 'Go early.', 'Take a picnic.', 'Stay away from ...'	To get persuasively closer to the reader, giving the effect of someone chatting informally to their friends.
Humorous	• Use of exaggeration or a series of exaggerations (also called hyperbole): 'He was so thin; I've seen more fat on a chip!' • Telling jokes/stories against the speaker or topic • Mixing formal and informal **style**s: 'Please refrain from asking for credit as a smack on the gob frequently offends.' • Pairing items/people that do not normally go together: 'What were they called ... them things like cucumbers ... Suffragettes.' (Victoria Wood)	To strive for comic effect, sometimes simply to amuse, but sometimes to underline and mock the absurd/pointless nature of some issue under discussion.

Emotive	• Use of words which stir up strong emotions such as anger or pity: 'weary pensioner', 'helpless infant', 'heartless thieves', 'terrified for their lives' • Rhetorical questions: 'When, oh when will this legal harassment end?'	To arouse extreme feelings in the face of fear, suffering, injustice, loneliness or cruelty.
Ironic/ tongue-in-cheek	• Often saying the opposite of what you mean: 'The concert lasts four hours? With no interval? How lovely!'	To criticise or mock something or somebody in a humorous way to make a critical point.
Persuasive	• Using comparatives/superlatives: 'A better way of banking, the best in its class, the newest sat-nav' • Words highlighting excellence: 'quality', 'perfection', 'integrity' • Words suggesting trustworthiness: 'for generations', 'the choice of experts' • Rhetorical questions: 'What kind of parent sends a child to school hungry?'	To win over readers to the author's point of view/beliefs.
Factual/ matter-of-fact	• Usually created by a series of statements which avoid any of the above slanting of information: 'Comets are more common than is popularly imagined. Astronomers believe that as many as one trillion could exist in the farther reaches of the solar system. Best known of all is Halley's Comet.'	To impart information in a neutral, unemotional manner. Sometimes used effectively to contrast with the more colourful tones described above.

DON'T FORGET

Tone can take many forms: sad, happy, angry, regretful, nostalgic, serious, etc. But whatever tone you detect, make sure you can back up your answer with evidence from the text and a comment of your own which explains your thinking.

How does that work?

Exhausted, the twins collapsed on the flat rock that marked the cliff's summit. Lee raised a badly bruised arm to ward off the burning glare of the sun. The little that remained of their meagre rations was a real temptation to them both now. Hunger wrenched their stomachs. But, wearily, they staggered to their blistered feet. There was still a way to go.

Suppose you were faced with a passage of this kind and asked to comment on how the writer has achieved the emotive tone here. You would need to:

- pick out an item which you feel is there to work on your emotions, and
- make your own comment on how this aroused your feelings.

Here, there is quite a choice: 'Exhausted' ... 'collapsed' ... 'a badly bruised arm' ... 'burning glare' ... 'meagre rations' ... 'Hunger wrenched' ... 'wearily'... 'staggered' ... 'blistered feet'. All of these words/phrases are calculated to arouse emotions. If the question was offering two marks, usually a quoted item and a comment would secure your two marks.

You might suggest:

'a badly bruised arm': Lee is not only exhausted by the climb but has had to do it with a quite serious injury, making us feel even sorrier for him

or you might have said:

'Hunger wrenched': the twins had had an exhausting climb and had had to do it while feeling agonisingly hungry, arousing even more pity in us.

When asked to look out for a certain tone, it's essential to find a feature which exemplifies it, quote it and then comment on the feelings this quotation is meant to arouse in you. This means knowing the common markers of tone really well.

Make sure you can identify tone with some precision. Know the common tone markers. **Tip**: examiners seem fond of humorous tone ...

DON'T FORGET

Classroom challenge

For practice, try these examples. Look out for tell-tale markers that will help you identify tone.

EXAMPLE	MARKERS	TONE
a) I wouldn't say John was mean but the last time he opened his wallet, moths flew out.		
b) Rents continue to rise, the national average being £790 per month and £1240 per month in London.		
c) Her future in politics began well: she came bottom of the poll.		
d) There's this bloke, see. He's like, 'I wanna travel, I wanna see the world.' Travel? Him! Him!		
e) Will this war-torn country ever find peace?		

You can download Teaching Notes for this at www.brightredpublishing.co.uk/Shop/national-5-english-course-book

TEACHING NOTES

EVALUATION

What's coming up?

- What is evaluation?
- What you might be expected to evaluate
- How to approach questions testing evaluation
- Practice with questions testing evaluation skills

INTRODUCING EVALUATION

What is evaluation?

The word itself might sound a bit off-putting, but it's something we do all the time. We see a trailer for a film, we hear a track from a new album – and we make a decision about whether to see the film or to buy the album. There were certain clues to content which we've understood, certain features of style which we've analysed, almost without noticing that we've done so. As a result, we come up with our evaluation.

The skills that we use to decide whether to see a film, or buy an album, are rather like those you need for tackling evaluation questions in your exam. There's a similar element of understanding and analysis involved. However, an evaluation question asks you to go a step further: you need to add an opinion of your own. And, as you did with the film trailer or album track, you're free to assess favourably or not. Provided, of course, you have the textual evidence to back up your case.

What you might be expected to evaluate

In two words: almost anything! You might be expected to say how 'successful', 'appropriate' or 'effective' you find:

- an opening or a concluding paragraph to the passage,
- a figure of speech (metaphor, simile, hyperbole, etc.),
- an item of word choice,
- an aspect of sentence structure (list, minor sentence, etc.), or
- any other interesting aspect of style which the passage suggests.

DON'T FORGET

The knowledge you have built up to answer analysis questions helps you answer evaluation questions. But you need to add your own comment.

The good news is that the knowledge you have built up to answer analysis questions will come in useful once again. If you know the features of style for answering analysis questions, you're well-placed to answer evaluation questions. But this time, you have to give something of yourself as well – your personal evaluation of how successful or effective you find the feature in focus.

DON'T FORGET

Be sure you know the meaning of 'effective' and 'appropriate'. They are words which often signal evaluation. 'Effective' = successful in producing a desired result. 'Appropriate' = suitable in the circumstances.

HOW TO APPROACH QUESTIONS TESTING EVALUATION

An opening paragraph

Introductions are constructed not only to catch your attention but to keep it for the rest of the article. Look out for a variety of means which you might call 'effective' or 'appropriate' in creating the 'read on' factor:

- A question to 'hook' your interest. A question also may be an appropriate lead-in to the article which answers that question.
- An example or **anecdote** to illustrate graphically (and connect to) the content of the article as a whole.
- Short/minor/one-word sentences. They add dramatic impact to the opening statements.
- Chatty/colloquial tone. Journalists like to get close to their readers, so you may notice them using the pronouns 'you' and/or 'we' quite a lot.
- Humorous tone. When an article tackles even a serious topic, the writer may employ elements of humour to invite us into that topic.

A concluding paragraph

Here, too, article-writers work hard. Their intention is to leave you with their various ideas planted firmly in your mind. Look out for:

- A re-visiting of the major points of the article. In a lengthy article, it's easy to forget what was said earlier. Making main points again in the conclusion reinforces them in the reader's mind.
- A connection with or a reference back to a statement, phrase, image or story used in the introduction. Writers often prize giving a satisfying cyclical feel to rounding off the article.
- A short/minor/one-word sentence as the final line. These lend a touch of drama to the conclusion and are intended punch home the writer's message.

Aspects of style

You may be invited to give your opinion on items selected by the examiner, saying how 'effective', 'successful' or 'appropriate' they are in conveying the writer's sense of wonder, delight, surprise, irritation, amusement or some such response. You may be asked to consider word choice, tone, sentence structure, images, etc. In short, all the items you have studied to answer analysis questions.

Or you may be invited to select your own items to say how 'effective', 'successful' or 'appropriate' these items are in their context, for example, a concluding paragraph or a passage describing a beautiful scene. You may end up discussing something you have used to answer an analysis question earlier. However, the essential thing now is to make sure you give your own opinion of this feature. In your opinion, IS it 'effective', 'successful' or 'appropriate'? You'll have to say, once you've discussed your evidence.

How does that work?

Here is the opening paragraph of an article which goes on to explore the side of Edinburgh which not all tourists see – lesser-known Edinburgh. Read the paragraph. How would you go about answering the question which follows? If you're not sure, check out the advice in this section on evaluating an opening paragraph.

Close Encounters of the 17th-Century Kind

'Edinburgh? Yes, been there, know it well.' But do you? Do you really? Yes, admittedly, it's a city which offers up many obvious goodies to first-time visitors: the Castle, the Royal Mile, Holyrood House and the International and Fringe Festivals. But take a few minutes off your stroll down the Royal Mile. Slip down an alleyway (or 'close' as we call them in Edinburgh) to time travel into the city's 17th-century past.

Explain fully why this paragraph is an effective opening to an article about lesser-known Edinburgh. 2

So, what could we say? There are two marks on offer, suggesting you need to point to an item of evidence and make a comment on it. You have quite a choice. You could choose items of evidence from the following:

- Three questions 'hook' the reader's attention: 'Edinburgh?', 'But do you?', 'Do you really?'
- Short sentences: 'But do you?', 'Do you really?' add impact to writer's chat with reader.
- One-word sentence: 'Edinburgh?' is a dramatic opening to the paragraph.
- Use of 'you' and 'we' set up a chatty tone and connection with the reader.
- Use of 'been there, know it well' and 'obvious goodies' continue the light-hearted, informal tone to make the subject matter approachable to readers.
- Chatty commands of the kind you find in informal tone – 'But take a few minutes' and 'Slip down' – are, again, there to get close to the reader.

It's essential to point to a piece of evidence from the text, then say what it is doing. Now give your opinion on it. Does this informal chatty style work for you? Would you want to read on? In other words, how 'effective' has this opening paragraph been for coaxing you into the article?

Classroom challenge

Here's the concluding paragraph to the same article about lesser-known Edinburgh. Have a go at answering how it might be a fitting conclusion to the article which the introduction hinted at.

So, as you go about your business in downtown Tokyo or uptown New York, spare a thought for the discoveries you made unexpectedly down those Royal Mile closes. Remember the peace and quiet of that 17th-century topiary garden at Dunbar's Close, or the graceful turreted mansion you found tucked away in Lady Stair's Close. Step back into the Tardis. Dr Who won't mind.

Explain fully how this final paragraph would make an appropriate conclusion to the article. 3

Tip: read the introduction again before you start.

TEACHING NOTES

You can download Teaching Notes for this challenge at www.brightredpublishing.co.uk/Shop/national-5-english-course-book

DON'T FORGET

If you should wish to make a negative evaluative comment on some point, you are at liberty to do so. But make sure you have convincing evidence from the text and a soundly argued case.

Homework helper

The writer here describes a hidden, highland loch. Read the passage and answer the question which follows.

The Loch of the Eagle was not large. It lay among the encircling hills like a fairy pool come upon in dreams; yet it had not the desolate quality of the high mountain tarns, whose black waters lie shoreless at the foot of precipices. At one end was a multitude of silver-stemmed birches, of whom some loved the loch (or their own reflection) so dearly they leaned over it until the veil of their hair almost brushed its surface; and with these court ladies stood a guard of very old pines, severe and beautiful, and here and there was the feathered bravery of a rowan tree.

Adapted from D.K. Broster, *The Flight of the Heron*, Heinemann, London, 1947

In the passage, the writer is keen to convey the beauty of the scene. Explain with reference to her language how successful you think she has been in achieving this. 3

TEACHING NOTES

You can download Teaching Notes for this challenge at www.brightredpublishing.co.uk/Shop/national-5-english-course-book

EXAM-STYLE TESTS

We have spent some time explaining the challenges of questions testing understanding, analysis and evaluation. We've also practised the skills required in some preliminary exercises. Now, it's time to practise these skills with some test questions of the kind you will be expected to meet in the exam itself.

If you're in any doubt about how to answer, look back over this chapter. Good luck!

TEST 1: TAX THE FAT

Read the passage below and then attempt questions 1 to 8.

In this passage, food writer Giles Coren puts forward the case for making people who are overweight pay more tax.

Tax the Fat

How many fat people have you seen today? Did the milkman waddle down your garden path on legs like giant kebabs? Did the chap in the newsagent where you bought this paper sweat as he put your money in the till with his pudgy hand?

Is your husband, even now, forking another sausage into his puddingy face? Perhaps you yourself are — how can I put this politely? — 'fuller-figured'. In which case, you may want to stop reading now. As for the rest of you, stop looking so smug.

Extra transport costs incurred as a result of our increasing weight ran to £250 million because the fatter we grow, the fewer people can fit on any given bus or train. (By 2020, when a third of Britons will be clinically obese, 2,500 extra buses will have to be built, at a cost of £100,000 per bus, to cart our bulkier frames around.)

There are 900 people in Britain so fat that they can do, almost literally, nothing at all. These super-whoppers cost the country £8million just on their own. And where does this money — almost £4billion — come from? From the taxes paid by thin, healthy people like me. People with a bit of self-control. People who are able to say 'no thanks, I'm full' when offered second helpings of pud. People who have the basic self-discipline required to walk past a High Street pie shop a couple of hours after lunch without nipping in for a couple of steak and kidneys and a gallon of fizzy pop.

I should stress at this point that there is a tiny percentage of people with genuine metabolic problems that cause them to pile on the pounds. They, of course, deserve sympathy rather than contempt.

But the vast majority of chubbies in Britain are big because they lack the willpower or incentive to maintain a healthier lifestyle. We're paying for their self-indulgence. And I'm sorry, but I just don't think it's fair. Smokers are expected to pay vast amounts in tax to fund their habit. Boozers are taxed in the same way; gamblers, too.

And I think it's high time the obese were made to stump up as well. The time has come to tax the fat. It may sound harsh. It may sound a bit 'nanny state'. It may even, in its apparently cavalier attitude to human rights, strike you as mildly fascistic.

We could follow along the path of cigarettes and alcohol and simply add tax to items of food that are particularly unhealthy. But I don't want to pay more for a bag of chips just because two-thirds of our population are unable to regulate their own consumption of them. The only way is to tax the fat directly, tailoring each individual's tax bill to reflect their girth, which is to say, their fat burden on the rest of us.

Not only would it raise the money we need to offset the economic burden of the fat (while lowering tax bills for the rest of us), it would also, as in the case of taxes on cigarettes and alcohol, act as a deterrent. Some people — all of them fat — told me during the course of filming that this was an infringement of their human rights. But so is insisting that people drive within the speed limit and avoid dropping litter.

Fat people tell me that I am prejudiced and that the overweight are a 'minority group' as deserving of respect as any other. I beg to differ. Being fat is a choice. A choice to consume dwindling resources, to use more energy, to take up more space.

If you can afford to do that, fine. You're free, in our society, to be antisocial, out of breath and physically unprepossessing if you can pay for the pleasure yourself. But if you can't afford it, I'm sure as hell not paying.

And, believe me, it is a choice. The fat people I interviewed for the film were always telling me they couldn't change their size. A moment's research soon proved this was tosh.

People said: 'I'm not fat, I'm just big-boned.' Nonsense. Have you ever seen a fat skeleton?

They said: 'I've got a slow metabolism.' Piffle. Fat people, if anything, have higher metabolisms than the rest of us because of the amount of effort it takes to haul their bulk around.

They told me: 'It's genetic.' Poppycock. What fat children inherit from fat parents is bad eating habits, not fat bellies.

They said: 'Obesity is a disease of the poor. The lower social registers cannot afford to eat healthily.'

How patronising. In making the show, I debunked this myth by taking £20 (the bottom end of what a person on the minimum wage or standard benefits spends on food in a week) and buying more than enough healthy food to last seven days.

I bought pounds of fresh vegetables (carrots, cabbage, beans), two pounds of organic beef, two salmon steaks, four pounds of whole-wheat pasta, two pounds of porridge, two pints of semi-skimmed organic milk, bags of pulses, four tins of tomatoes, two sacks of oranges and a sack of apples. And where do you think I bought all this? An open-air market in the East End? A discount warehouse in Glasgow? No, Sainsbury's in Islington. And I've got the receipt to prove it.

All you have to do is a little cooking. We did it for 10,000 years, so why stop now? Why do people instead prefer to spend £20 on two giant takeaway pizzas and a lethal torpedo of fizzy pop?

Britain is dying of fat. And while tax may be a bitter pill for tubbies to swallow (nothing like as yummy as an extra helping of treacle pud) I believe it's the only cure that will work.

Adapted from Giles Coren, writing in The Times

Total Marks – 30

Attempt ALL questions

1. Look at paragraph 1 (lines 1–6). Explain fully why this paragraph is an effective introduction to the article. 4

2. Look at lines 19–24. How does the writer use sentence structure to emphasise his feelings about people who are overweight? 2

3. Look at paragraph 7 (lines 32– 34). Explain what is meant by 'mildly fascistic' and why this phrase is surprising. 3

4. Look at lines 35–39. Explain how the writer uses imagery to make his point about tax. 3

5. Look at lines 40–47. The writer explains his justifications for taxing overweight people, as well as some objections to his proposal.

a) Using your own words as far as possible, what are the two benefits described of taxing fat directly outlined in lines 40–42? 2

b) Explain the objections to this idea **and** the reasons Coren disagrees with these objections. Answer using your own words. 4

6. Look at lines 51–63. How does the writer use language to dismiss the excuses people gave him for being overweight? 6

7. Look at lines 64–69. How does the writer use language to emphasise how much healthy food he was able to buy? 4

8. Look at the paragraph beginning on line 73. Explain fully why this paragraph is an effective conclusion to the article. 2

You can download Teaching Notes for this Topic Test at www.brightredpublishing.co.uk/Shop/national-5-english-course-book

TEACHING NOTES

TEST 2: TRAINS

Read the passage below and then attempt questions 1 to 8.

In this passage, comedian Nish Kumar laments the state of Britain's rail network.

Schoolmates used to ask me about Indian trains. I can now confirm British ones are worse.

Last week Southern Rail staff went on strike, leaving thousands of commuters facing a slightly improved service. Southern's non-stop calamities this summer have added support to the idea of renationalisation. This debate is something I watched with great interest. I'm a stand-up comedian who can't drive. I have never learned. I don't trust my hand-eye coordination. You're looking at someone who once dropped a cricket ball on to his own head during a routine catching practice; I don't think it's a great idea to have me in control of a high-speed metal death robot.

So I rely on the train system in this country. And I can tell you from firsthand experience that our train system is a mess. Carriages are full of unhappy travellers packed together like sardines, who have inexplicably paid for the privilege of being incarcerated. Periodically, everyone has to flee for cover, either by lying across the laps of the passengers lucky enough to have a seat, or by climbing into the luggage racks on the ceiling to allow the optimistically named 'buffet' cart to pass through just in case anyone wants to spend £50 on a packet of crisps or a single fruit pastille.

And it's not cheap, either. Train fares have increased way out [of] step with inflation, meaning the percentage of our salaries we spend on train fares is now six times higher than many of our European counterparts – and that's if you plan ahead. If you want to travel from London to Manchester, and have not booked a ticket, be prepared to sell a kidney or stay at home. Frequent train travellers have to plan ahead, booking months in advance to avoid massive fares. But there is still the risk that you will turn up on the day and the train will have lost its seat reservations for no apparent reason, and you will end up wedged between the door and the bathroom. Other than a music festival, a train is the only thing you might have to buy a ticket for and still end up spending an hour standing next to a toilet.

I feel sorry for the commuters affected by the Southern Rail chaos, especially because I hail from Croydon and have experienced that mayhem firsthand. As if being from Croydon wasn't bad enough. When I was growing up, and periodically going to India to visit my grandmother, my classmates would often ask me about the trains. There was an exotic fascination with people sitting on top of the carriages. Well, just to clear this up, British trains are now worse than Indian trains. Even if you're sat on the roof, at least you get a seat.

I was once ejected from a Southern train for sitting in first class when the train was full. I informed the guard that, as the section was empty and I would have happily moved for people with first-class tickets, I didn't see what the problem was. He said: 'It's far more serious than that – you have to keep that area clear in case people in wheelchairs get on.' I apologised and said: 'I didn't realise people in wheelchairs were allowed in that section'

He replied: 'Yeah – only if they have a first-class ticket. Otherwise we kick them off as well.'

It's interesting how far we have moved on in our attitude to renationalisation. In the 1980s and 1990s, we consistently elected governments that essentially based their economic policies on the boardgame Monopoly, where public services were flogged off to the highest bidder. We were in thrall to Rich Uncle Pennybags, the moustachioed, monocle-wearing mascot we now call Mr Monopoly. (This is clearly a terrible name, by the way. It's like me changing my name to Grandpa Nishy Mouthjoker.)

But there has been a change in public opinion, if not in government policy. A 2015 poll revealed nearly 60% of us support public ownership of the railways. Last year, the East Coast service was reprivatised. The government had taken over the running of the line after the collapse of the previous private ownership and, in public control, it had become profitable to the Treasury and reported positive customer satisfaction. It is now run by Virgin Trains and, on Friday morning, staff announced strike action over two weekends in August. This means that I can't get back to London from the Edinburgh Fringe. Once again, comedians are punished. Truly we are the most oppressed people in society.

Frustration with the trains is inevitable, given the daily difficulties commuters face. In France, a near fully publicly owned rail system managed to give its passengers fares far lower than the UK for almost exactly the same amount of public rail subsidy between 1996 and 2010. Furthermore, the French government has invested profits in private rail companies, which then invest in companies that run British trains. Including – surprise! – Southern. As we haemorrhage money, we are lining the pockets of Riche Oncle Sacs d'Argent.

Nationalisation might seem like the preserve of old-fashioned, duffel-coat-wearing, Red-Flag-singing socialists, but it also appears to be economically efficient.

Adapted from Nish Kumar, writing in The Guardian

Total Marks – 30

Attempt ALL questions

1. Look at paragraph 1 (lines 1–9). Explain fully why this paragraph is an effective introduction to the article. 4

2. Look at paragraph 2 (lines 10–16).

a) Explain what is meant by 'the privilege of being incarcerated' and why this phrase is surprising. 3

b) How does the writer use language to suggest the service on trains is bad? 4

3. Look at paragraphs 3 and 4 (lines 17–31). Using your own words as far as possible, what are the problems the writer identifies with the trains in Britain? 4

4. Look at paragraph 5 (lines 32–36). Explain in your own words why the writer felt he should be able to sit in First Class. 2

5. Look at paragraph 8 (lines 46–51). Using your own words as far as possible, explain the writer's point about the East Coast service. 4

6. Look at paragraph 9 (lines 52–57). How does the writer use language to suggest the French system is better? 2

7. Look at the final paragraph (lines 58–59).

a) Explain, using your own words, the writer's point about nationalising the railways. 3

b) Explain fully how the writer's use of language makes this paragraph an effective conclusion to the article 4

You can download Teaching Notes for this Topic Test at
www.brightredpublishing.co.uk/Shop/national-5-english-course-book

TEACHING NOTES

OVERVIEW

WHAT'S INVOLVED?

Encouragingly, the skills you are acquiring for your RUAE work will serve you well again in the 'Critical Reading' paper. Here again, your final score will be determined by:

- how well you **understand** what is going on in the text,
- how well you **understand** what the question is asking you to do,
- your ability to **analyse** how the author creates their effects, and
- your ability to **evaluate** the significance of the evidence presented.

Whether you are writing a critical essay on a class text, or answering questions on a Scottish set-text, these are skills which you will draw on time and time again.

However, successful critical reading depends on one further important element. You need to be alert to the fact that the different **genre**s which you are studying all have very different features. Drama, poetry, novels and short stories all have their own characteristics. Writing about or answering questions on these genres requires you to know what these differences are and how to respond to them appropriately in your essays and answers.

To help you do this successfully, let's take a look at some key points to help you identify the various genres.

What's coming up?

- What to look out for in drama
- What to look out for in novels and short stories
- What to look out for in poetry
- Identifying features in your own study texts
- Familiarising activities for literary techniques

STUDYING DRAMA

What to look out for

In studying drama, we need to be alert to the fact that, unlike a novel, short story or poem, a play is much more than words on a page. Since it is meant to be acted out on a stage, we have to take into consideration all the resources writers have at their disposal to bring the narrative alive for the audience.

The primary resource is, of course, dialogue between the characters. But, in addition to this, we must remember the contribution of stage presentation, stage directions, costume, lighting, props, music and sound effects: all are vital to communicating a

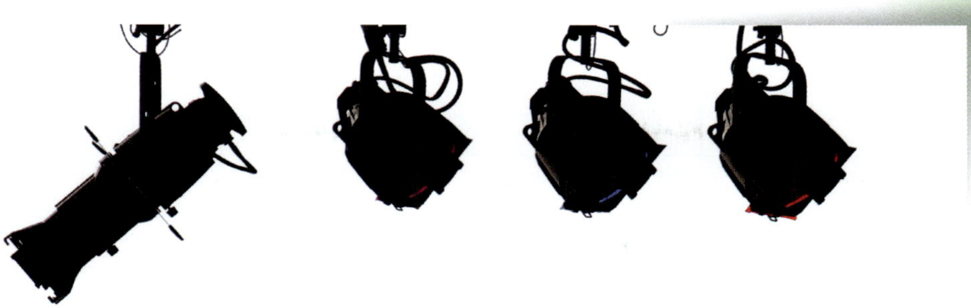

rounded experience to the audience. In short, when writing about or commenting on drama, don't limit your evidence simply to the text. The choice available to you is much greater than that.

Character presentation

THE CAST	THEIR PERSONALITY	HOW IS THIS REVEALED?
Personal characteristics	What are the character's strengths?	• Dialogue with others • Speech characteristics • Soliloquies • Asides • Actions in key scenes • Costume • Stage directions
	What are the character's weaknesses?	
	How does the character view the world?	
	What motivates the character?	
Relationship to others	With whom is the character close?	• Dialogue • Speech characteristics • Soliloquies • Asides • Actions in key scenes • Costume • Stage directions
	With whom is the character in conflict?	
Development throughout the play	Does the character change over the course of the action?	Resulting from: • own actions • actions by others • fate

Staging

	SETTING	HOW IS THIS CONVEYED?
In the text	Where does the action take place?	• Stage directions
	In what period does it happen?	• Language/period references
	Over what time scale does the action take place?	• Time references
On the stage	What are the characters' social/financial situations?	• Stage décor • Stage props • Costumes • Music/sound effects • Lighting
	Do the characters' fortunes change?	

Structure

Exposition: setting the scene	This introduces us to the characters, their social situation and their relationships with each other.
Development: when things start to change	This usually happens when a new character arrives or something happens to change the existing situation.
Climax: as a result of growing tension	The development section is usually marked by emerging tensions between the characters, often caused by the arrival of the new character or changed circumstances. A crisis or confrontation will often painfully sweep away previously held views of people or situations.
Resolution: a changed perspective	As a result of the crisis or confrontation, a new, clearer view of reality emerges. Previous misunderstandings or misconceptions are replaced, however painfully, by much more realistic appreciations of characters and relationships.
Key scenes: furthering understanding	These may happen at any point in the play. It is often in key scenes that we see the above situations being made clearer for the audience and the play's characters. It is in key scenes, too, that themes may clarify themselves and develop significantly.

Themes

	POSSIBLE MATERIAL FOR THEMES	HOW IS THIS REVEALED?
A **theme** is what the play is **about**. A plot is how this theme (or themes) is gradually revealed. A play may have several themes and sub-themes as the plot unrolls.	Personal relationships involving love/revenge/ambition/jealousy/etc.	• Dialogue • Soliloquies • Pairings • Confrontations • Key scenes
	Political engagement: what is being said about the outside world of great events as it affects the circle of the play's characters?	• Dialogue • Historical references • Reactions to historical events • Results of historical events
	Social theme: what is being said about the way people interact in, or react to, society around them?	• Dialogue • References to social conditions • Effects on human behaviour

DON'T FORGET

When writing about or commenting on a play, don't overlook the evidence that comes from stage directions, lighting, costumes, etc. A change of costume can say a great deal about a character's changing fortunes; and two characters at opposite ends of a family kitchen can say much about a failing relationship. Facts like this can sometimes be easier to memorise than a long quotation. And just as effective as evidence!

Classroom challenge

1. Once you've completed reading your play's first few scenes, you're well placed to start an evidence file on key characters.

- Choose a character to whom you've been introduced. (Think about selecting a different character from your neighbour.)
- Start to answer the questions in the second column of the 'Character presentation' grid by finding evidence of the kind described in the third column.
- Take care to note down page references for the evidence you are presenting. You'll find evidence in more than one place.
- Now make your own comments on your character based on the evidence you have collected. Keep them on file to be added to later.

2. Read the section on 'Staging' again, then consider the opening scene of the play you are reading.
   - Start to answer the questions in column two by thinking about the suggestions made in column three.
   - Note down page references for the evidence you find. Often, you'll discover evidence in more than one place.
   - Prepare your own personal comments on what this setting makes you feel about the characters' situation. You may want to repeat this exercise should the setting change at some point.
3. Use the evidence you've collected on different characters and the play's setting to discuss, as a group or class, what you now know and feel about your characters and their circumstances. Make notes as others talk to help with revision nearer the exam. You may wish to repeat this process once you've read further on in the play.

Homework helper

When you've read two or three scenes of your play, read the section on 'Themes' again. By using possible clues from column three, make notes on what you see as the play's theme or themes. Remember, the suggestions in column two are just some of many possibilities. Maybe your play has another, quite different theme? Maybe it has several?

Again, find evidence and page numbers to back up what you think your play is 'about'. Use your notes as the basis for a class discussion.

STUDYING PROSE

What to look out for

In writing novels or short stories, writers all share one major aim: to create an experience for readers which mirrors exactly what the writer felt as they imagined the story. Their aim is the creation of a wholly convincing world in which readers lose themselves entirely until the very last page.

Unlike writers for the stage or film, writers of novels or short stories cannot call on lights, music, stage décor or special effects to create this all-absorbing experience. Words are their only tool, so imagery, word choice and sentence structure become vitally important in creating this world.

Great care must be taken to ensure that characters and settings are created in such a way that they come truly alive for the reader. We need to feel that we're there with the characters, and that we truly know these characters, as well as we know our friends and family. Being able to do this successfully is just as important as devising a clever plot.

As we read, we'll also become aware that the writer – through the characters, setting and plot – is saying something about the world they, and perhaps we, inhabit. In other words, we'll discover that there's also a theme (or themes) holding the narrative together.

Let's look in some detail at what writers can do with characters, setting, plot and themes.

Character presentation in novels and short stories

Characters	Role	• Are they the narrator? • Are they the hero/heroine? • Are they the villain? • If neither narrator/hero/villain, why are they present in story? • What is their initial impact on the reader? • What creates this impact? Behaviour to others/treatment by others/author's description? • Does our view of them change?
	Personality	• What are their strengths? • What are their weaknesses? • Do they change throughout the action? • Age? • Appearance?
	Relationships	• Who are their friends? • Do they *have* friends? • Are they contrasted with anyone else? • What contrasts do you observe? • Are they in conflict with anyone? If so, who and why?
	Behaviour in key incidents	• How do their actions here reveal character? • What are their private thoughts here? • How do their actions affect others? • Are we told anecdotes about past behaviour?

Setting

Setting	Physical	• When do the events happen? • Over what time scale? • Is landscape/townscape important to the narrative? • How do word choice, imagery and sentence structure contribute to the setting's description? • What changes of scene are there? • Are weather conditions important? • Does changing weather affect the morale of the character(s)? • Are there recurring references, for example, to heat, cold, water, colour, etc.? • Why might the writer have used these?
	Society	• What level of society does the character find themselves in? Rich? Poor? Does this change? • What kind of society surrounds the character? Settled? Conflicted? • Do they fit in? • Do they encounter other types of society? • How do they react to them?

Plot

Plot	Organisation	• Does the narrative unfold chronologically? • Does the narrative employ flashbacks? • Is there a cyclical movement? That is, does the narrative end where it started? • Are all loose ends tied up?
	Narrative style	• From whose viewpoint is the story told? The author? A character? • Is there more than one narrator? • How formal or informal is the narrator's tone? • Are there important action-provoking key scenes? • Why are they important? What do we learn from them? What are the consequences for the characters – and the plot?

Presentation of theme(s)

Theme	Social/historical	• What is being suggested about the society (or societies) described? Greedy, narrow-minded, prejudiced, etc.? • What evidence have you for saying this? • How does this evidence emerge? Key incidents/events? Conversations? Conflicts?
	Personal/moral	• Are there personality characteristics that people may share in their dealings with others? What might these be? Generous, tolerant, repressed, etc.? • What evidence do you have for saying this? How does this evidence emerge? Key incidents/events? Conversations? Conflicts?

Classroom challenge

Once you've read a few chapters of your novel, or several of your short stories, divide the class into four groups. One group (probably the largest) should look at key characters; one should look at setting; one should look at plot; and a fourth group should look at theme(s).

Set each group the task of examining the third column of our grids on prose fiction and trying to answer the questions which they pose about the short story or novel you're reading. Point to specific incidents/conversations/descriptions to support your answers (with page references).

Get a spokesperson to report back to the group on their findings. Take notes to add to your revision file.

DON'T FORGET

Make a decision early on in your novel, or selection of short stories, about how you're going to organise your revision file. Will it be by chapter/story? Or by character? Will you have a separate section for themes with page references for evidence? It's a good idea to make a decision on all this before you get too far into the text.

STUDYING POETRY

What to look out for

Of all the genres you'll study for National 5, poetry is perhaps the most difficult to define. A dictionary might tell you that a poem is a 'literary work in which the expression of feelings and ideas is given intensity by the use of distinctive style and rhythm.' But this doesn't get us very far.

What is certain, however, is that it's the most economical of genres. A moment, an idea, a feeling is brought to life in just a few lines. There's no room for vaguely selected words. Each single word will be present either for its specific sound or associations; each combination of words forming metaphors, similes, alliteration, onomatopoeia, etc. is there to appeal not only to our intellects but also to our emotions and senses – sometimes touch, smell, taste and hearing as well as sight. The chosen rhythm will also add to the effect the poet is targeting.

It's a good idea to ask yourself three questions about any poem that you encounter:

- What is the poem about?
- What effect does it have on me?
- How has the poet created these effects?

The first question requires you to think about the theme of the poem – the challenges of love, the pain of regret, the pity of war or whatever you find it to be saying. The second question requires you to think about your personal reaction to the poem – amused, moved, surprised, or perhaps provoked into thinking about something familiar in a new way. Your response to the first two questions will depend to a great extent on your answer to the third question – how did the devices and techniques of poetic language, rhythm and rhyme create a convincing experience for you?

So, what are some of the forms, devices and techniques which you need to be on the lookout for?

Form or structure

	CHARACTERISTICS/EFFECT	EXAMPLE
Is it written in a set poetic form? (Ballad, sonnet, ode, etc.)	A recognised poetic form with a pre-determined shape and regular rhyme scheme creates a tight framework for the poet's ideas and the reader's expectations. Often, the verses or **stanza**s within the framework will each deal with a specific aspect of the topic. Formality of this kind gives a reassuring sense of organisation to the topic.	*The king sits in Dunfermline town,* *Drinking the blude-red wine;* *'O whare will I get a skeely skipper,* *To sail this new ship of mine?'* *O up and spake an eldern knight,* *Sat at the king's right knee, –* *'Sir Patrick Spens is the best sailor,* *That ever sailed the sea.'* 'Sir Patrick Spens', Sir Walter Scott

Is it written in free verse?	Here, poets dispense with fixed patterns of rhythms and rhymes. Instead, to make their ideas memorable, they employ many poetic techniques such as alliteration, assonance, imagery, repetition, personification. Often, they use enjambment to capture the rhythms of everyday speech.	*Through the ample open door of the peaceful country barn,* *A sun-lit pasture field, with cattle and horses feeding;* *And haze, and vista, and the far horizon, fading away.* 'A Farm Picture', Walt Whitman

Techniques and devices

Here are some of the more common members of the figurative language family we've already looked at on page 33. These form the lifeblood of poetic language, so they're well worth looking at again. They fall broadly into two categories: those which conjure up visual pictures, and those which create pictures in sound – aural pictures, so to speak.

VISUAL IMAGERY	SOUND TECHNIQUES
Simile: a comparison between two items using 'like' or 'as' – 'My love is like a red, red rose.' The effect of similes and metaphors is to add pictorial emphasis/impact to the written description.	**Alliteration:** the repetition of a particular consonant – or consonant sound – at the beginning of a group of words to create a certain sound effect. 'Cold clay clads his coffin.' Here the harsh sound of the letter 'c' matches the grimness of the description. 'Soft sighing of the southern seas.' Here the soft 's' mimics the gentleness of the water's sound.
Metaphor: also a comparison but this time the two items being compared are not 'like' each other since one item becomes the other – 'The eyes are the window to the soul.'	**Assonance:** the repetition of a certain group of similar-sounding vowels in words close to each other, again used to create a certain aural effect – 'And murmuring of innumerable bees ...'
Personification: yet another way of making a comparison. Similes and metaphors can become examples of personification when an inanimate (without life) object is spoken of as if it were human and alive – 'In the June heat, the peonies collapsed like exhausted ballerinas.'	**Onomatopoeia:** here the sound of the word mimics its meaning. 'Clink', 'fizz', 'rip', 'honk', 'boom', 'purr' suggest their meaning in their sound.
Hyperbole: an exaggerated image to create a certain effect (sometimes humorous) or to emphasise a point or intensify an emotion. *I'll love you, dear, I'll love you* *Till China and Africa meet.* 'As I walked out one evening', WH Auden	**Enjambment:** in poetry this is the running on of one line into another or into several others, often to give either a conversational feel to the content or sometimes to suggest a speeding up for an effect of urgency. It can also make the reader wait for a key point to be made when the sentence finally stops. *...for my purpose holds* *To sail beyond the sunset, and the baths* *Of all the western stars, until I die.* 'Ulysses', Lord Tennyson

It's not enough to know the names of the various literary devices and to be able to spot them at work. You must always be able to make a comment on how these devices **affected** you as a reader.

DON'T FORGET

Rhythm and rhyme

The techniques and devices described in the previous section help create powerful sound effects. In poetry, sound is often as important as the meaning of the words in conveying the poet's intentions. If devices such as alliteration, assonance and onomatopoeia create what we might call the 'melody' of a poem, **rhythm** and **rhyme** help create the poem's underlying 'beat'.

HOW CAN RHYTHM HELP ME UNDERSTAND A POEM?

1. Look for the stress pattern

A stress pattern in a line of poetry is a series of recurring stressed or unstressed syllables. It can often help you understand the mood of a poem:

I ***leant*** *upon a* ***copp****ice* ***gate***
When ***Frost*** *was* ***spec****tre* ***grey***
And ***Win****ter's* ***dregs*** *made* ***des****olate*
The ***weak****ening* ***eye*** *of* ***day.***

'The Darkling Thrush', Thomas Hardy

The first syllable of the line is unstressed, the second stressed, which makes for a steady, movement forward. This deliberate pace suits and creates a thoughtful, reflective mood.

But here is a very different stress pattern and pace:

Fast*er than* ***fair****ies,* ***fast****er than* ***wit****ches,*
Bridg*es and* ***hous****es,* ***hedg****es and* ***dit****ches;*

'From a Railway Carriage', R.L. Stevenson

This pattern of stressed and unstressed syllables, when said aloud, creates the fast rhythm of excited forward movement, very different indeed from the preceding reflective pattern.

2. Say the lines aloud

Saying the words aloud helps you identify the pulse and pace of the lines. These, in turn, give you a strong 'feel' for what the poem might be about.

Does the rhythm suggest a lively, sad, angry, or contented mood? For poets, rhythm is a basic tool for creating a multitude of moods and atmospheres.

3. Look out for disturbances in the pattern

Sometimes, poets deliberately break the patterns they have set up to draw attention to a change of mood or atmosphere. This first verse below tells how a soldier in war follows orders and fires at the enemy. It follows a regular stress pattern:

But ranged as infantry,
And staring face to face,
I shot at him as he at me,
And killed him in his place.

The next verse, however, has a broken, halting stress pattern, suggesting the soldier's growing doubt about his orders:

I shot him dead because —
Because he was my foe,
Just so: my foe of course he was;
That's clear enough; although [...]

'The man he killed', Thomas Hardy

HOW CAN RHYME GUIDE MY RESPONSE TO A POEM?

Rhyme is when a poet deliberately repeats the end-sound of certain lines to match the sound of other lines in a verse. We usually call this pattern a rhyme scheme. We identify it giving the end-words the same letter:

There lived a wife at Usher's Well, — *a*
And a wealthy wife was she. — *b*
She had three stout and stalwart sons, — *c*
And sent them oe'r the sea. — *b*

They hadna been a week from her, — *d*
A week but barely ane, — *f*
Whan word cam tae the carlin wife — *g*
That her three sons were gane. — *f*

'The Wife of Usher's Well', Anon. Ballad

Even the very youngest children seem to derive pleasure from the sound of rhymes, as the lasting popularity of nursery rhymes suggests.

1. Listen for the music

One critic has suggested that 'Rhythm is the pulse of poetry, and rhyme is its echo.' Once you have detected the mood of the rhythm, you may find that the sound of the rhyme intensifies that mood. As such, rhyme supports rhythm to make a poem a musical, as well as an emotional, experience.

2. Look at the actual rhymes

Quite often, the **sense** of the words that perform the rhyme add much to the atmosphere of the verse. For instance, in the first poem in the first column: *grey* rhymes with *day; gate* with *desolate,* most of which emphasise a grim bleakness of mood.

3. Check for focus

Sometimes rhyme can concentrate the focus on a particular point to great effect. Here unattractive actions are associated with the least attractive plants in a garden.

For sweetest things turn sourest by their deeds;
Lilies that fester smell far worse than weeds.

'Sonnet XCIV', William Shakespeare

4. Be aware of half rhyme

Sometimes poets like the framework of a rhyme scheme but they don't want the rhymes to dominate too much. They 'tone down' the rhyme by using half rhyme at line ends to make the ends of lines less noticeable.

A half rhyme is a rhyme in which the rhyming words are close but not identical to each other. At times, poets will also use enjambment to add a conversational tone to these lines which are not 'end-stopped' by full rhyme.

When have I last looked ***on***

The round green eyes and the long wavering ***bodies***

Of the dark leopards of the ***moon?***

All the wild witches, those most noble ***ladies...***

'Lines Written in Dejection', W. B. Yeats

ONLINE

Want to increase your confidence when discussing poetry? Type 'The Close Reading of Poetry uvic.ca' into your browser for a very readable and informative account that will help you further explore the technical side of poetry.

Classroom challenge

The more precise you can be in spotting and naming figurative language at work, the greater your confidence will be in answering questions on poetry come exam time.

Let's check your technical knowledge.

Here are the definitions of some key poetic terms. Match the examples on the next page with their definition. To make life more interesting, be alert to the fact that several examples could apply to more than one term!

TERM	DEFINITION	EFFECT	EXAMPLE?
Simile	A comparison between two items using 'like' or 'as'.	Adds pictorial/aural emphasis/impact to the written description.	1.
Metaphor	A comparison between two items. There is no 'like' or 'as' since one item is said to *be* the other.	Adds pictorial/aural emphasis/impact to the written description.	2.
Personification	Similes and metaphors become this when an inanimate object is spoken of as if it were alive.	Makes objects seem like living things.	3.
Hyperbole	A deliberately over-exaggerated image.	Often to create a memorable / startling effect. At times, the effect may be humorous.	4.
Alliteration	The repetition of a particular consonant – or consonant sound – at the beginning of a group of words.	To draw attention to the meaning by the use of consonant sound – harsh or soft, according to context. It may also make the word group easily memorable.	5.
Assonance	The repetition of a certain group of similar-sounding vowels in close proximity to each other.	To draw attention to the meaning by the use of vowel sounds – harsh or soft – according to context.	6.

Onomatopoeia	When the sound of the word captures or mimics its meaning.	To create a picture in sound of an action or event.	7.
Enjambment	The running of the sense of one line on to the next or several others without end-line punctuation.	To give a sense of forward movement, to give a conversational feel to content, or to suggest a speeding-up for an effect of urgency.	8.

a.

The holy time is quiet as a Nun
Breathless with adoration; the broad sun
Is sinking down in its tranquillity;

William Wordsworth

b.

It shushes
It hushes

Gwendolyn Brookes

c.

A host, of golden daffodils;
Beside the lake, beneath the trees,
Fluttering and dancing in the breeze...

William Wordsworth

d.

When I see birches bend from left to right ...

Robert Frost

e.

The sea is a hungry dog,
Giant and grey.

James Reeves

f.

I'll love you till the ocean
Is folded and hung up to dry.

WH Auden

g.

I wandered lonely as a cloud
That floats on high o'er vales and hills.

William Wordsworth

h

... and my regret
Becomes an April violet,
And buds and blossoms with the rest.

Lord Tennyson

What you now know

- Different genres such as drama, novels and short stories, and poetry all have different identifying characteristics.
- Discussing each genre requires you to think about how these differences will affect the evidence you produce in your essays and answers.
- Convincing essays and answers require more than knowledge of literary techniques; they need you to comment on how the techniques you noted affected your response as a reader.

SCOTTISH TEXTS

WHAT'S INVOLVED?

Answering questions on a Scottish text which you have studied accounts for 20 of the 70 marks in the final exam. The skills you're already acquiring as you work on 'Reading for Understanding, Analysis and Evaluation' will again prove helpful here.

In the 'Critical Reading' exam, you'll be asked to read a short extract, or a short complete text, from your selected text(s) and answer a brief series of questions on the extract. As in RUAE, you'll be asked to look at technical features such as word choice, sentence structure, tone and imagery, and to demonstrate summarising skills. Here again, your final score will be determined by:

- how well you **understand** what is going on in the extract,
- how well you **understand** what the question is asking you to do,
- your ability to **analyse** how the author creates their effects, and
- your ability to **evaluate** the significance of the evidence presented.

In addition to all this, a final high-value question will ask you:

- to examine a particular feature of the extract,
- to relate it to at least one other part of the text(s) or other texts, and
- to discuss similarities or differences in their commonality.

Do not be put off by the word 'commonality'. It's simply a technical term for seeing how a particular aspect of the extract relates to a feature(s) elsewhere in your chosen text(s) and discussing similarities or contrasts. For a worked example, see page 70–71.

- In a play, novel, short story or poem, this aspect might be a theme as it's explored in the extract and elsewhere; **characterisation** variations/similarities in the extract and elsewhere; or the language (word choice, imagery, sentence structure, tone, etc.) here and as it appears elsewhere. This 'commonality' question might also ask you to relate how an idea, issue, challenge or problem encountered here is dealt with in the extract and in another area of the text(s).
- In a play, you need to be alert to all these things, as well as other key features such as stage directions, lighting, props, costume changes and changes of location. You must always remember that a play is much more than words on a page: it's a combination of words, colour, sound, light and movement. These are rich areas to examine in an answer.

DON'T FORGET

Spotting areas of commonality requires truly in-depth knowledge of your selected text(s). This means that regular reading of it/them is vital. In the exam room, you have precious few minutes to make a mental survey of your text(s). Your knowledge needs to be at your fingertips, not just in your file.

This unit will be your guide in studying how best to optimise your performance. You will find four of the selected Scottish texts explored in some detail.

What's coming up?

- Analysis of the play *Bold Girls*
- Analysis of four short stories from *Hieroglyphics*
- Analysis of six poems by Edwin Morgan
- Analysis of *The Strange Case of Dr Jekyll and Mr Hyde* by Robert Louis Stevenson
- Outline summaries of the texts
- Study notes on themes, characterisation, style
- Familiarisation activities on the text(s)
- Dealing with commonalities
- Exam-style tests on each text

BOLD GIRLS BY RONA MUNRO

What's coming up?

- Profile of the author
- Background to the play
- Outline of the action
- Character studies
- Themes and sub-themes
- Familiarisation activities
- Dealing with commonalities
- Exam-style tests

Profile of the author: Rona Munro

Born in Aberdeen in 1959, the daughter of a radiotherapist and a geology lecturer, Rona Munro was fascinated by playwriting from an early age. After studying history at Edinburgh University, she quickly established herself as a rising star in drama circles with commissions for plays, screenplays and radio plays.

In a recent interview she underlined her interest in 'representing voices or people that have been under-represented' which, of course, is well illustrated in her portrayal of the four women here. In media terms, the wives, mothers and daughters of prisoners were the forgotten people of the Northern Irish 'troubles'.

At first glance, examining as it does the fallout from political turmoil, *Bold Girls* might appear to be overtly political, but Munro is keen to dispel this idea. In the same interview, she remarked:

'If you put characters on stage that people are not familiar with seeing centre-stage or carrying a narrative, that is political. Just putting women centre-stage when I started out was a fairly political act. By making the audience have that act of empathy with someone whose experience isn't theirs is political. But within that I don't think plays should be arguing a case one way or another.'

Written in 1991, *Bold Girls* won Munro the 1991 London Critics Circle Theatre Award for Most Promising New Playwright. It is a powerful 'act of empathy' which deals with the everyday lives of four women, whose men-folk have been either killed or imprisoned for their roles in the 'troubles' in Northern Ireland.

Outline summary

The action takes place over the course of a late afternoon, evening and early morning in the West Belfast of what Munro, writing in 1991, calls 'today'. Three neighbours, Marie, Nora and Cassie have their already difficult lives disrupted by the arrival of the mysterious young girl, Deirdre.

Despite presenting the appearance of mutually supportive closeness, the trio pursue various consoling dreams which highlight their underlying isolation and which camouflage hidden tensions. Deirdre, in her search for the truth about her father, serves as a catalyst to revealing these cracks. Despite its many humorous moments, its searing examination of the stereotypical roles of men and women in the material-driven society of today gives it a significance which transcends Northern Irish boundaries.

Character studies

Marie

Marie is the 'cheerful, efficient, young' widow of Michael, whose image looks out on the living room. A jealous guardian of his memory, she's bringing up her sons Mickey and Brendan to see their father as a pillar of virtue. She's increasingly disturbed by the young girl in white who has begun to haunt her house.

The picture of the Virgin Mary that hangs in Marie's kitchen helps suggest her Christian values in the audience's mind before she ever appears. She reacts with unquestioning generosity to Deirdre's arrival, in contrast to Nora and Cassie. She's regularly associated with acts of kindness to birds throughout the play, a kindness which finds its final expression in the welcoming into her home of Deirdre, seemingly her late husband's love-child.

Classroom challenge

Here are some details from the opening stage directions for Marie's house (p.1). They serve to tell us much about her and the life she leads before we even meet her. Add a comment beside each detail to suggest what each one tells us about her character, as a woman and mother.

TEACHING NOTES

You can download Teaching Notes for this challenge at www.brightredpublishing.co.uk/Shop/national-5-english-course-book

'toys that are new and gleaming and flashing with lights [...] have swallowed up the year's savings'	
'the kettle always hot for tea'	
'it's furniture bald with age'	
'the coal fire that's gleaming clean'	
'a small picture of the Virgin on one wall'	
'a large grainy blow-up photo of a smiling young man'	

Note: all page references, in this section, are from the Hodder & Stoughton 2004 edition of Bold Girls.

Cassie

Daughter of Nora, 'sceptical, sharp-tongued' Cassie is the long-term friend of Marie. She enjoys an uneasy relationship with her mother due partly to their conflicting views on Nora's dead husband and Cassie's father, Sean. The truth about Sean – violent brute of a husband, or a man provoked beyond endurance by nagging – remains elusive throughout the play.

Cassie dreams of fleeing Belfast to start a new life, free from the drabness of provincial life and from the guilt of knowing she had an affair with Marie's husband, Michael. This is a secret which emerges late in the play partly due to the arrival of Deirdre. While Marie strives to maintain a rosy view of her late husband (but finally slashes his image when she accepts the truth of his rumoured infidelities), Cassie views her husband, Joe, with undisguised contempt. Joe's imminent release from prison is yet another reason for Cassie's wish to flee Belfast.

Classroom challenge

Here are some key quotations which help us understand the complex character of Cassie. Add a comment beside each quotation to suggest what you learn about her from it.

'Are you still on for the club tonight?' (p.5)	
'a heart of flint and a tongue to match' (p.8)	
'I fell out with my mummy on the delivery room floor.' (p.9)	
'And here's me never stopped dancing since they took mine away.' (p.25)	
'*(With sudden vehemence)* Oh Marie, I wish I was out of this place!' (p.31)	
'Lying hounds every one of them.' (p.31)	
'I've two hundred pounds saved. I'm going, Marie.' (p.57)	

TEACHING NOTES

You can download Teaching Notes for this challenge at http://www.brightredpublishing.co.uk/Shop/national-5-english-course-book

Nora

Source of much of the play's humour, Nora protects herself from the pain of a failed marriage, her judgemental daughter and the daily trials of living in strife-torn Belfast by retreating largely into a world of interior decoration.

A victim of domestic and political violence, she's a rich source of stories told about her past experiences (which Cassie and Marie appear to have heard many times). Nora has crafted stories such as the one about the night she lost her bamboo suite to the British army and the arrest of her son-in-law Joe into humorous yarns – her way, perhaps, of living with the pain of such incidents.

Classroom challenge

Nora is the character perhaps most associated with objects. But objects, in the form of stage props or personal property, also play an important part elsewhere in the play. Sometimes they're symbols underlining a theme or idea; often, they help advance the story line. Comment on each of the following. Remember that some are mentioned more than once. Consider later mentions as well as an earlier one.

	SYMBOLIC USE	HOW IT ADVANCES THE STORY LINE
Nora's peach-coloured polyester		
Cassie's £200 behind the picture		
Michael's picture		
Deirdre's knife		
Michael's blue car		
Breadcrumbs		

You can download Teaching Notes for this challenge at www.brightredpublishing.co.uk/Shop/national-5-english-course-book

TEACHING NOTES

Deirdre

Deirdre emerges out of the 'darkness' of the violence around her, seeking the truth about her father, probably Michael, and the chance to come in from the cold, possibly by finding a home with Marie. Nurtured in violence, she has no qualms initially about revenging herself on society by stealing and destroying whatever comes to hand.

Underneath this violence – stemming from the dark places of her mind – Deirdre, like others in the play, clings to a consoling dream. Hers is the natural desire of a child for caring parents, recognition of her status as Michael's child and the security of a proper home. The play ends in the hope of a new life for her with Marie, perhaps the only dream in the play which is likely to be realised by events.

Classroom challenge

Deirdre is presented convincingly as a troubled teenager. Examine the following quotations and stage directions, then comment on what each reveals about her personality, life and behaviour.

'Marie: "Cassie – do you believe in ghosts?"' (p.9)	
'I'm wet, I'm cold. I want to get inside.' (p.13)	
'She has heavy black make-up on, smudged slightly [...] as if she's been crying.' (p.18)	
'I need a knife. [...] I thought I'd like that. A wee bit of hard truth you could hold in your hand and point where you liked.' (p.24)	
'Brick in your hand, hard in your hand, hit skin and it'll burst open and bleed ...' (p.49)	
'No one will tell you the truth to your face.' (p.74)	
'Marie touches Deirdre's shoulder. Deirdre flinches [...] Marie turns her gently. She looks at her bruised body.' (p.77)	
'I'll get the other fiver for you.' (p.79)	

TEACHING NOTES

You can download Teaching Notes for this challenge at www.brightredpublishing.co.uk/Shop/national-5-english-course-book

Themes

According to Professor Douglas Gifford,

'Munro's main theme is a satire on the way ordinary people live now – not just in Northern Ireland, but in the West, and indeed in any culture which imbalances the sexes in their social roles, encouraging stereotyping of male dominance and social privilege and female subservience to that behaviour.'

This we see in the way the men – who never appear – are pandered to by the women, even though from what we hear of their gambling, drinking, fighting and promiscuity, they are hardly worthy recipients of this attention.

DON'T FORGET

When analysing drama, it's important to consider how the play's themes are conveyed not only through the characters' dialogue and interaction, but through stage props, lighting, costume, setting and other stage effects.

Read Douglas Gifford's full article, 'Making Them Bold and Breaking the Mould' at www.brightredbooks.net

ONLINE

There is, however, another major theme which helps inform the action of the play. In Scene 2, Deirdre comments:

The whole town's a prison, smash chunks off the walls 'cause we're all in a prison.

When we examine the lives of the three women, we see that Deirdre is not far from the truth. While a number of their men are certainly in Long Kesh prison, the women, too, are similarly confined – not simply in a society that privileges men, but in one where their lives are caught in a web of television game-shows, films and soap-operas; the cheapening materialism of peach-coloured polyester; Mickey's raspberry ice-cream syrup; magi-mixes; and Black-and-Decker drills ... the world of contemporary Western culture, Munro seems to suggest.

But, it could be argued, this materialism is as much refuge as prison for these women, as they struggle with the difficulties of reconciling their lives with a version of the truth that they can live with – one of the play's several sub-themes.

Homework helper

To start you off thinking about finding links or commonalities scattered through the play, here's a research activity to help you find related material. The column on the left suggests a key characteristic of someone, or an idea running through the text. The column on the right gives you a page reference to help you find a shared commonality. Try to find a quotation or detailed reference for the central column to illustrate this. There are, of course, other possibilities which you may wish to add to your list as you read.

FEATURED ITEM	COMMONALITY	PAGE REFERENCE
Cassie's unrealistic mind-set: 'I'm going anyway, money or no money.' p.66		16
Nora's capacity to turn painful events into humorous yarns: 'Oh do you remember the night they took Joe?' p.26		46
Marie's kindness to birds: 'I just like to feed them.' p.29		80
The women live in a close-knit community: '... there was a Deirdre McMahon used to live up there – sure but she'd be twenty-five now at least.' p.24		35
Nora's humour coming from exaggeration: 'Foam right up to the walls.' p.6		39
At times, Deirdre appears aggressive: *'There is a thunderous knocking at the door.'* p.17		49
Deirdre also appears like an insecure little girl at times: *'She stands uncertain in the centre of the room.'* p.18		74

You can download Teaching Notes for this challenge at www.brightredpublishing.co.uk/Shop/national-5-english-course-book

TEACHING NOTES

The troublesome truth

Truth is often a troublesome commodity and nowhere more so than in this play. What IS the truth behind Sean's violence towards Nora: a violent drunk or a good man provoked beyond endurance? And what are we think of Joe, Cassie's husband? To Nora, he's a sound provider; to Cassie, a drunken oaf. To what extent exactly did Marie suspect Michael of carrying on with other women? This difficulty in negotiating the truth drives the women into different positions.

Marie, whatever her suspicions, studiously **avoids confronting the truth**, telling her sons that:

> *Your daddy was a good man and a brave man and he did the best he could and he's in heaven watching out for you and that's what [...] keeps me going, keeps me strong ...*

This mental image – and the physical image of Michael on the wall – comforts and sustains her as she goes about her life.

Cassie has spent some effort in **concealing the truth** about her relationship with Michael from Marie, which adds to her desire to escape what she sees as the grim, restricting provincial life of West Belfast.

Nora **flees the truth** of her bleak existence – her husband dead, a son in prison and herself the victim of military and domestic violence – by seeking comfort in maintaining and decorating her home, a trim retreat from reality. With a new roll of cut-price peach-coloured polyester she is convinced:

> *That'll be my front room just a wee dream again.*

Deirdre is the only one of the quartet who is actively **seeking the truth**: the truth about her paternity. A truth that will give her a home with Marie, she hopes, and allow her into a family life of the kind she has, up until now, been deprived of, thereby escaping from the circle of violence and theft which seems to have been her life so far.

DON'T FORGET

As you read, stay alert to links you notice between what's being said and a similar reference elsewhere. Remembering an image, a personal characteristic, a stage direction, and/or a recurring idea could help you pick up marks in the final high-value question on the extract.

Talking without communicating

There's no shortage of chat and banter in the play. Indeed, its robust interchanges are at the heart of the play's appeal. But there are various points when we hear Marie, Cassie and Nora talking completely at cross-purposes, with no one really listening to anyone else. The effect can at times be humorous, as in the play's opening lines. But, at others, it emphasises the distance between the women.

Despite a surface appearance of closeness and solidarity, they are essentially three lonely women who often fail in daily life to communicate to one another their doubts and fears. When they do, as happens in Scene 4, the results are disastrous, although it finally leads to the air being cleared.

This stifling of real communication is a sad but very necessary means of papering over the underlying cracks in the relationship between Marie and Cassie, and between Cassie and her mother. These recurring 'cross-talks' are one of Munro's ways of signalling their essential isolation in what appears to be a mutually supportive quasi-family.

DON'T FORGET

Don't overlook the importance of the soliloquies on pages 1, 13, 14, 31, 32 and 43 by Deirdre, Marie and Cassie. These monologues are vital for understanding how life's experiences have shaped these troubled women. They share with the audience an insight into their behaviour and character which isn't always clear to the other women.

The consoling dream

To sustain them in their lives, the four women have forged their own consoling dreams.

For Cassie, it is, Marie suggests, escaping to Spain with a toyboy – hence her preoccupation with diets, her appearance in a bikini and the £200 she has stolen from Nora. Nora's dream, as we've seen, concerns escape into a world of peach-coloured polyester. Marie's dream is less materialistic, anchored as it is in a vision of Michael's essential goodness as she goes about tending to her family and feeding the birds.

Deirdre, like Marie, is less materialistic in her dream, seeking only a refuge from the streets into a family life of which she feels deprived. It's her 'wee bit of hard truth' which helps puncture the dreams of the other three, but there is – in the play's final pages – a hint that Marie and Deirdre may find consolation together, a consolation based on a reality stripped of distracting illusions.

ONLINE

For more insight into the setting of *Bold Girls*, read 'A Brief History of Belfast' at www.brightredbooks.net

Classroom challenge

Organise a classroom debate on an idea which underlies much of the play:

- Have the women been diminished or trivialised by a society obsessed by materialism (peach-coloured polyester, raspberry ice-cream syrup, *The Price is Right*, etc.), or does materialism offer them welcome relief from an unpleasant reality?

Make sure you have plenty of textual evidence (page references, quotations) to back up your viewpoint. This might form a useful outcome for assessment.

Homework helper

The play is rich in themes and sub-themes of the kind we have discussed.

Here are some quotations and a list of the themes that they illustrate. The lists have been deliberately mixed up. Match the quotation with the theme which it helps to exemplify.

1. 'I never once got my dinner before he'd his in his mouth.' p.42

2. 'Your daddy was a good man and a brave man and he did the best he could and he's in heaven watching out for you ...' p.30

3. 'Marie: "I didn't know him."
Cassie: "There's that cramp again, in my leg, I'll wobble."' p.34

4. 'No one will tell you the truth to your face.' p.74

5. 'Cassie: "Computer games. Eighteen pounds, ninety five."
Nora: "Twenty-five pounds."
Cassie: "Eighteen ninety five. I've seen them in a catalogue."' p.41

a) Talking without communicating

b) The troublesome truth

c) The dominance of the consumer society

d) Inequality of men and women

e) The consoling dream

TEACHING NOTES

You can download Teaching Notes for this task at www.brightredpublishing.co.uk/Shop/national-5-english-course-book

Dealing with commonalities

How does that work?

We have already defined at the beginning of this chapter what a commonality is and suggested what the aim of the commonality-seeking final question is. (See page 61.) You've also had a chance to start practising the skills necessary for an effective answer. (See page 67.)

In the upcoming Topic Test, you'll be able to try answering a full commonality question in the extract. But what exactly is a marker looking for in this kind of answer?

Let's take a practice example. Suppose you were faced with a question similar to this:

This is a play in which women have to face up to many difficulties. By referring to this extract and at least one other example from the play, discuss what these difficulties are. 8

The safest way to go about this is to adopt a simple formula.

Step 1: Say what difficulty arises in the extract (1 mark), then mention another difficulty faced in another part of the play (1 mark). This might read as:

Deirdre finds herself outside, frightened of the black smoke of a nearby violent explosion, showing the difficulty of living with sectarian violence. (1) The women's night out is later threatened when shooting in the street makes going out a problem. (1)

So, you already have 2 marks.

Step 2: Now select a brief quotation from the extract which illustrates this difficulty (1 mark), then make your own comment on this (1 mark). This might read as:

'There's burning making the sky black.' (1) The women live with the constant threat of violence and/or explosions around them. (1)

Now you have 4 marks.

Step 3: Now find another quotation from elsewhere in the play which illustrates yet another difficulty for the women, then add your comment on it. This might read as:

'Wallop! Knocked her straight through the hedge.' (1) The women are sometimes victims of physical violence during raids, as when Nora faces up to a British soldier. (1)

(If you cannot remember a quotation from elsewhere in the play to illustrate a difficulty, refer in detail to the difficulty you have in mind and then comment on it.)

That's 6 marks.

Step 4: You now need some final reference/quotation to a difficulty and a comment.

'Oh, the paper's hanging off the wall in there.' (1) Adding to their difficulties is the fact that the houses they have to live in are of poor quality, riddled with damp. (1)

(Again, if you don't have the quotation to hand, refer to it in detail and then comment on the detail.)

And there are your 8 marks.

From this exercise, you can see that the way to maximise your score is to know your text(s) thoroughly. You need to be able to make an instant mental survey of your text(s) and select appropriate material in very few minutes. This can only be done if your text knowledge is absolutely secure. That comes from multiple readings.

Exam-style tests

Topic Test 1

Read the extract below and then attempt the following questions.

***Bold Girls* by Rona Munro**

In this extract, Marie and Cassie have returned from their night out at the club and are discussing their differing attitudes to coping with daily life.

CASSIE: How do you stand it here, Marie?
MARIE: Sure, where else would I go?
CASSIE: How do you keep that smile on your face?
MARIE: Super-glue.
CASSIE: There's not one piece of bitterness in you, is there?
MARIE: Oh, Cassie.
CASSIE: You see, you're good. And I'm just wicked.
MARIE: Aye, you're a bold woman altogether.
CASSIE: Is it hard being good?
MARIE: I took lessons.
CASSIE: Well, tell me what you've got to smile about, Marie, because I'm sure I can't see it.
MARIE: I've a lot to be thankful for. I've my kids, my job, a nice wee house and I can still pay for it.
CASSIE: You've two wee boys growing out of their clothes faster than you can get new ones, a part-time job licking envelopes for a wage that wouldn't keep a budgie and three red bills on your mantelpiece there.
MARIE: That's what's great about a Saturday out with you, Cassie, you just know how to look at the bright side of things, don't you?
CASSIE: Well, just tell me how you can keep filling that kettle and making folk tea without pouring it over their head?
MARIE: Ah well you see, I'm a mug.
CASSIE: I think you are.
MARIE: I didn't marry Joe, but ...
CASSIE: No. You did not. That mug was me.
MARIE: See, Cassie, I've had better times with Michael than a lot of women get in their whole lives with a man.
CASSIE: And that keeps you going?
MARIE: It's a warming kind of thought.

1. Marie demonstrates a range of responses to Cassie's criticisms of her life. With close reference to the text, explain what **two** of these are. **4**

2. Cassie does not share Marie's positive view of her situation. With reference to word choice and/or sentence structure, explain clearly how Cassie regards it. **4**

3. Men are held in low esteem by Cassie, although she appreciates how they may have their uses and attractions. With close reference to her language, show clearly **two** ways in which they might have attracted Cassie. **4**

4. The extract refers to Marie's consolation in her difficult life. With close reference to the extract and at least one other place elsewhere in the text, explain how the idea of consolation is explored. **8**

TOTAL – 20 marks

TEACHING NOTES

You can download Teaching Notes for this test at www.brightredpublishing.co.uk/Shop/national-5-english-course-book

Topic Test 2

Read the extract below and then attempt the following questions.

***Bold Girls* by Rona Munro**

In this extract, Marie, Nora and Cassie are on a night out at the club where there's a minute's silence for a man recently killed in the troubles.

Scene Two

The Club

This could be a community hall or even an ancient warehouse but it has been jazzed up with glitterballs and spots. The chairs and tables are cheap and battered. There are double doors at the back of the room. Marie, Nora and Cassie have got themselves a table overlooking the small dance floor. There is a small stand, like a lectern, on one side of it. The place is crowded, bright with the colours of the women's dresses and great misty clouds of cigarette smoke whirling in the fans. Cassie's dress is quite revealing though not extravagantly so. It is silent. The three women are standing by their chairs, heads bowed as if by a grave-side. No one moves, they speak in whispers.

MARIE: I didn't know him.

CASSIE: There's that cramp again, in my leg. I'll wobble.

NORA: That's his aunty there, is it not? She shouldn't be here drinking sure she shouldn't.

MARIE: Can't put a face to him at all.

CASSIE: My shoes, a size too small and I've swelled with the heat. Oh God, don't let me fall off them.

NORA: His mother's sister-in-law's sister, it's close enough. She should be with that poor woman.

MARIE: Was he young?

CASSIE: Just a boy too.

NORA: Is that not a minute over?

MARIE: Is that not a minute now?

CASSIE: Can I get off my feet?

There is a sudden burst of music and a loud buzz of talk. The women shout over this as they claim their seats with jackets and handbags.

MARIE: Did you get my ticket for the competition, Cassie?

CASSIE: I got us all ten.

NORA: Ten?

MARIE: Money to burn.

CASSIE: I'm feeling lucky.

MARIE: So it's a gin and lime and a black Russian for you, Nora?

NORA: No, I'll get these.

CASSIE: Sure I'll get them.

MARIE: *(waving a fiver at the waitress)* No you're all right. I've my money in my hand.

CASSIE: Let's have a kitty then, fiver in and start us with doubles, Marie.

MARIE: I can't catch her eye.

NORA: Did you know him then, the poor wee boy?

CASSIE: It was him with the dog.

NORA: At the chemist's?

CASSIE: His brother.

MARIE: Always seems such a long minute.

NORA: I was just in that chemist's today.

MARIE: I hate it. Never know what to fill my head with.

NORA: They still hadn't got my prescription in.

MARIE: I didn't know him. What can you fill your head with if you can't picture his face?

CASSIE: You'd know him if you saw him. Just nineteen, trying to grow a moustache like dust on a ledge.

NORA: His mother's youngest. The last one at home.

MARIE: *(shivering)* I still can't see him. I just think of coffins.

NORA: She's all on her own now. All on her own.

CASSIE: Marie, will you hurry up getting that drink, it's the only nourishment I've got coming to me today. This is going to be the wildest of nights. I'm telling you, Mummy, all the times I've been here, the best ones have always been when we've come on our own, just the three of us.

Marie waves her money for the waitress again.

Marie exits.

NORA: Remember the first we knew of what happened to Michael was when they asked us to stand for him?

CASSIE: Marie had never been out of her house, never told a soul till we came in to her.

NORA: Oh, but he was well respected.

CASSIE: Just sitting by the fire and the fire dead for hours and the baby crying and crying ...

NORA: They sang for him as well, do you remember?

CASSIE: Her just sitting there.

NORA: He's still missed; there's some men you don't forget.

CASSIE: He was popular, I'll say that for him.

NORA: He was.

1. Using your own words as far as possible, summarise what this extract tells us about the women's lives in West Belfast. You should make at least **four** key points. **4**

2. By referring to an example for each woman, show fully how

a) Marie reacts to the minute's silence **3**

b) Cassie reacts to the minute's silence. **3**

3. By referring to one example from Nora's dialogue, show how her reaction to the death of the boy might appear surprising. **2**

4. By referring to the extract and to elsewhere in the play, show how the writer explores humour. **8**

TOTAL – 20 marks

TEACHING NOTES

You can download Teaching Notes for this test at www.brightredpublishing.co.uk/Shop/national-5-english-course-book

ONLINE

Have a look at the 'National Library of Scotland's Description of Bold Girls' at www.brightredbooks.net

HIEROGLYPHICS AND OTHER STORIES BY ANNE DONOVAN

What's coming up?

- Profile of the author
- Outline of the anthology
- Themes
- Stories under the spotlight
- Familiarisation activities
- Exam-style tests

Profile of the author: Anne Donovan

Originally from Coatbridge, Anne Donovan studied English and Philosophy at Glasgow University before becoming an English teacher. She taught in various secondary schools until 2003 when, after the publication of her first novel, she made the transition to full-time writing.

Her collection *Hieroglyphics and Other Stories* was published in 2001 to considerable critical and popular acclaim. In 2003 the publication of her first novel *Buddha Da* was followed soon after by its inclusion on the shortlist of potential winners of the prestigious Orange Prize for Fiction. It was later nominated for the Whitbread First Novel Award, sealing Anne Donovan's place as one of the leading writers of her generation. The same year saw Donovan adapting the short story *Hieroglyphics* into a one-act play which was staged at Oran Mor in Glasgow and later published in an Association for Scottish Literary Studies (ASLS) anthology, *Plays for Schools.*

Outline of the anthology

The anthology consists of eighteen short stories, eleven of them written in Glaswegian Scots with a twelfth alternating between Standard English and Glaswegian Scots. With the exception of one, all are told in a female voice. Six of them (and part of a seventh) are voiced by a young girl, two by elderly women.

The collection follows female experience from childhood to old age: the first six explore the world through young girls' eyes; the seventh bridges the child–woman divide; the following four depict various mother–child relationships; the later ones focus on various aspects of adult relationships, with the final two highlighting the world of older women.

The N5 selection

The four short stories you are asked to explore in National 5 offer a cross section of Anne Donovan's concerns in this anthology. To help you spot the links between them, here is an outline guide to some of the recurring themes, ideas and relationships which connect them.

Themes

Themes in short stories and novels are ideas which underlie the story line. In an anthology of this kind, the alert reader will begin to see that there are certain themes which keep recurring and which help bind the anthology together.

Without ever being stated directly by the writer, the theme(s) emerge gradually through everyday events in each story's action. We see that certain preoccupations of the writer appear in different guises from story to story. *Hieroglyphics and Other Stories* is particularly rich in these ideas which unite the various titles. According to their perspective, different readers may find different themes. Some of the more interesting are explored below, although not all appear in every story.

Finding empowerment

Empowerment is the ability to achieve your aims and desires. A number of the stories end with the main character finding her own particular way to achieving her goal(s), thus finding personal fulfilment. This change in personal circumstances might have come about despite an unfavourable surrounding situation. Sadly, there are stories in which, despite her best efforts, the main character fails to find empowerment to change her circumstances for the better.

DON'T FORGET

As you read through the stories, stay alert to spotting themes which make a link between each of them. As well as making the reading experience more enjoyable, this will serve you well in answering the final commonality question in the exam. We've outlined three possible uniting themes. Have you noticed any others?

Being spontaneous

Empowerment in several of these stories comes about through characters being true to themselves and to their deepest feelings and insights. This often happens in the face of pressures to conform to some other set of values.

Communication across the generations

Several of the stories present us with interaction between family members of different generations. In some, we see that there is a gap in the way each generation views the world, and each other, leading to a certain tension between them which may or may not be resolved by the story's end.

Stories under the spotlight

'All that glisters'

For the young girl Clare, the discovery of brightly coloured glitter pens is a joyful revelation. She shares her delight with her invalid father, a victim of asbestosis. Her plans to do something colourful with them for his Christmas are abruptly cut short when her father suddenly dies.

Left somewhat alone in preparations for the funeral, Clare decides to wear a red outfit for the event, knowing her father loved to see her in it. Her aunt is scandalised by what she thinks is a wholly inappropriate idea and insists she wear her rather drab school uniform. Clare concedes, but takes her glitter pens and covers herself and her clothes with them so that she was 'bleezin wi light' – her own very personal and unconventional tribute to her father's memory.

This is the first of several stories highlighting the relationship between a young girl and her parent(s), a thematic link in the collection. The girl, who throughout is associated with light and colour, brings with her, literally, a sparkle and brightness to her dying father. Once a ghostly figure in his white asbestos-covered clothes, he's now drained entirely of colour in his own life, only cheered by the colour his daughter brings him. The story celebrates the colour and spontaneity of young people in the face of the darker, drabber adult world.

ONLINE

For a 6-minute dramatisation of parts of this story and an interview with Anne Donovan, watch the BBC's video 'All that glisters' in the Anne Donovan section of N5 English at http://www.brightredbooks.net. There's another abridged version of the story by Claire Lamond at vimeo.com.

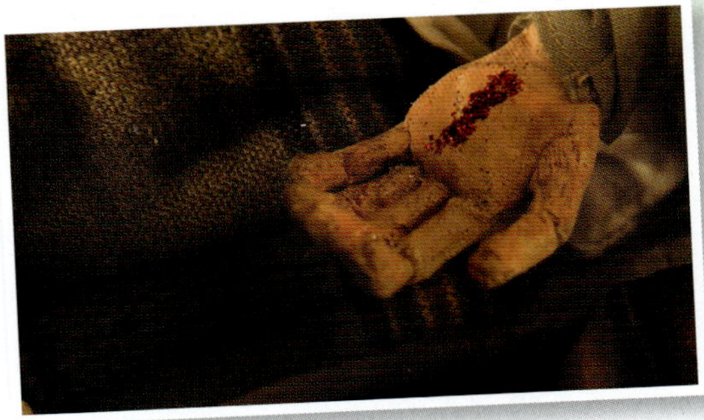

REVISION POINTS	
LANGUAGE:	Glaswegian Scots
NARRATION:	By Clare, a young girl Clare (corruption of French 'claire' *light*); constantly associated with colour and sparkle; adults either drained of colour or associated with dull/drab ones.
RELATIONSHIPS:	Adult–child Father–daughter: fully supportive on both sides Mother–daughter: less developed but seemingly supportive Aunt–niece: lack of mutual understanding
CONNECTING THEMES	
Finding empowerment	Clare, despite her shortage of money, manages to find a way of purchasing the pens she so desperately wants. Clare, despite her aunt, succeeds in finding her own way of marking her father's passing.
Being spontaneous	Clare defies conventional thinking on the need for sombre funeral clothes to express herself in her own colourful way.
Communication across the generations	Despite her close relationship with her father, Clare is at odds with the way adults mark death.

Homework helper

Beside each of these quotations from 'All that glisters', make your own comment about what each one illustrates about the character, situation or theme:

'... the glitter jist brought everythin tae life, gleamin and glisterin agin the flat cardboard. It wis like the difference between a Christmas tree skinklin wi fairy lights an wan lyin deid and daurk in a corner.' (p.13)	
'It's good tae find sumpn that cheers him up even a wee bit because ma daddy's really sick.' (p.14)	
'[he] stares at a patch on the downie cover where there's a coffee stain that ma ma cannae wash oot.' (p.14)	

'In the end ah sellt ma dinner tickets tae big Maggie Hughes and all week ah wis starving...' (p.17)	
'Blue veins criss-crossed the back of her haun. Why were veins blue when blood wis red?' (p.18)	
'*You cannae wear red tae a funeral. You have tae show respect fur the deid.*' (p.19)	
'Then ah stood and looked in the mirror at the glowin figure afore me and ah smiled.' (p.21)	

Note: all page references, in this section, are from the Canongate 2004 edition of Hieroglyphics and Other Stories.

TEACHING NOTES

You can download Teaching Notes for this at www.brightredpublishing.co.uk/Shop/national-5-english-course-book

DON'T FORGET

When you jot down what you think are key quotations in your notes, make sure you include page numbers; it will save you a great deal of time when you come to revise.

'Dear Santa'

This is another story featuring the parent–child relationship; this time, that of a mother and her eight-year-old daughter, Alison, the narrator. Here, the mother's preference for her younger daughter, Katie, leaves Alison desperately yearning for her mother's affection, while her mother seems curiously oblivious of her elder daughter's devotion and hunger for her love.

The story's title stems from Alison's struggle to write a letter to Santa; its narrative highlights her feeling of being unloved by her mother as Christmas approaches, normally a time when parents and children draw closer.

So painful is it for her to put down on paper her overwhelming need, she ultimately fails to articulate her desire in her letter. (The fact that she only half believes in Santa but is willing to give the idea a try is testimony to her desperation.) Lamely, instead of asking for her mother's love, she asks for a Barbie doll and a toy dog. She had similarly failed to voice her request to the department-store Santa from whom she got the idea of writing down her 'secret' desire.

REVISION POINTS	
LANGUAGE:	Glaswegian Scots
RELATIONSHIPS:	Mother–daughter Losing out in her mother's affections to her blonde-haired younger sister, dark-haired Alison struggles even to mention her deepest desire.
NARRATION:	By eight-year-old Alison Alison's sadness is underlined by various references to darkness surrounding her, contrasting with the 'sparkle' of the Christmas shops.
CONNECTING THEMES	
Finding empowerment	Alison fails to obtain what she wants most. In this case, evidence of her mother's love. She seems unable to articulate this desire to her mother directly, in her letter to Santa, or even to the store Santa. She is one of the characters who fails to find empowerment.
Communication across the generations	Here is another story in which there seems to be a communication gap between the generations. The mother and daughter talk but the mother seems emotionally aloof and the daughter cannot express her feelings.

Classroom challenge

For exam success, being able to point to evidence to support your answers is a key skill to acquire. Here's an opportunity for you to try your skills at tracking down evidence for yourself.

In the grid below, the column on the right makes comments about Alison's situation and feelings. The column on the left offers clues as to where to find the evidence to support the comment.

Your evidence may take the form of a direct quotation or a reference to relevant information.

p.43	Alison appears to have had rather un-sisterly feelings towards Katie at an early age.
p.44	Katie appears to be admired by outsiders and family members alike.
p.44	Alison is compared unfavourably with Katie by her mother.
p.45	Alison appears to be of an age when she is beginning to think for herself.
p.46	The task of writing to Santa appears to cause Alison considerable difficulty.
p.47	Alison's mother may be undemonstrative in her reactions to others in the family.
p.47	Anne Donovan hints that there may be some hope for some future improvement in the mother–daughter relationship.

TEACHING NOTES

You can download Teaching Notes for this at www.brightredpublishing.co.uk/Shop/national-5-english-course-book

ONLINE

You can enjoy another perspective on these stories by checking out 'The Short Review – *Hieroglyphics and Other Stories*' at www.brightredbooks.net

'Away in a Manger'

Once again, Anne Donovan re-visits the mother–child relationship. This time it takes on a new poignancy as the Christmas setting ends with Sandra and Amy adopting a quasi-Madonna-and-Child position on their journey home.

Shop-worker Sandra arranges for Amy to join her in central Glasgow to see the lights and nativity scene in George Square. Seemingly a single mum, Sandra is tired and jaded after doing extra hours in the shop where she works in order to give Amy 'nice things'. Her heart isn't really in this Christmas jaunt around the lights and she wonders at people sitting and enjoying it all on such a cold night.

By contrast, Amy is enchanted, particularly when she sees an addition to the nativity scene which she mistakes for an angel. The young man in question is clearly a homeless person but Sandra is reluctant to elaborate on the concept of homelessness to protect the child's innocence. Amy, however, seizes on the idea of offering the man a home with them. The child seems intuitively to understand the real spirit of Christmas in a way denied to the more worldly and practical adult.

Although a kindly and protective mother, Sandra seems cut off from the broader humanity of the child who reaches out instinctively to the homeless young man. Perhaps aware of her rather uncharitable attitude, Sandra offers three pounds to a passing paper-seller before mother and child make their way home on the bus, staring out 'intae the dark night.'

REVISION POINTS	
LANGUAGE:	Glaswegian Scots
RELATIONSHIPS:	Mother–daughter Sandra is a rather care-worn mother who fails to find either the true spirit of Christmas or real enjoyment in their outing. Amy, by contrast, is delighted and intuitively seems to understand what the true spirit of Christmas should be.
NARRATION:	Interior monologue by Sandra Sandra's interior monologue is interspersed with dialogue with her boss, Amy and a woman on the bus.
CONNECTING THEMES	
Finding empowerment	Amy is determined to offer the homeless man a bed. Sandra, however, thwarts the idea quite firmly. Amy is powerless to persuade the older woman to implement her charitable intention.
Being spontaneous	Amy instinctively feels what a reaction to homelessness ought to be. Her desire to offer a bed at Christmas is wholly in keeping with the spirit of her favourite carol, 'Away in a Manger'. The mother's practicality and world-weariness have robbed her of the spontaneous generosity of her child.

Classroom challenge

Here are some quotations from, and possible comments about, 'Away in a Manger'. These will help add depth to your knowledge of the text.

Fill in the grid's blanks; quotations are in the left-hand column, comments in the right. Sometimes you'll need to find a quotation; sometimes you'll need to make your own comment about what the quotation suggests about the situation or the character.

p.77	Amy's human warmth is hinted at early in the story.
p.78 'Late night shoppers, trippin ower wan another tae buy presents that'd be returned on Boxin Day, everybody in a bad mood, trachled wi parcels.'	
p.82	Sandra is keen to protect Amy from the harsh facts of homelessness.
p.82 'He could come and stay wi us.'	
p.83	Sandra perhaps has a conscience about squashing Amy's idea of helping the young man.
p.83 'This is murder, so it is. Ah'll be glad when it's all over. Gets worse every year.'	
p.83	Anne Donovan suggests that Sandra's weary view of Christmas may stem from a rather sad life. Perhaps we should not judge her too harshly.

TEACHING NOTES

You can download Teaching Notes for this at www.brightredpublishing.co.uk/Shop/national-5-english-course-book

'Hieroglyphics'

Mary Ryan lives in Drumchapel with her mother and sisters, Catherine and Elizabeth. She suffers from dyslexia and the isolation which this brings from her peers. Several half-hearted attempts are made at primary and secondary school to deal with her problem but to no avail.

We first meet her at the age of eight and follow her progress into lower secondary school. It's a throwaway insult from the unpleasant Mr Kelly which, ironically, opens a gateway to a new world for Mary: the language of hieroglyphics. Freed from having to use conventional methods of creating texts, she finds her own method of depicting her world and expressing her feelings – things that standard spelling and writing procedures have denied her. Through hieroglyphics, she rescues herself from marginalisation to participate in the world and work of her peer group.

REVISION POINTS	
LANGUAGE:	Glaswegian Scots
NARRATION:	By Mary, a young girl with learning difficulties
RELATIONSHIPS:	Teachers–pupil: the relationships range from feebly supportive to frankly unsympathetic Mother–daughter: mother not particularly supportive Peer group–Mary: unsupportive
CONNECTING THEMES	
Finding empowerment	Mary, from a throwaway sarcastic remark by Mr Kelly, finds empowerment to communicate through her own imagination. She ends by participating fully in her essay-writing task.
Being spontaneous	She succeeds in describing her world and expressing her feelings effectively in a way alien to conventional education.
Communication across the generations	Adults here fail entirely to appreciate the underlying intelligence of a child struggling with learning challenges.

Classroom challenge

Beside each of these quotations from 'Hieroglyphics', make your own comment about what each one illustrates about the character, situation or theme.

'Ah mind they were birlin and dancing roond like big black spiders.' (p.1)	
'But they didnae follow oany rules that ah could make sense of.' (p.1)	
'They gave me aw these tests an heard ma readin and tellt ma ma ah hud a readin age of 6.4 an a spellin age of 5.7 and Goad knows whit else, but naebdy ever asked me whit wis gaun oan in ma heid. So ah never tellt them.' (p.3)	
'She's a poor wee soul but she tries very hard.' (p.5)	
'And there seemed tae be an empty space aw roond me in the class, fur naebdy sat next tae me if they could help it.' (p.6)	
'And gradually ah progressed fae writin wee messages tae writin whole stories in pictures.' (p.7)	
'So ah drew a wee picture of masel wi a cheery face on it, pit ma story right on tap ae the pile and planted the whole doon in the centre of his desk.' (p.11)	

TEACHING NOTES

You can download Teaching Notes at www.brightredpublishing.co.uk/Shop/national-5-english-course-book

Homework helper

When revising, make sure you have the characters' names and the story in which they appear at your fingertips. Knowing the story means being able to name the characters and their story quickly and accurately. Here's a quick test to remind you of some key names.

CHARACTERS	NAME	APPEARANCE IN WHICH STORY?
Heroine with sharp intelligence who struggles with reading and writing.		
A girl whose mother does not love her.		
Heroine who loved glitter pens.		
Woman who worked extra hours to make more money for Christmas.		
Girl who feels isolated from class mates.		
A girl with whom a heroine is unfavourably compared.		
A girl who feels compassion towards a homeless man.		

TEACHING NOTES

You can download Teaching Notes at www.brightredpublishing.co.uk/Shop/national-5-english-course-book

Classroom challenge

For all their differences, the Anne Donovan stories which you've read have certain recurring themes which help bind the collection together. We have seen there are at least three key themes at play here. Here are some quotations which help illustrate these themes in the stories.

1. In the second column of grid below, say from which story each quotation comes.

1. 'So ah drew a wee picture of masel wi a cheery face on it, pit ma story right on tap ae the pile and planted the whole lot doon in the centre of his desk.'	
2. '*Whit the hell dae you think you're daein? Go and get changed this minute.*'	
3. 'Once and for all, he's no comin hame wi us. And if you don't stop gaun on aboot it Santa'll no come this year either.'	
4. 'Ah love stroking her hair, it's that soft and fuzzy but she cannae be bothered wi that and jerks her heid away, sayin *don't you'll mess it up.*'	
5. 'Amy stared at the man, her heid tae one side. "He could come and stay wi us."'	
6. 'In the end ah selt ma dinner tickets tae big Maggie Hughes [...] But on Friday it wis worth it when ah went doon the shops tae buy the pens.'	
7. 'Ah kin see it in her eyes, no the way she looks at me, but the way she looks through me ...'	
8. '*But if you were an Egyptian you could read hieroglyphics, sur.*'	
9. 'Then ah stood and looked in the mirror at the glowin figure afore me and ah smiled. Subtle, daddy? Aye, hen, subtle.'	

2. Now, in the grid below, place each of the quotations from the first grid in the column you think it belongs to.

FINDING EMPOWERMENT	BEING SPONTANEOUS	COMMUNICATION ACROSS THE GENERATIONS

Once you've allocated the quotations, try to think of other quotations which you might add to each column. This will help you to prepare yourself to discuss themes in a commonality question.

TEACHING NOTES

You can download Teaching Notes at www.brightredpublishing.co.uk/Shop/national-5-english-course-book

DON'T FORGET

Be prepared to make connections of your own in this collection of fascinating characters and situations. In addition to uniting themes, there may well be family situations, personal difficulties, narrative styles, language choices about which you could make sound points in a commonality question. To pick up top marks for this, it's vital to know the connections between the stories.

Exam-style tests

Topic Test 3

Read the extract below and then attempt the following questions.

'Hieroglyphics' by Anne Donovan

Anither brand new jotter. Anither set a rules tae copy. This is the last period a the day and the sixth time ah've hud tae dae it. Could they no jist huv wan lot a rules fur every class? It takes me that long tae copy the rules oot that the lesson's nearly finished and ah've missed it. The French teacher took wan look at the dug's dinner ah wis producing and tellt me no tae bother. And the Maths teacher asked me ma name an looked me up in a list.

You're Mary Ryan, are you? Mmm.

Must of been the remmy list. Ah'm no remmy at Maths right enough – it's jist ah cannae read the stuff. If sumbdy tells me whit tae dae ah kin usually dae it, ah jist cannae read it masel in thae wee booklets. It's funny how the numbers never seem tae birl aroond the way the letters dae; mibby it's because there urny usually as many numbers in a number as there are letters in a word, if ye know whit ah mean. Or is it because ye read them across the way and ye dae Maths doon the way? Mibby if ah lived in wanny thae countries where they wrote doon the way ah'd be aw right. Ah mean no evrbdy writes like we dae. We done a project on it in Primary Five and there's aw kinds a ways a writin in the world. Some folk read right tae left and some up and doon. And they Egyptians drew wee pictures fur aw their writin. Ah hink ah should of been an Egyptian.

And what's this supposed to be – hieroglyphics?

Ah hated that sarky bastard, Mr Kelly. Skelly, we cried him though he wisnae actually skelly; he used tae squint at ye through wan eye as if he wis examinin ye through a microscope an hid jist discovered some new strain a bacteria that could wipe oot the entire population a Glasga. He wis the Latin teacher but he hud hardly oany classes because naebdy done Latin noo so they'd gied him oor class fur English, and then every time a teacher wis aff sick he used tae take the class, so ah began seein a loaty him. And that wis bad news.

Ye see ah'd never felt like this afore wi oany ither teachers. Ah knew whit they were thinkin of me right enough, ah could see it in their eyes, but maisty them jist thoat ah wis a poor wee sowl that couldnae learn oanythin, so whit wis the point a them tryin tae teach me? Sometimes they even said it oot loud, like when the heidie wis his wee dauner roon the classes tae make sure we were aw workin hard and no writin graffiti on wer jotters. (Chance wid of been a fine thing.)

And how are they settling in, Miss Niven?

Oh very well, Mr McIver, they're all working very hard on their projects on the Egyptians. Amir has produced a wonderful imaginative piece on the last thoughts of Tutenkhamun and look how neatly Mary's coloured in the borders of the wall display.

She's a poor wee soul but she tries hard.

Obviously no bein able tae read makes ye deif.

But that big skelly bastard wis different. Tae start wi ah thoat he wis jist borin and boredom is sumpn that disnae bother me, ah'm used tae it, ah hink maist weans are. The furst few days he rambled on aboot grammar and wrote stuff up on the board an we didnae really huvty dae oanythin bar keep oor mooths shut. Which is easie-peasie tae me. But then he startit tae dictates notes tae us and he could time his pace jist so. If ye kin imagine the class like a field a racehorses then he wus gaun at such a pelt that only the furst two or three could keep up wi him. The rest wur scribblin furiously, their airms hingin oot thur soackets, sighin an moanin ower their jotters, and then he'd tease them wi a pause that wis jist a toty bit aff bein long enough tae let them catch up, an then, wheech, he wis aff again lik lightning.

Me, ah wis the wan that fell at the furst fence.

1. Look at paragraph one. ('Anither brand ... in a list.')

   Show **two** examples of Anne Donovan's language which suggest Mary's frustration with classroom administration. **4**

2. Look at paragraph three. ('Must of been ... an Egyptian.')

   Explain using your own words as far as possible why Mary feels success is more possible for her in Maths than in English. You should make **two** main points. **2**

3. Using your own words as far as possible, summarise Mary's reasons for disliking Mr Kelly.

   You should make **four** main points. **4**

4. Look at the final paragraph. ('But that big skelly ... furst fence.')

   Explain how any one example of the writer's use of language in these lines reveals that Mary, despite self-doubts about her writing ability, is a skilled observer of classroom life. **2**

5. Young girls in Donovan's stories are often faced with difficulties in their lives. With reference to this extract and to at least one other story, show how these problems are explored. **8**

TOTAL – 20 marks

Topic Test 4

Read the extract below and then attempt the following questions.

'Away in a Manger' by Anne Donovan

In this extract from 'Away in a Manger', Sandra and her daughter, Amy, visit George Square, Glasgow, to see the Christmas lights.

This year the nativity scene was bigger than life-sized. The figures were bronze statues, staunin on a carpet of straw and surrounded by what looked like a hoose made of glass. It was placed tae wan side of the square, inside a fence. Sandra thought it was quite dull lookin. Weans liked bright colours and these huge people were kind of scary. She minded the wee plastic figures of Mary and Joseph she used tae set carefully in place every Christmas, leavin the baby Jesus tae last. They'd fitted intae the palm of her haund. She'd need tae get a crib for Amy. Sandra wisnae very religious, no religious at all, really, but still, it was nice for wee ones tae have a crib.

'Is that the manger, Mammy?' Amy pointed.

'That's right. D'you know who all the people are?'

Amy sucked at her mitt and looked carefully at the figures. 'That's Mary and that's Joseph – and that's the baby Jesus. And that's a shepherd wi his sheep. But who's that, Mammy?'

'They're the three wise kings. Look – they've got presents for the baby Jesus.'

'But who's *that*, Mammy? Behind the cow.'

Huddled in the straw, hidden in a corner behind the figure of a large beast, lay a man. He was slightly built, dressed in auld jeans and a thin jacket. One of his feet stuck round the end of the statue and on it was a worn trainin shoe, the cheapest kind they sold in the store. Sandra moved round tae get a better look at him. He was quite young, wi a pointed face and longish dark hair. A stubbly growth covered his chin. He seemed sound asleep.

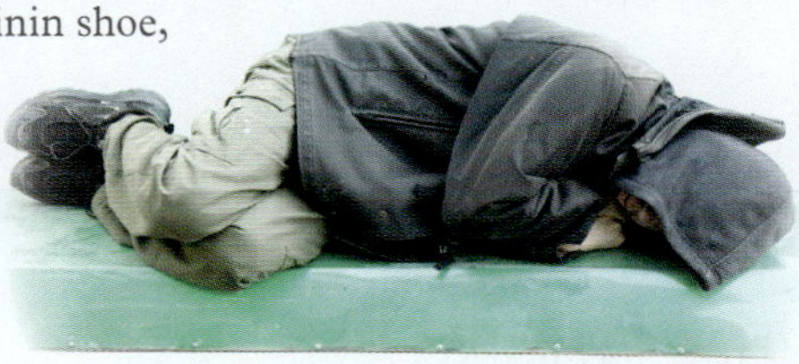

'Is he an angel, Mammy?'

Sandra didnae answer. She was lookin at the glass structure wonderin how on earth he'd got in. One of the panels at the back looked a bit loose, but you'd think they'd have an alarm on it. Lucky for him they never – at least he'd be warm in there. She was that intent on the glass panels that she'd nearly forgotten he wisnae a statue. Suddenly he opened his eyes. They were grey.

Amy grabbed her mother's arm and started jumpin up and down.

'Mammy, look, he's alive! Look Mammy. He's an angel!'

'Naw, he's no an angel. He's a man.'

But, Mammy, what's he daein in there wi the baby Jesus?'

'Ah don't know, Amy. Some folk don't have anywhere tae stay.'

Sandra didnae want her tae know, she was too young. She wished she could of thought of a story – he's a security guard havin a sleep, he's a councillor checkin how they've spent the ratepayers' money, he's an art student examining the statues.

Amy stared at the man, his head tae one side. 'He could come and stay wi us.'

'Naw, he cannae.'

'How no?'

'Because we havenae got room.'

'We have so, Mammy, we've got a spare room.'

'Aye but that's where your granny sleeps when she comes tae stay. She's comin for Christmas soon.'

'Ah can sleep wi Granny. Ah like sleepin wi ma granny. She's fat.'

'Don't tell her that.'

'How no? She's like a big hot-water bottle.'

Sandra laughed. 'C'mon.'

She took Amy's haund but Amy stayed where she was.

'If ah slept wi ma granny the man could have ma bed.'

'Naw, he couldnae. Ye cannae just take anybody intae your hoose. We don't know him.'

'If he came tae stay wi us we would know him.'

'Once and for all, he's no comin hame wi us. And if you don't stop gaun on aboot it Santa'll no come this year either.'

She took Amy by the haund and led her away oot the square.

1. Summarise what happens in this extract from the short story. Make at least **four** key points. **4**

2. Choose **two** examples of Anne Donovan's use of language which help show Sandra in a good light as a caring mother. **4**

3. With close reference to the text, explain the reactions to the young man of:

a) Sandra

b) Amy **4**

4. By referring to this extract and at least one other short story by Anne Donovan, show how the writer explores the difficulties children may face. **8**

TOTAL – 20 marks

TEACHING NOTES

You can download Teaching Notes for this at www.brightredpublishing.co.uk/Shop/national-5-english-course-book

SIX POEMS BY EDWIN MORGAN

What's coming up?

- Profile of the author
- Poems under the spotlight
- Themes
- Familiarisation activities
- Exam-style tests

Profile of the author: Edwin Morgan

Born in 1920 in Glasgow, Edwin Morgan attended Rutherglen Academy and Glasgow High School before entering Glasgow University in 1937. He read English Language and Literature there until his studies were interrupted by the Second World War, when he enrolled as a conscientious objector in the Royal Army Medical Corps.

He returned from service in the Middle East to complete his degree with First Class Honours. On graduating, he took up a post as titular professor of English at the University, which he held until he retired in 1980 to devote the rest of his life to writing. He was the recipient of many honours, including the Queen's Gold Medal for Poetry in 2000. He was appointed Scotland's first Scots Makar of modern times, the Scottish equivalent of Poet Laureate, in 2004. He died in 2010.

Morgan was among the most inventive, adventurous poets of his age, seeing poetry 'as an instrument of exploration, like a spaceship, into new fields of feeling or experience'. The poems you study for National 5 give only a tiny indication of the depth and breadth of his output.

Here is an example of Morgan's 'concrete' style at its most playful. Shape and content are one here. The poem is called 'Siesta of a Hungarian Snake'. This is the whole poem.

s sz sz SZ sz SZ sz ZS zs ZS zs zs z

In terms of language, he ranges widely from Glaswegian Scots, to attempts to create the language of the Loch Ness Monster, the men from Mercury, Hungarian snakes or even an African hyena. Complementing this desire to give a voice to others is a drive to intensify the power of his own, often through a series of complex verbal effects, a process which appears to have fascinated him and which we see at work in several of the poems for study here.

In terms of topics, he ranges widely, often finding material in the urban cite of his native Glasgow or the history and geography of Scotland. But he also ventures into the worlds of computers, inter-planetary travel, Bible history, and even pre-history.

Poems under the spotlight

'Good Friday'

At what is usually a time on Good Friday (3pm) when, in biblical history, a darkness was said to cover the land, this Glasgow Good Friday is bathed in sunshine and the tipsy man is happily celebrating and off to buy Easter eggs for the 'kiddies'.

Morgan cleverly captures the speech patterns of the man which, like the bus itself, are given to lurches and sudden changes of direction. Note how Morgan avoids any direct comment on his fellow traveller but listens, uncritically, and seems to find the man's chatter inoffensively amusing, even picturing his descent from the top deck in 'concrete' terms, with a word for each descending step.

REVISION POINTS	
LANGUAGE:	Glaswegian Scots
FORM:	Dramatic monologue Free verse (avoiding regular rhythm and rhyme)
TONE:	Chatty/amused Speaker is a good-natured, tipsy man. Note, there is also a 'me' in the poem, presumably the 'educatit' Morgan.
SUBJECT MATTER:	A bus journey along Bath Street, Glasgow, on a Good Friday afternoon. Topics covered include Christ's crucifixion and resurrection; the meaning of Easter; and the speaker's drinking habits, lack of education and immediate intentions once off the bus.

KEY FEATURES:

- Tipsiness caught in many places by word choice, repetition and incomplete sentences.
- Final lines mimic visually downward steps of the traveller.
- Bus movement and traveller share similar lurching movement for comic effect.
- Original way of exploring a religious festival.

Homework helper

When exploring a poem, being able to pick out language features such as imagery, word choice or sentence structure is important, but it's not the whole story.

Being able to comment in your own words on the effect each technique has on the reader is equally important. In the grid below, you'll find some ways to familiarise yourself with the content of 'Good Friday'. Sometimes, you'll need to find a brief quotation as evidence for a given comment; sometimes, you'll need to make a comment of your own on the evidence's effect.

TEXTUAL EVIDENCE	POSSIBLE COMMENT
	The poet's verb choice helps us understand that the man seems not in control of his movements at the start and end of the poem.
'Oh tha's, tha's ...' and 'ye understand – ye understand?'	
	Morgan's use of Scots gives the poem an informal, chatty tone.
'The bus lurches' and 'The bus brakes violently'	
	The repetition of this phrase at the start and end of the poem seems the reverse of the weather associated with the original Good Friday.
	The man seems generous and seeks to give pleasure to others.
	The fact that the man sometimes seems unable to complete sentences is one way the poet indicates the man is not quite sober.
'On very Nearly Steady Legs.'	

TEACHING NOTES

You can download Teaching Notes for this at www.brightredpublishing.co.uk/Shop/national-5-english-course-book

DON'T FORGET

These six Morgan poems differ greatly in topics and techniques. Make sure your notes are full enough to allow you to make connections between the six.

'In the Snack-Bar'

Here, as in 'Good Friday', we have another casual Glasgow encounter. There are, however, sharp differences. This time, the effect is far from cheery and light-hearted as before; and the speaker, again presumably Morgan, describes the setting, the action and his response to it.

In a detailed realisation of a 'crowded evening snack-bar' with its formica, hissing coffee machine and fixed stools, the old man is presented almost as a species from another world, 'like a monstrous animal caught in a tent / In some story'. The speaker helps the old man to the toilet. Skilfully, Morgan captures the slow progress of the pair as they descend the stairs to the toilet by effective use of repetition and inversion:

And slowly we go down. And slowly we go down.

This is a technique which Morgan returns to again in the poem to mirror the man's painfully slow progress in carrying out any action. His helplessness and clumsiness in coping with the simplest action is frequently further underlined by Morgan's word choice: 'He **shambles uncouth**', 'he **clings** to me', 'to **haul** his blind **hump**'.

Morgan is not only an active, compassionate helper here – one whose strength serves not only to emphasise in comparison the frailty of the old man – but presents himself as a moved, distraught commentator also:

Dear Christ, to be born for this!

REVISION POINTS	
LANGUAGE:	Standard English
FORM:	Free verse (avoiding regular rhythm and rhyme) The incident is recounted by an 'I', usually taken to be Morgan himself.
TONE:	Seemingly objective in its description, yet word choice and sentence structure betray speaker's compassion. Direct comment delayed until last line.
SUBJECT MATTER:	Casual encounter in a Glasgow snack-bar. Three of Morgan's N5 poems stem from casual encounters in Glasgow's city centre.

KEY FEATURES:

- Atmosphere of café on a wet August evening carefully captured through word choice, alliteration and onomatopoeia.
- Blind man's 'other worldliness' contrasted with everyday nature of life in snack-bar.
- Blind man's painfully difficult movement well captured by sentence structure and word choice.

Homework helper

Look at some possible comments which could be made about Morgan's handling of 'In the Snack-Bar'. Once you've studied the poem, try to find textual evidence to support the comments in the column on the right.

TEXTUAL EVIDENCE	POSSIBLE COMMENT
	The poet uses alliteration to picture in sound the sudden harsh disruption that the blind man's clumsy attempt to rise causes in the café.
	This simile conveys effectively how alien the blind man seems in this city-centre setting.
	Whenever the blind man speaks, Morgan shows his insecurity in his hesitant sentence structure.
	Morgan uses repetition and inversion to convey how the two men tackled the descent to the toilet.
	The painfully hesitant yet determined nature of the blind man's ascent is well conveyed through Morgan's seemingly contradictory word choice.
	The poet conveys effectively the contrast between his view of the distance from stairs to front door with that of the blind man through word choice that seems to contradict itself.
	The bleakness of the blind man's life is suggested by what the speaker supposes he said to the bus conductor.
	The burden of the blind man's painful progress through life is captured in the final lines by Morgan's word choice and use of alliteration.

TEACHING NOTES

You can download Teaching Notes for this at www.brightredpublishing.co.uk/Shop/national-5-english-course-book

'Trio'

While 'In the Snack Bar' records the darker side of city life in Glasgow, in 'Trio' we see Morgan delighting mightily in a casual encounter in Buchanan Street one 'sharp winter evening' just before Christmas.

Here the speaker, like the drunk man in 'Good Friday', appears to have doubts as to the credibility of the Christian myth ('Whether Christ is born, or not born ...'). Nevertheless, there's no doubting the sheer joy the trio of two young girls and young man inspire in the speaker as he describes in detail their sighting, the gifts they carry and the 'cloud of happiness' that surrounds them. Here, Morgan cleverly uses these three young people and their surroundings to draw modern-day parallels with the three kings of the Christmas legend. They carry gifts, not the gold, frankincense and myrrh of the magi, but a guitar, baby and a chihuahua; they appear, not under a star, but the Christmas lights of Buchanan Street; and a child is central to the encounter.

The speaker dips into yet another myth (of Orpheus and his lute) to salute in mock heroic terms the guitar-carrying young man as an 'Orphean sprig', hailing also the baby and the chihuahua in equally delighted exclamations of joy. This happiness may be the outcome of a commercially driven Christmas rather than a religiously inspired one, but the speaker sees it having the power, no less than a Christian one, to drive away the gloom of 'the vale of tears' which is the world, and which 'abdicates / under the Christmas lights'. It is a joy which lingers even after they have passed out of sight, marking the 'end of this winter's day'.

Morgan employs a contrast of styles here: in the early lines his language is matter-of-fact, conversational in its use of enjambment and simple word choice to describe the physical appearance of the trio. Then, with 'Orphean sprig!', Morgan seeks to underline the significance he places on the encounter by adopting a more rhetorical, lofty tone and language as he mulls over its lasting power to inspire. What began as a snapshot of three ordinary young people carrying Christmas gifts in a Glasgow street ends as a more philosophical celebration of the great power of joy to enrich the lives of those observing it.

REVISION POINTS	
LANGUAGE:	Standard English
FORM:	Free verse (avoiding regular rhythm and rhyme)
TONE:	Lines 1–14 adopt a conversational tone to capture a snapshot of the three young people. From line 15 onwards, the tone becomes more lofty as Morgan expands on what the encounter means to him.
SUBJECT MATTER:	An encounter between the speaker and three young people in Glasgow city centre. Morgan develops parallels and contrasts with this Glasgow Christmas scene and the biblical nativity.

KEY FEATURES:

- Shares Glasgow city centre setting with 'Good Friday', 'In the Snack-Bar', and 'Glasgow 5 March 1971'.
- Shares with 'Good Friday' an unconventional way of interpreting Christian festivals.
- Poem leaves Morgan with a happiness independent of religious belief.
- Simple word choice and enjambment underline the conversational tone in first part.
- Tone becomes more philosophical from line 15 as Morgan draws inspiration from the scene.

Homework helper

Use the grid below to help you familiarise yourself with the content of 'Trio'. Sometimes, you'll need to find a brief quotation as evidence for a given comment; sometimes, you'll need to make a comment of your own on the evidence's effect.

TEXTUAL EVIDENCE	POSSIBLE COMMENT
	The poet is precise about the time and place of the encounter.
'... their breath rises / in a cloud of happiness ...'	
'... a tiny Royal Stewart tartan coat like a teapot-holder ...'	
'Orphean sprig! Melting baby! Warm chihuahua!'	
	The misery of daily life melts away when brought face-to-face with such happiness.
'Whether Christ is born, or is not born ...'	
'it [fate] abdicates under the Christmas lights.'	
'And the three have passed, vanished in the crowd (yet not vanished ...)'	

TEACHING NOTES

You can download Teaching Notes for this at www.brightredpublishing.co.uk/Shop/national-5-english-course-book

'Winter'

Here Morgan exploits his English lecturer's knowledge of Tennyson's 1833 poem 'Tithonus', a man who in Greek mythology sought immortality but forgot to wish for eternal youth as well. Tennyson's poem begins:

The woods decay, the woods decay and fall,
The vapours weep their burthen to the ground,
Man comes and tills the field and lies beneath,
And after many a summer dies the swan.

Tithonus is, consequently, left as a lonely, solitary character, a fate which seems to be shared by the speaker here as, at the end of the poem, he gazes at the 'grey dead pane'.

Is that 'pane' a play on 'pain'? By altering the punctuation subtly, Morgan achieves a complex verbal effect in his opening lines, drawing as he does the reader away from classical Greek myth and Tennyson to his own more mundane world of Great Western Road and Bingham's Pond, local home of mute swans.

The altered punctuation leads in its shortened phrases to a fractured forward movement, far from the smoothly flowing melancholy of the earlier poem. The halting progress continues in the fragmented phrases as Morgan describes the frozen winter scene, insisting on hardness and sharpness as 'swan-white ice glints only crystal beyond white'. This is intensified as the 'stark scene' is 'cut' by 'cries' in the 'warring air' and the 'hiss of blades'. The harshness of the alliteration and onomatopoeia add to the bleakness of the scene.

Gradually, the skaters disappear into the fog as, eventually, do the lights themselves. Now the scene is left to the fog which takes over and 'drives monstrous down the dual carriageway' like some demonic driver, leaving the speaker solitary, staring blankly at only greyness. And greyness stares back at him. In its rich poetic effects which underline the bleaker aspects of winter, this is a poem in which the speaker's emotions seem as frozen as the external landscape.

REVISION POINTS	
LANGUAGE:	Standard English
FORM:	Free verse (avoiding regular rhythm and rhyme)
TONE:	Reflective
SUBJECT MATTER:	Bleak thoughts on the annual dying of nature. Lines 1–9 convey an impression of the coming of winter around the speaker's home. Lines 10–23 focus on one particular winter scene that illustrates the full bleakness of the speaker's thoughts.

KEY FEATURES:

- With mention of Bingham Pond and 'the dual carriageway / out to the west', the poem has Glasgow as its setting.
- Nature – and its annual decay and death – provides inspiration for the poem.
- The sentence structure is often choppy and awkward, offering fractured forward movement, which suggests the emotional disturbance of the speaker.
- Harsh onomatopoeia and alliteration underline the sharpness of the speaker's bleak thoughts.
- Speaker exploits the frozen landscape of winter as a symbol of the numbness of his own feelings.

Homework helper

Once again, use the grid below to help you familiarise yourself with the content of 'Winter'. You'll have to either find the textual evidence or make a comment of your own on the evidence's effect.

TEXTUAL EVIDENCE	POSSIBLE COMMENT
	In lines 1–2, the speaker's word choice suggests that the passing of time is very much on his mind.
	The speaker uses the swan to intensify the idea that the year has died completely.

TEACHING NOTES

You can download Teaching Notes for this at www.brightredpublishing.co.uk/Shop/national-5-english-course-book

	The abruptness of the change from liquid pond to frozen ice has an effect on wildlife as well as the speaker.
'the swan-white ice glints only crystal beyond white'	
	The speaker employs alliteration on harsh consonants to illustrate the bleakness of the sight and sound of one particular evening.
	Repetition is useful in creating a sense of the sounds vanishing into the gloom.
'when fog drives monstrous down the dual carriageway out to the west.'	
	Repetition helps emphasise the sheer emptiness which the speaker feels at the end of the poem.

DON'T FORGET

These six poems give the poet's varied response to the city of Glasgow. At times, he sees Glasgow as life-affirming, in poems such as 'Good Friday' and 'Trio'. At others ('In the Snack-Bar', 'Glasgow Sonnet No 1', 'Winter' and 'Glasgow 5 March 1971'), the city presents a darker side of itself and of people. Complementing this variety of moods are the various styles and forms that Morgan employs to capture his vision: formal sonnet form and free verse; simple conversational tone and more elaborated use of language; and Standard English and Glaswegian Scots. Despite their differences, they enjoy considerable areas of commonality. Make sure you're familiar with them all.

'Glasgow Sonnet No 1'

The sonnet is a 14-line poetic structure most commonly used in the past for poems of love and romance. Here, Morgan harnesses it to a much bleaker task.

Camera-like, the poet's description moves relentlessly in from a broad focus on the 'backcourt' in the first quatrain (four lines) to an increasingly narrower one until it alights, finally, on the unemployed man. The opening panorama personifies a world of desolation; weirdly, only inanimate items show any sign of life: 'a mean wind wanders', 'Hackles on puddles rise', 'mattresses puff'. The bleakness is intensified by alliteration ('wind wanders', 'bricks and bric-a-brac') and the hissing consonance of the internal 's' of 'mattresses' and 'fortresses' which, together with the equally hissing rhyme of 'trash' and 'ash', suggest the sound of the rain that created those backcourt puddles.

The second quatrain moves upwards from the courtyard onto the building itself. The mother and daughter seem besieged in the crumbling building, with only a 'cracked sill' to buttress them against their hostile environment. Again, we have the harsh sounds created by the hissing 's' in 'buttresses', 'mistresses' and the rhyming 'smash' and 'crash'.

The 'mistresses' of the semi-derelict building seem more like victims, marooned as they are in this desolate scene where (in the first three lines of the **sestet**) they are surrounded by 'cracks', 'rats' and 'roses of mould'. So grim is the scene that even 'The kettle whimpers on a crazy hob'.

The final three lines arrive at the bedside of the sick, unemployed man. The focus has moved steadily from a wide exterior angle to a close-up focus on this figure of despair coughing out his life. From urban desolation, we have moved on to its human counterpart, a man as derelict as the building he inhabits. With its final reference to 'an air too poor to rob' the sonnet has come full circle, having begun noting a faintly menacing, prowling 'mean wind' in the courtyard. Now, the evident poverty is such that it makes any robbery pointless.

REVISION POINTS	
LANGUAGE:	Standard English
FORM:	Petrarchan (Italian) sonnet Octave (8 lines) followed by sestet (6 lines) in the rhyme scheme abba, abba, cdc, dcd.
TONE:	Objective description intensified by rich use of poetic devices. Frequent use of enjambment softens the formal sonnet rhyme pattern. No direct comment by poet.
SUBJECT MATTER:	A portrayal of urban decay and poverty in the Gorbals of the '70s. The poem uses its octave/sestet structure to explore, in turn, urban and human destitution.

KEY FEATURES:

- Shares the harsher side of Glasgow city centre setting with 'In the Snack-Bar' and 'Glasgow 5 March 1971'.
- Only poem of these six to employ a formal structure.
- Alliteration, consonance, onomatopoeia and personification are key poetic techniques employed here by Morgan to re-create the squalor and desolation of the scene.

Classroom challenge

Here's a chance to try your skills on making comments of your own on selected textual evidence or finding evidence to support comments that could be made in class.

TEXTUAL EVIDENCE	POSSIBLE COMMENT
'Hackles on puddles rise,'	
	Morgan emphasises the grim atmosphere by sometimes placing end-rhymes on words whose meaning is unattractive and whose sound is harsh.
	Mother and daughter sound as if they are besieged in their home.
'condemned to stand'	
'The kettle whimpers'	
	Morgan's use of enjambment makes end-rhyme less obvious and maintains the forward flow of the poem.

You can download Teaching Notes for this challenge at www.brightredpublishing.co.uk/Shop/national-5-english-course-book

TEACHING NOTES

'Glasgow 5 March 1971'

This is a poem which, like 'Trio', features a city-centre street encounter. But, here, the stark brutality of the scene highlights a very different side of city life. It is one of several 'Instamatic' poems which, named after a cheap camera of the period, give an instant picture of a single moment in time, hence the precise nature of the title. Morgan uses this 'moment-in-time' technique, however, to present us with more than a simple snapshot; we are offered a thought-provoking image which says much about Morgan's society – some might say it's changed very little since 1971.

The poem is structured around three couples: the two victims of the attack, the two thieving thugs and the two passing drivers. The frequent use of enjambment throughout the poem helps establish an almost conversational tone, seemingly at odds with the horrific nature of the attack. But it's the very ordinary language describing outrageous brutality which is perhaps Morgan's point: such behaviour has, sadly, become quite commonplace. However, at moments, his word choice bursts out of this matter-of-fact, black-and-white language to underline the horror of the moment with graphic vividness.

The scene is not some dark alley, stereotypically home of much crime, but city-centre Sauchiehall Street, 'on a sharp clear night'. A young couple is being used as a battering ram by 'two youths' to smash a shop window in order to steal goods. Dehumanised, the couple have become merely a tool to assist a theft. Against the 'ragged diamond of shattered plate-glass', the couple show 'surprise, shock/ and the beginning of pain.'

Morgan's methodical description comes most vividly alive when he describes the actual violence, when we hear that the young man's beard, horrifically, is bristling not with stubble but with 'fragments of shattered glass' and the girl's leg, caught on the shattered window 'spurts arterial blood/ over her wet-look white coat.' The arms of these human beings are 'starfished out' to meet the impact with the glass, their predicament caught in shockingly vivid terms.

In contrast, the thugs are described matter-of-factly as they 'are about to complete the operation/ reaching into the window/ to loot what they can smartly./ Their faces show no expression.' This act of savagery is to them merely an 'operation'. Meanwhile, two passing motorists, good drivers but poor citizens, 'keep their eyes on the road'. Morgan's meaning is clear: witnesses to such acts (perhaps readers included) do not wish to become involved. And so, violence in society continues.

This hard-hitting message about the casualness of violence has been made with no direct authorial comment; powerfully, Morgan leaves the snapshot to speak for itself.

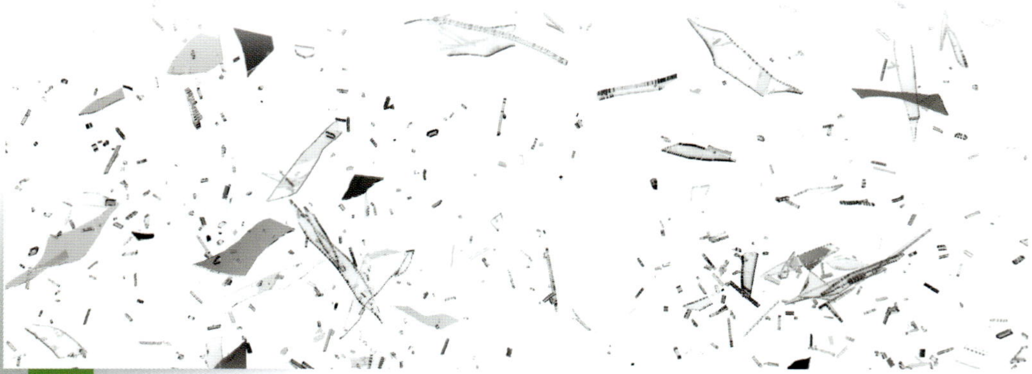

REVISION POINTS	
LANGUAGE:	Standard English
FORM:	Free verse (avoiding regular rhythm and rhyme)
TONE:	Matter-of-fact, objective recital of facts. Frequent enjambment contributes an almost conversational tone to events. Word choice is richest at moments of extreme violence.
SUBJECT MATTER:	An 'Instamatic' snapshot of a violent city-centre encounter.

KEY FEATURES:

- Shares the harsher side of Glasgow city-centre setting with 'In the Snack-Bar' and 'Glasgow Sonnet No 1.
- Language of factual reporting for the most part. Graphic word choice at moments of violence.
- As in 'Trio', the central characters are young: 'a young man and his girl'/'two youths'
- As in Trio, the action takes place at night.
- Insistence on present tense emphasises the 'Instamatic' immediacy of the assault.

Classroom challenge

Now get to know the poem better by looking at it some detail. Find textual detail to back up the comments or make a comment of your own on the textual evidence.

TEXTUAL EVIDENCE	POSSIBLE COMMENT
	Morgan employs a matter-of-fact tone for the narrative elements of the poem.
	At moments of intense violence, Morgan's word choice becomes startlingly vivid.
	Morgan's extensive use of the present tense heightens the drama of the moment.
'the girl's leg [...] spurts arterial blood'	
'Their faces show no expression.'	
'In the background two drivers keep their eyes on the road.'	

TEACHING NOTES

You can download Teaching Notes for this challenge at www.brightredpublishing.co.uk/Shop/national-5-english-course-book

Homework helper

How well do you know your Morgan poems? From which poems do these twelve quotations come?

1 'I find one stark scene
cut by evening cries ...'

2 'Whether Christ was – crucified or was he –
Rose fae the dead like, see what I mean?'

3 'I notice now his stick, once painted white
but scuffed and muddy, hanging from his
right arm.'

4 'Three o'clock. The bus lurches
Round into the sun.'

5 'Roses of mould grow from ceiling to wall.'

6 'A cup capsizes along the formica,
slithering with a dull clatter.'

7 'Whether Christ is born, or is not born, you
put paid to fate ...'

8 'their faces show surprise, shock,
and the beginning of pain.'

9 'Around them the cracks deepen, the
rats crawl.'

10 'It is a sharp clear night
In Sauchiehall Street.'

11 'Monsters of the year
go blank, are scattered back ...'

12 'At last the lamps go too, when fog
drives monstrous down the dual carriageway
out to the west ...'

Homework helper

Being able to spot connections between poems is a necessary part of your study if you're to do well in the commonality question. What connections have you noticed in these six poems of Morgan?

1. Which poems see central characters facing difficulties/troubles of some kind?
2. In which poems does a speaker (or a 'me') appear?
3. Which poems have young people as central characters?
4. Which city poems have a happy, life-affirming atmosphere?
5. Which poems show city-centre life's darker aspects?
6. Which poems employ free verse, and which a formal rhyme scheme?
7. Which poems take place at night or evening?
8. Which poems employ Standard English or Glaswegian Scots (fully or in parts)?

TEACHING NOTES

You can download Teaching Notes for this task at www.brightredpublishing.co.uk/Shop/national-5-english-course-book

Exam-style tests

Topic Test 5

Read the poem below and then attempt the following questions.

'Winter' by Edwin Morgan

The year goes, the woods decay, and after,
many a summer dies. The swan
on Bingham's pond, a ghost, comes and goes.
It goes, and ice appears, it holds,
bears gulls that stand around surprised,
blinking in the heavy light, bears boys
when skates take over, the swan-white ice
glints only crystal beyond white. Even
dearest blue's not there, though poets would find it.
I find one stark scene
cut by evening cries, by warring air.
The muffled hiss of blades escapes into breath,
hangs with it a moment, fades off.
Fades off, goes, the scene, the voices fade,
the line of trees, the woods that fall, decay
and break, the dark comes down, the shouts
run off into it and disappear.
At last the lamps go too, when fog
drives monstrous down the dual carriageway
out to the west, and even in my room
and on this paper I do not know
about that grey dead pane
of ice that sees nothing and that nothing sees.

1. Look at lines 1–3. Explain how the poet uses **two** examples of word choice to develop the idea of time. **4**
2. Look at lines 4–8. Using your own words as far as possible, explain what we learn about winter at the pond. You should make **four** points. **4**
3. Look at lines 10–17. Comment on the effectiveness of **two** features of the poet's use of language in conveying the winter scene. **4**
4. By referring closely to this poem and to at least one other poem, show how Morgan uses night to explore a theme. **8**

TOTAL – 20 marks

You can download Teaching Notes for this at www.brightredpublishing.co.uk/Shop/national-5-english-course-book

TEACHING NOTES

Topic Test 6

Read the poem below and then attempt the following questions.

'Glasgow Sonnet No 1' by Edwin Morgan

A mean wind wanders through the backcourt trash.
Hackles on puddles rise, old mattresses
puff briefly and subside. Play-fortresses
of brick and bric-a-brac spill out some ash.
Four storeys have no windows left to smash,
but the fifth a chipped sill buttresses
mother and daughter the last mistresses
of that block condemned to stand, not crash.
Around them the cracks deepen, the rats crawl.
The kettle whimpers on a crazy hob.
Roses of mould grow from ceiling to wall.
The man lies late since he has lost his job,
smokes on one elbow, letting his coughs fall
thinly into an air too poor to rob.

1. Look at the first four lines of the poem. By referring to **two** examples of imagery, explain how they help make these lines an effective opening to the poem. **4**
2. Look at lines 5–8. By referring to one example of the poet's use of language, explain fully how the poet makes clear how the building and its tenants seem to be under threat. **2**
3. Look at lines 9–11. By referring to **two** examples of the poet's use of word choice or imagery, explain fully how the poet makes clear the disturbed nature of life in the flat. **4**
4. Look at the poem's last line. Explain, referring to the words 'air too poor to rob', why they make an effective close to the poem. **2**
5. In Morgan's poetry the challenges of city-centre life is a recurring theme. By referring to this poem and to at least one other poem by Morgan, show how the poet uses word choice and/or imagery to explore this theme. **8**

TOTAL – 20 marks

TEACHING NOTES You can download Teaching Notes for this at www.brightredpublishing.co.uk/Shop/national-5-english-course-book

THE STRANGE CASE OF DR JEKYLL AND MR HYDE BY ROBERT LOUIS STEVENSON

What's coming up?

- Profile of the author
- Background to the novel
- Narrative structure
- Section commentaries
- Character studies
- Themes and motifs
- Familiarisation activities
- Exam-style tests

Profile of the author

Son of a famous engineer, Robert Louis Stevenson was born on 13th November 1850 in Edinburgh. Relations with his father were not the best. Although he entered the University of Edinburgh to study engineering with a view to following a career path similar to his father's, his heart wasn't in it. His real desire was to become a writer, an ambition his family disapproved of.

A victim of ill health from his childhood, he began to spend as much time as possible away from the harsh Scottish weather. By the 1870s he was beginning to have some success as a writer, which allowed him to travel extensively in Europe. While travelling in France, he met the American who was later to become his fiercely protective wife.

1886 was a breakthrough year for the writer when his short novel, or novella, *The Strange Case of Dr Jekyll and Mr Hyde*, was published to great acclaim. In the same year, he had another success with *Kidnapped*. Literary success allowed him to travel to warmer climates for his health. Enjoying travel in the South Pacific, he visited many of the islands, including Tahiti and Hawaii, before settling finally in Samoa where he died suddenly on 3rd December 1894.

Background to the novel

Although a resident of Edinburgh's prosperous New Town, the young Stevenson enjoyed spending his leisure time in the more disreputable Old Town, where the constraints of respectable society were far less limiting. No stranger to wild nights in the Old Town's drinking dens, he would return in the early hours to the respectability of the family home in fashionable Heriot Row. But in pursuing two contrasting lifestyles in 19th-century Edinburgh (although in Stevenson's case, the more disreputable one was fairly innocent), he was by no means unique.

As a native of Edinburgh, he would be familiar with the tale of the 18th-century Edinburgh town councillor Deacon Brodie who led a double life – respectable cabinet-maker by day and burglar by night – in order to support his gambling habit and mistresses. Another Edinburgh worthy who was not all he seemed was the 17th-century Major Weir who presented an impeccably virtuous and pious façade to the public. In secret, however, he and his sister had practised witchcraft for many years. Found out eventually, he was executed and his body burned. In short, Stevenson would be no stranger to ideas of a divided self, the starting point for the novella which we are studying here.

But the divided self was by no means a phenomenon which demonstrated itself in civic life solely in Edinburgh. In Victorian middle- and upper-class society at large, the outward forms of morality and respectability were highly prized. But behind these upright façades, personal instincts and behaviour were often quite different.

While vice of all kinds was deplored by respectable society, many 'respectable' men fell far short of the moral standards they claimed in public. In the back streets of cities like London, crime and various forms of moral depravity flourished, as is hinted at here in Mr Hyde's nocturnal activities. In polite society, any direct reference to such unpalatable truths would be hypocritically repressed, as indeed they are by Utterson and Enfield in the opening chapter. Although each seems to be mulling over the probability of Jekyll's involvement with the evil Hyde, it takes a long time for Utterson to draw out Hyde's name from Enfield – and neither mention Jekyll by name to the other.

It's a striking fact of the whole text that its bachelor cast, most of whom have known each other from earlier years, seldom directly voice their worries or concerns. They may suspect much, but they say little. Comment, like society itself, appears repressed throughout.

The idea of the divided self (sometimes referred to as 'duality') crops up in many places in this text – and not simply in the character of Dr Jekyll. Look out for this duality in other characters (and even in places) as you read and take notes.

DON'T FORGET

At this point, decide how you're going to organise your study file for *The Strange Case of Dr Jekyll and Mr Hyde*. Are you going to keep notes chapter by chapter – noting key events, character information and themes as they emerge? Experiment during the first chapters to see what works best for you.

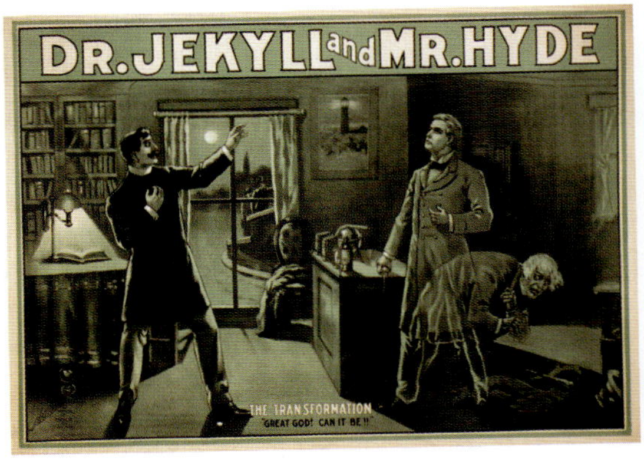

Narrative structure

In this novel, the respectable Dr Jekyll longs to be free of the restraints of respectability to indulge his hidden evil desires. A skilled scientist, he devises a potion to transform himself into Mr Hyde, a wicked character who lives out Jekyll's evil ambitions. However, instead of finding lasting release, Jekyll finds he's on the path to ruin.

The novel takes the form of a fact-finding quest by Dr Jekyll's lawyer and friend, Gabriel Utterson. By clever structuring, Stevenson ensures that the reader, too, is involved in answering the question which bothers the lawyer: what exactly is the truth about this respectable doctor and his strange friend Edward Hyde?

To give this quest a feeling of investigative authenticity, Stevenson employs testimony from various important witnesses – Enfield, Utterson, Lanyon and finally Jekyll himself.

In addition, there are letters and diary entries which give the reader the impression of being directly involved in sifting through fragments of factual evidence. As well as adding authenticity, this approach both draws the reader further and further into the mystery and heightens the tension.

Adding to the 'real world' credibility of this investigative approach, is the fact that the disparate ten sections of 'evidence' are of uneven length: the final one in which Dr Jekyll gives his own testimony occupies a fifth of the novella; the seventh is barely two pages long. In other words, Stevenson has marshalled his material into something which, in its fragmentary structure, tends to resemble the format of a police file, hence the significance of the 'Case' in the novella's title.

Let's take a look at each of the sections, or chapters, now.

Commentary: 'Story of the Door'

Key chapter elements:

- Utterson's description
- Enfield's narrative
- London at night
- Hyde's environment
- Hyde's introduction
- The repressed society

Utterson's description

While the novella is famously centred on the divided character of Jekyll/Hyde, we learn in the first chapter that there is more than one character with divisions and contradictions in his personality. Utterson, the text's second most important character, also manifests a number of puzzling contradictions.

We learn he is 'lean, long, dusty, dreary, and yet somehow lovable'. We also discover he enjoyed fine wines but drank only gin; he enjoyed the theatre but had not been for twenty years; he claims to 'let my brother go to the devil in his own way yet'; and is described as being 'the last good influence in the lives of down-going men'. For all his claimed disinterest in the fate of others, he will become seriously concerned by what he thinks might be the 'disgrace' of his client and friend, Jekyll.

Hyde's environment

Hyde's environment will turn out to be closely connected to that of Jekyll. But at the moment, all we know is that his base is 'a sinister block' which 'bore in every feature the marks of prolonged and sordid negligence. The door, which was equipped with neither bell nor knocker, was blistered and distained'. Yet, dismal though building and entrance might be, they stood out in their sordid nature as a sharp contrast to the rest of the street whose 'shop fronts stood along that thoroughfare with an air of invitation, like rows of smiling saleswomen'. This street, in its turn, 'shone out in contrast to its dingy neighbourhood, like a fire in a forest; and with its freshly painted shutters, well-polished brasses, and general cleanliness and gaiety of note, instantly caught and pleased the eye'.

So, it's not only people but places, too, which can display contrasting and contradictory characteristics: Hyde's grim, grubby home is in an attractive, well-tended street – and that street itself contrasts with its surrounding dingy neighbourhood.

Enfield's narrative

'Well-known man about town' Richard Enfield, although a distant relative, seems an unlikely friend for dull Mr Utterson. But their Sunday walk is for each man 'the chief jewel of each week'. (Here, again, we see in their friendship the coming together of contrasting elements.)

As they pass the door of Hyde's abode, Enfield begins a strange tale. Returning home late one night he had witnessed nearby 'a little man' collide and then violently trample over a young girl. Outraged witnesses order the man to pay compensation, whereupon he disappears behind the door and returns with a sum in gold and a cheque from the account of Henry Jekyll.

Hyde's introduction

On Enfield and on the witnesses, Hyde has a powerful negative effect. 'I had taken a loathing to my gentleman at first sight. So had the child's family.' Even more disturbing was the reaction of the attending doctor who, Enfield supposes, was normally was 'as emotional as a bagpipe'. But when faced with Hyde the doctor 'turned sick and white with the desire to kill him.' (Yet another character with two sides to his personality.)

The surrounding women 'were as wild as harpies. I never saw a circle of such hateful faces'. Such is Hyde's effect on people. He, in his turn, met all this 'with a kind of black sneering coolness – frightened too, I could see that – but carrying it off, sir, like Satan'. Enfield is at something of a loss to give a physical description of Hyde, feeling simply that he was 'not easy to describe. There is something wrong with his appearance; something displeasing, something downright detestable. I never saw a man I so disliked and yet I scarce know why ...'. Nevertheless, we learn important facts about his attitude to and effect on people.

London at night

The city itself, particularly in its night-time aspects, will appear several times in the text. Hyde first appears at night when Enfield is returning 'from some place at the end of the world, about three o'clock of a black winter morning'. Here, London takes on an almost nightmarish nature, devoid of people entirely: 'there was literally nothing to be seen but lamps. ... street after street, all lighted up as if for a procession, and all as empty as a church – till at last I got into that state of mind when a man listens and listens and begins to long for the sight of a policeman'.

The cinematic nature of Stevenson's description presents the city as a desolate, lonely place whose bleakness is only interrupted by an act of violence which unleashes a torrent of hatred. Watch out for further nightscapes in the text. London at night is almost itself a character in the novella.

The repressed society

It is only towards the end of this story that Utterson elicits a name from Enfield for the strange creature. Furthermore, both Utterson and Enfield appear to know the identity of the owner of the property behind the door. Yet both are reluctant even to articulate Jekyll's name or query his connection with Hyde.

Enfield has a deep-seated aversion to asking potentially embarrassing questions: 'I feel very strongly about putting questions ... You start a question, and it's like starting a stone'. Utterson shares Enfield's unwillingness to mention the name of the property's owner (on whose bank account the compensation cheque was drawn) : '"Enfield"', said Mr Utterson, "that's a good rule of yours."' Jekyll's name is in both their minds; both fear blackmail may lie at the root of the connection; yet both repress any desire to enquire into the private life of their friend. Who knows where the questions might lead, what embarrassments might be exposed? The mask of respectability must be maintained.

These two are not alone, as we shall see, in observing much but commenting little. Repression doesn't just take the forms of restricted conversation; it emerges in forms such as the windowless building of Hyde, locked doors, barred windows, lockfast drawers and safes – all fine features for keeping secrets.

DON'T FORGET

Although this novella is famous for the Jekyll/Hyde split, there are other people here who, to perhaps a lesser extent, also demonstrate contradictory or conflicting aspects in their personalities.

Classroom challenge

In this opening section, Stevenson makes some key points on character and themes which are developed later. Here are some quotations which illustrate these aspects of character and themes. Make a comment on each quotation or pair of quotations.

TEXTUAL EVIDENCE	POSSIBLE COMMENT(S)
'I let my brother go to the devil in his own way.' '... it was frequently his fortune to be [...] the last good influence in the lives of down-going men.'	
'... the street shone out in contrast to its dingy neighbourhood like a fire in a forest ...'	
'... a certain sinister block of a building thrust forward its gable on the street. It [...] showed no window, nothing but a door on the lower storey and a blind forehead of discoloured wall on the upper, and bore in every feature the marks of prolonged and sordid negligence.'	
'He was the usual cut-and-dry apothecary [...] about as emotional as a bagpipe.' 'I saw that Sawbones turned sick and white with the desire to kill him.'	
'He must be deformed somewhere; he gives a strong feeling of deformity, although I couldn't specify the point.'	
'Let us make a bargain never to refer to this again.'	

TEACHING NOTES

You can download Teaching Notes for this challenge at www.brightredpublishing.co.uk/Shop/national-5-english-course-book

Homework helper

Stevenson begins this tale with a chapter heading which draws attention not to a building or person but to a door. In your own words, explain as fully as you can:

a) Why reference to a door might usually be an effective way to open a story.

b) Why this particular door contradicts our expectations.

c) Why a door is an effective symbol in a novel where people seem reluctant to discuss disturbing information.

TEACHING NOTES You can download Teaching Notes for this task at www.brightredpublishing.co.uk/Shop/national-5-english-course-book

Commentary: 'Search for Mr Hyde'

Key chapter elements:

- Jekyll's will
- Hyde encountered
- Utterson's obsession
- Jekyll's environment

Jekyll's will

When Enfield mentioned Hyde's name, it was already known to Utterson since he was the holder of Jekyll's will, wherein the doctor left his entire estate to Hyde should he disappear for more than three months. (We later learn that the inheritance comes to a quarter of a million pounds.) Utterson was 'offended' by the will's terms since he was 'a lover of the sane and customary sides of life'. In other words, this will was 'fanciful' and out of keeping with his lawyerly ways. Now he knew what kind of character Hyde was, he was doubly troubled. He fears the worse: does Hyde have some hold over Jekyll? Blackmail? 'I thought it was madness' [...] 'and now I begin to fear it is disgrace.'

Utterson's obsession

So troubled is Utterson he goes from his 'dusty, dreary' self to a man possessed. He must find out more about this Hyde. He first visits a mutual friend of Jekyll and himself, Dr Lanyon. He discovers little except that, interestingly, Lanyon has had no contact with Jekyll for years – since Jekyll had, in the doctor's words, begun 'to go wrong, wrong in mind'.

Utterson's imagination becomes 'enslaved' about what hold Hyde may have on Jekyll. He has nightmares thinking of the threat of this evil man to his friend. 'From that time forward, Mr Utterson began to haunt the door at all hours.' But it is only at night that he finally comes face to face with Hyde.

Hyde encountered

After seemingly many 'nightly patrols' Utterson finally encounters Hyde at ten o'clock one night. Like Enfield, he remarks on his small stature. Tapped on the shoulder, Hyde 'shrank back with a hissing intake of the breath'. (This animal imagery we will come across again with reference to Hyde.) They confront each other; Hyde initially avoids eye contact (perhaps flustered to see his old friend) but finally lets Utterson see his face 'with an air of defiance'.

But, even within the persona of Hyde, there are still contradictions in that he was 'a murderous mixture of timidity and boldness'. Keen to know how he was recognised, he is angered when Utterson mentions descriptions from common friends, such as Jekyll. Outraged by this slight extension of the truth, he snaps, 'I never thought you would have lied.' He finally departs with 'a savage laugh'.

Utterson, like Enfield, finds it hard to articulate a description of Hyde. He was 'pale and dwarfish; he gave the impression of deformity without any namable malformation'. He struggles to put his finger on what alarms him so: '... the man seems hardly human! Something troglodytic, shall we say?' He concludes by seeing 'Satan's signature' on his face. In revising, pay attention to the imagery here (and elsewhere) that suggests Hyde is less than human.

Jekyll's environment

Jekyll's home is 'on a square of ancient handsome houses, now for the most part decayed from their high estate'. But Jekyll's house stands out from these in that it 'wore a great air of wealth and comfort'. Once again, we are confronted with an environment which reveals a divided personality. Furthermore, we know this grand house connects to the sordid, sinister door of Chapter One. The property manifests the same duality we have seen in other people and places earlier.

Classroom challenge

We have seen by now how Stevenson is beginning to develop characters and themes. Read the comments below then try to find textual evidence which might support the point(s) being made. You may find more than one quotation!

TEXTUAL EVIDENCE	POSSIBLE COMMENT(S)
	The concerns which Utterson once had about Jekyll's strange will now appear much more serious after hearing Enfield's story.
	Utterson's fears for the safety of his friend bring about a change in his personality and behaviour.
	Utterson, like Enfield, has a problem in describing Hyde.
	This encounter is rich in imagery which suggests Hyde is less than human.
	The presentation of Jekyll's home makes it seem a fitting environment for the Jekyll/Hyde personas.
	Despite the warmth and comfort of Jekyll's hall, Utterson is curiously depressed.

TEACHING NOTES

You can download Teaching Notes for this challenge at www.brightredpublishing.co.uk/Shop/national-5-english-course-book

DON'T FORGET

In *The Strange Case of Dr Jekyll and Mr Hyde*, places – as well as people – are seen as manifesting contrasting/conflicting personalities.

Homework helper

How well do you know the characters and places you have already encountered in Chapters 1 and 2? Try to identify the people or places to which these quotations refer.

1. 'His friends were those of his own blood, or those he had known the longest'
2. 'the well-known man about town'
3. 'the street shone out [...] like a fire in a forest.'
4. 'a sinister block of a building thrust forward its gable on the street.'
5. 'I was coming back from somewhere at the end of the world ...'
6. 'There are three windows looking on the court on the first floor; none below; the windows are always shut.'
7. 'But it is more than ten years since [he] became too fanciful for me.'
8. 'And still the figure had no face by which he might know it ...'
9. 'He was small, and very plainly dressed ...'
10. 'Round the corner from the by street there was a square of ancient, handsome houses ...'
11. 'We have all orders to obey him.'
12. '... he was humbled to the dust by the many ill things he had done ...'

TEACHING NOTES

You can download Teaching Notes for this task at www.brightredpublishing.co.uk/Shop/national-5-english-course-book

Commentary: 'Dr Jekyll was Quite at Ease'

Key chapter elements:

- Jekyll at home
- The repressed society

Jekyll at home

Jekyll is presented to us as a genial host at one of his pleasant dinners attended by 'five or six old cronies, all reputable men'. No one could be more different to the dwarfish Hyde: 'a large, well-made, smooth-faced man of fifty' with 'every mark of capacity and kindness'. Yet, there is a lurking contradiction to this very positive presentation for he had also 'something of a slyish cast perhaps'. Jekyll may not be all he seems.

When Utterson brings up the subject of the will, Jekyll is quick to try to deflect the topic, by referring to his irritation with Lanyon, whom he describes as 'an ignorant, blatant pedant. I was never more disappointed in any man than Lanyon'. (We wonder why. What has disrupted their long-standing friendship?) Utterson refuses to be deflected and comes back to the will, receiving short shrift from Jekyll who responds 'a trifle sharply' as he 'grew pale to the very lips, and there came a blackness to his eyes'.

He closes the matter by telling Utterson 'I have really a very great interest in poor Hyde' and appeals to Utterson to 'get his rights for him' when Jekyll is no longer there. Perhaps the most interesting thing Jekyll says about Hyde is: 'the moment I choose, I can be rid of Mr Hyde'. We shall see if he's correct in his prediction.

The repressed society

Utterson and Jekyll have been friends since childhood. Utterson, as well as being his lawyer, is a man whom Jekyll would trust 'before any man alive'. The relaxed post-dinner atmosphere is an ideal moment for confessions between old friends who are also lawyer and client. Yet Jekyll steadfastly refuses to talk of the nature of his relationship with Hyde: 'this is a private matter, and I beg you to let it sleep'. Utterson, for his part, won't spell out fully the nature of his fears. Free conversations are impossible, even between long-standing friends, in the repressed, tight-lipped society they live in.

Classroom challenge

Fill out the missing gaps with either a quotation or a comment of your own as part of your revision of Chapter 3.

TEXTUAL EVIDENCE	POSSIBLE COMMENT(S)
	Dr Jekyll is introduced positively, but there is a worrying aspect to his description.
'I never saw a man so distressed as you were by my will; unless it was that hide-bound pedant, Lanyon, at what he called my scientific heresies.'	
	Just as direct reference to Jekyll angered Hyde, so too does direct reference to Hyde anger Jekyll.
	Jekyll has unbounded faith in Utterson.
'... the moment I choose, I can be rid of Mr Hyde.'	
	Jekyll is determined to repress any further discussion of his connection with Hyde.

TEACHING NOTES

You can download Teaching Notes for this challenge at www.brightredpublishing.co.uk/Shop/national-5-english-course-book

DON'T FORGET

This is a story about a circle of friends, most of whom have known each other since childhood. Notice how little they say directly to each other, particularly if there's the threat of anything potentially embarrassing coming out. What does this suggest about the society they live in?

Homework helper

Examine closely these extracts from the language of Mr Utterson and Dr Jekyll in this chapter. Show how sentence structure is used to illustrate the personalities and aims of the two men. You may answer in bullet points.

TEACHING NOTES

You can download Teaching Notes for this task at www.brightredpublishing.co.uk/Shop/national-5-english-course-book

MR UTTERSON	DR JEKYLL
'I have been wanting to speak to you, Jekyll,' began the latter. 'You know that will of yours?' 'You know I never approved of it,' pursued Utterson ...' 'What I heard was abominable,' said Utterson. 'Jekyll' said Utterson 'you know me. I am a man to be trusted. Make a clean breast of this in confidence, and I make no doubt I can get you out of it.'	'My poor Utterson,' said he, 'you are unfortunate in such a client. I never saw a man so distressed as you were by my will; unless it were that hide-bound pedant, Lanyon, at what he called my scientific heresies. O, I know he's a good fellow – you needn't frown – an excellent fellow, and I always mean to see more of him; but a hide-bound pedant for all that; an ignorant, blatant pedant.'

Commentary: 'The Carew Murder Case'

Key chapter elements:

- Hyde's new victim
- Utterson and the police
- Duality in minor characters
- The murder's setting
- Hyde's Soho home
- Fog and the city

Hyde's new victim

A year has passed since Hyde's last eruption of violence. In the interval, his capacity for evil has only strengthened, as this attack is much more ferocious than the previous one, leaving its victim dead. Hyde 'broke out in a great flame of rage and clubbed him to the earth. And the next moment, [...] he was trampling the victim under foot'. The victim's bones were 'audibly shattered' and we note that all this was done 'with ape-like fury'. (Here again we have animal imagery applied to Hyde.)

The first victim was a little girl; this one is an old man. Stevenson stresses the innocence of the latter who, to the watching maid's eyes, had 'such an innocent and old-world-kindness of disposition'. While the little girl and the old man may share innocence, their social positions are very different; Sir Danver's prominence 'will make a great deal of noise', as Inspector Newcomen comments. (We later learn he is an MP.) The social standing of Hyde's new victim, to say nothing of his violent death, will intensify interest in finding the perpetrator, thus placing Hyde/Jekyll under much more pressure than he felt after the assault on the girl.

The murder's setting

Again, we see Hyde prowling about at night, but this is night seen from the perspective of the maid-servant, a night 'brilliantly lit by the full moon. [...] never had she felt more at peace with all men or thought more kindly of the world'. The moon is significant not only in allowing the maidservant to view the crime clearly and identify Hyde; it also helpfully illuminates the crime-scene for Hyde.

Moonlight, as well as being an object of great beauty and peace to the maid, is also, in folk-literature, a time when evil creatures of all kinds (here including Hyde) emerge to create havoc in the world. Moonlight, like much else in the text, presents us with a certain duality of nature.

Utterson and the police

A letter in the pocket of Sir Danvers leads Inspector Newcomen to Mr Utterson. Utterson is now in a tricky situation: the letter connects him to Sir Danvers and the maid has identified Hyde as his murderer – and the murder weapon is a walking stick he had given to Jekyll. To a certain extent, Utterson is helpful to the police: he gives Hyde's Soho address to Newcomen and accompanies him there. But what's much more significant is what he doesn't say: he fails to mention Hyde's base in the by street, knowing full well its connection to Jekyll.

A lawyer, of all people, should surely help the police as fully as he can? Since, after all, Hyde is missing from his Soho haunt, perhaps he could be found at the laboratory? But Utterson's tight-lipped loyalty to his friend transcends his loyalty to even the law which he serves.

Hyde's Soho home

Here, reminding us of the earlier Hyde/Jekyll building complex, is yet another environment that presents a dual nature. The house is in 'a dingy street' with, as its neighbours, 'a gin palace', and 'a low French eating-house' with 'many ragged children huddled in the doorways'. The contrast inside, however, is startling, for it is 'furnished with luxury and good taste. A closet was filled with wine; the plate was of silver, the napery elegant; a good picture hung upon the walls [...] and the carpets were of many plies and agreeable in colour.' Once again, we have the sordid and the smart brought together by Stevenson.

But there's yet another contrast to be noted in this tasteful home. It's in a state of great disarray: 'the rooms bore every mark of having been recently and hurriedly ransacked; clothes lay about the floor, [...] lockfast drawers stood open; and on the hearth there lay a pile of grey ashes, as though many papers had been burned'. They find a half-burned cheque book and the other half of the murder weapon. All this suggests Hyde/Jekyll is in a considerable panic to cover his tracks. This time, the crime cannot be brushed aside with £10 in gold and a Coutts cheque; Hyde has had to flee his home.

Duality in minor characters

Inspector Newcomen and Hyde's housekeeper, while of secondary importance to the plot's development, help to underline a key theme at the heart of the novella – the duality existing in human nature.

Newcomen is initially presented as an unexceptional professional officer of the law, calmly unmoved by the viciously brutal murder of Danvers Carew. Until, that is, the victim is identified as a person of some social standing. At the mention of the victim's importance 'his eyes lighted up with professional ambition'. He views the 'deal of noise' which it will generate as professionally useful, seeing solving crime as suddenly much more interesting when it's married to career advancement.

Hyde's housekeeper is another character with dual aspects to her character: 'She had an evil face, smoothed by hypocrisy, but her manners were excellent'. The manners slip a little when she has a 'flash of odious joy', hearing Hyde might be in trouble. The housekeeper's underlying personality is perhaps more obvious than Newcomen's, but both characters embody a certain duality.

Fog and the city

Fog 'rolled over the city' in the hours following Carew's murder; it is also present when Utterson and Newcomen arrive at Hyde's Soho address with 'the first fog of the season. A great chocolate-coloured pall lowered over heaven.' Fog, gloomy light and twilight add much to the setting in a tale of this kind, conveying as they do an appropriately creepy atmosphere. Wealthy, prosperous London, leading world city, has become 'like a district of some city in a nightmare'.

But fog has a metaphorical use here also. For if a literal fog cloaks London at key moments, there's also a metaphorical fog around both Hyde and Jekyll for much of the novel. It obscures from people who they really are and what they're up to. In vain, Utterson toils to disperse it. Interestingly, here it's also seen as a 'pall' (a covering for a coffin) concealing these deadly activities from the very eye of heaven itself.

DON'T FORGET

Think about why the attack on Sir Danvers Carew is so much more violent than the earlier attack.

Classroom challenge

To familiarise yourself with the text, try matching these comments with quotations from this chapter. There are some where you will have plenty of choice. In these cases, list as many as you can.

TEXTUAL EVIDENCE	POSSIBLE COMMENT(S)
	From the maidservant's description, Sir Danvers Carew appears to be a thoroughly unthreatening character.
	Stevenson captures effectively but economically the sheer brutality of the act of murder.
	Hyde's behaviour appears to go beyond that of a human being.
	Stevenson makes clever use of the weather in this chapter.
	Even minor characters are used to explore the theme of duality.
	There is difficulty in creating Hyde's wanted poster for two particular reasons.

TEACHING NOTES

You can download Teaching Notes for this challenge at www.brightredpublishing.co.uk/Shop/national-5-english-course-book

Homework helper

We don't have much information about Hyde so far. Those who have encountered him so far tend to speak of him under the five headings below. Go through the four chapters we've looked at so far to find textual evidence to support these descriptions. Try to find at least two examples for each descriptor.

small | **young** | **violent** | **difficult to describe** | **seeming less than human**

You can download Teaching Notes for this task at www.brightredpublishing.co.uk/Shop/national-5-english-course-book

TEACHING NOTES

Commentary: 'Incident of the Letter'

Key chapter elements:

- Jekyll's changed environment
- Jekyll's altered attitude
- Jekyll's deceit?
- The repressed society

Jekyll's changed environment

When last we met Dr Jekyll, he was playing host 'at one of his pleasant dinners' in his handsome home. Now, he has retreated to the 'dingy windowless structure' of the laboratory from which Hyde come and goes. The premises are 'gaunt and silent with the light falling dimly through the foggy cupola'. Jekyll is now found in a room 'looking out upon the court by three dusty windows barred with iron'. Such is the outcry at the murder of Carew that he feels the need of this grim refuge with its barred windows and where there are, in places, no windows at all. Dr Jekyll by day is already in physical retreat from Hyde's actions by night. In fact, this room sounds as much like a prison as a refuge.

Jekyll's altered attitude

Dr Jekyll is certainly no longer at ease as he was at his dinner party. He sits huddled up to the fire 'looking deadly sick. He did not rise to meet his visitor but held out a cold hand and bade him welcome in a changed voice'. Hyde's murder has taken a physical and mental toll on Dr Jekyll.

Gone is the assurance with which he dismissed Utterson's earlier worries. He had earlier maintained that Hyde could be got rid of but now, rather feverishly, tells Utterson: 'he is safe, he is quite safe; mark my words, he will never more be heard of'. But Jekyll is shaken to the core: 'I have had a lesson – O God, Utterson, what a lesson I have had.'

Jekyll's deceit?

It is testimony of the panic in the Jekyll/Hyde persona that some deceit is undertaken to take the heat out of the situation. Jekyll produces a 'letter' which purports to come from Hyde indicating that he has gone away and will not bother Jekyll again. When the writing is examined by Guest, Utterson's head clerk and a handwriting expert, he places it beside Jekyll's handwriting and remarks: '... it's a very interesting autograph'. He notes that there is 'a singular resemblance: the two hands are in many points identical; only differently sloped'.

Given that the butler reports to have received no mail either by hand or by post that day, the conclusion which Utterson makes is that Jekyll has written the note himself. Lacking the courage to present it to the police in person, Jekyll leaves it to Utterson's judgment as to what to do with it, knowing full well that his discreet friend would probably behave true to form. And, of course, he did, since he promptly 'locked the note in his safe'.

But Jekyll's good friend Utterson is shocked by what he sees as Jekyll's moral degradation: 'Henry Jekyll forge for a murderer!' Hyde may be 'gone' in one sense, but his corrupting effect, in Utterson's eyes, is already affecting the once highly respected Dr Jekyll. But if Jekyll and Hyde are one and the same person, can the letter be, strictly speaking, a forgery? From Utterson's currently limited perspective, it is just that.

The repressed society

This is a novel in which the characters suspect much but discuss little. Even in this moment of crisis, Utterson and Jekyll never mention the word 'murder', simply 'the news'; Hyde is 'he' or 'this fellow' for much of the chapter, his name being only mentioned once (by Jekyll). Only when he is alone does Utterson articulate the word 'murderer'. It's as if by not mentioning 'murder' or the murderer's name in their conversation, they're distancing the crime and criminal from their once comfortable lives.

DON'T FORGET

Be alert to any reference to fog in *The Strange Case of Dr Jekyll and Mr Hyde*. Think about which theme it's there to support.

In conversation with Guest, Utterson's trusted head clerk, both men are careful not to articulate the word 'forgery'. Again, we see the repressed society at work: unpleasant facts are avoided and the outward signs of this closed-off world – barred windows, windowless rooms and safes – are all present in this chapter. And, metaphorically speaking, obscuring the crime still further, 'even in the houses the fog began to lie thickly'. And above them 'The fog slept on the wing above the drowned city ...'

Cutting through to the truth will not be easy in a society where awkward facts and disturbing thoughts are systematically obscured or repressed.

Classroom challenge

By matching the comments in the column on the right with short quotations from the text, you will usefully add depth to your study of this chapter. Try to extend the given comment to support your choice of quotation.

TEACHING NOTES

You can download Teaching Notes for this challenge at www.brightredpublishing.co.uk/Shop/national-5-english-course-book

TEXTUAL EVIDENCE	POSSIBLE COMMENT(S)
	Stevenson makes clever use of physical setting to support a character's state of mind.
	Jekyll's outward appearance suggests inner troubles.
	Utterson and Jekyll both avoid any mention of murder in their conversation.
	Jekyll confidently declares his connection with Hyde has now reached a new stage.
	Utterson and Jekyll are not the only people here to avoid mentioning unpleasant facts directly.
	Utterson's behaviour at the end of the chapter is perfectly true to form.

Homework helper

This chapter contains some important quotations for a full understanding of key characters and themes. Explain in your own words how these quotations develop characters and themes you may have encountered earlier.

TEXTUAL EVIDENCE	POSSIBLE COMMENT(S)
'"And now," said Utterson, as soon as Poole had left them, "you have heard the news?"'	
'I have grounds for certainty that I cannot share with anyone.'	
'I was thinking of my own character, which this hateful business had rather exposed.'	
'The lawyer liked this letter well enough; it put a better colour on the intimacy than he had looked for, and he blamed himself for some of his past suspicions.'	
'"This is a sad business about Sir Danvers," he said.'	
'"I wouldn't speak of this note, you know," said the master. "No, sir", said the clerk. "I understand."'	

You can download Teaching Notes for this task at
www.brightredpublishing.co.uk/Shop/national-5-english-course-book

TEACHING NOTES

Commentary: 'Remarkable Incident of Dr Lanyon'

Key chapter elements:

- Jekyll becomes erratic
- The death of Lanyon

Jekyll becomes erratic

With the disappearance of Hyde, Jekyll gradually returns to form and to his former sociable self:

> 'He came out of his seclusion, renewed relations with his friends, became once more their familiar guest and entertainer. But he goes even farther: whilst he had always been known for charities, he was now no less distinguished for religion. He was busy, he was much in the open air, he did good; his face seemed to open and brighten, as if with an inward consciousness of service ...'

Deeply shaken by Hyde's devilish deed, he now seeks out God; after his dark days behind barred windows, he relishes the open air; after seclusion, he pursues company. For two months, all seems to be going well until, suddenly, everything changes. On the 8th, Jekyll was entertaining happily; on the 12th, Utterson was faced with a closed door. Something extraordinary clearly has happened between the 8th January and 12th January, according to Utterson's diary entries. After the same thing happens on the 14th and 15th, he consults their mutual friend, Dr Lanyon.

The death of Lanyon

Physically, Lanyon is a totally changed man: 'The rosy man had grown pale; his flesh had fallen away; he was visibly balder and older'. Even more shocking to Utterson than Lanyon's medical condition is the fact that in his eyes he sees 'some deep-seated terror of the mind'. Both Utterson and Lanyon himself accept that he is 'a doomed man'.

Death is near and the comments of this once happy man are chilling: 'I sometimes think if we knew it all, we should be more glad to get away.' Mention of Jekyll intensifies his anguish. At the mention of his one-time friend his facial expression changes and he holds up 'a trembling hand: "I wish to see or hear no more of Jekyll"'. What has happened during these crucial four days? Lanyon clearly knows something about Jekyll's new-found seclusion, but for the moment refuses to say anything.

After his death, Utterson receives a letter marked for his attention alone. This is to be destroyed unread should Utterson predecease Lanyon. Inside is yet another sealed letter 'not to be opened only till the death or disappearance of Dr Henry Jekyll'. Tormented as he is by curiosity, Utterson refuses to succumb to temptation and, true to form, locks it away. For now, 'the packet slept in the innermost corner of his private safe'. The silence of a dying man, a letter within a letter, both locked away in a private safe: here we have more examples of the repressed society and its secretive ways.

Classroom challenge

What comments can be made concerning characters and themes from these quotations from this chapter?

TEXTUAL EVIDENCE	POSSIBLE COMMENT(S)
'Much of his past was unearthed, indeed, and all disreputable: tales came out of the man's cruelty, at once so callous and violent, of his vile life, of his strange associates, of the hatred that seemed to have surrounded his career …'	
'… for more than two months the doctor was at peace.'	
'"I have had a shock," he said "and I shall never recover."'	
'I mean henceforth to lead a life of extreme seclusion; you must not be surprised, nor must you doubt my friendship, if my door is shut even to you.'	
'If I am the chief of sinners, I am the chief of sufferers also.'	
'He went to call indeed; but he was perhaps relieved to be denied admittance …'	

DON'T FORGET

Dr Lanyon is a particularly distinguished and experienced medical man. Think about why Stevenson would want another doctor in this story.

TEACHING NOTES

You can download Teaching Notes for this challenge at www.brightredpublishing.co.uk/Shop/national-5-english-course-book

Homework helper

Search this chapter to see if you can find supporting quotations to back up the following statements.

TEXTUAL EVIDENCE	POSSIBLE COMMENT(S)
	Jekyll is not the only character to find new-found peace after the departure of Hyde.
	When Jekyll rejects Hyde, he seems to have expelled the tormenting evil from himself to become his former sociable self.
	Whatever has happened to Jekyll has happened over a comparatively short time interval.
	Lanyon is entirely convinced that Jekyll has put himself beyond the pale of human decency.
	There was a particular word in one of Lanyon's letters which also appeared in Jekyll's will which greatly disturbed Utterson.
	Poole's news of Jekyll suggests the doctor is gravely troubled.

You can download Teaching Notes for this task at
www.brightredpublishing.co.uk/Shop/national-5-english-course-book

TEACHING NOTES

Commentary: 'Incident at the Window'

Key chapter elements:

- The repressed society
- Duality in action

The repressed society

Although only two pages long, this is a key chapter because, in it, Utterson begins to understand the mystery surrounding his friend Jekyll; and we begin to understand even more the repressed nature that engulfs this society of bachelors.

On their usual Sunday walk, Enfield and Utterson chance on Hyde's laboratory retreat. Now, we know Utterson and Enfield are best friends (even related) and that they walk together every Sunday; but it appears that even after the enormous outcry surrounding Hyde's criminality, Utterson has apparently never mentioned over the course of many Sundays that he had encountered Hyde in person: 'Did I ever tell you that I once saw him ...? Enfield clearly has been equally economical with information on these walks: 'And, by the way, what an ass you must have thought me, not to know that this was a back way to Jekyll's!' Hyde and the Jekyll connection are potentially embarrassing topics – so they have never been discussed.

After the appalling reality of Jekyll's situation is made horrifically clearer this particular Sunday, they once again adopt a typically close-lipped response: '... they turned and left the court without a word. In silence, too, they traversed the by street ...' It is some time before anything is said at all and, even then, it's merely: '"God forgive us!" said Utterson'.

What they've seen is truly mind-shattering, yet there is no discussion of it whatsoever and they 'walked on once more in silence'. For who knows what discussion might do to the reputation of their friend? As Enfield earlier had remarked: 'the more it looks like Queer Street, the less I ask.' (Queer Street is an old-fashioned, colloquial expression suggesting someone is in extreme difficulty.)

Duality in action

Enfield and Utterson encounter Jekyll displaying 'an infinite sadness of mien' at a half-open overlooking the courtyard of the laboratory. So despondent is he that he looks 'like some disconsolate prisoner' and confesses: 'I am very low, Utterson'. Somewhat ambiguously, he adds: 'It will not last long'. (Does he mean the mood will pass or does he feel death approaching?)

Kindly Utterson suggests a walk together, but Jekyll counters with: 'I dare not'. What he fears becomes only too clear 'when an expression of such abject terror and despair' struck his face. He immediately slams shut the window, but the men have caught a glimpse of something in his face which 'froze the very blood' of the two friends. Stevenson, tantalisingly, does not articulate what it was the two men saw but we deduce it was the changing of Jekyll into Hyde.

This implied cross-over between the two characters is the first public hint that Hyde and Jekyll are one and the same. Suggestively, Stevenson has the scene play out at sunset in the courtyard which was 'full of premature twilight'. Just as the day is ending, so, too, perhaps is Jekyll's life. And prematurely, too, due to his illicit tampering with nature. Not surprisingly, the next chapter is entitled 'The Last Night'.

Classroom challenge

Weather and/or the time of day play a significant part as the backdrop to this strange tale. Now that we've looked at seven chapters, go back and note details of the times of day and weather conditions for the following events. Suggest why Stevenson may have selected these particular times and conditions to enrich the setting.

1. Enfield's encounter with Hyde
2. Utterson's meeting with Hyde
3. Carew's murder
4. Newcomen's visit to Hyde's Soho home
5. Presentation of the 'Hyde' letter
6. Utterson/Enfield's encounter with Jekyll in the courtyard

TEACHING NOTES

You can download Teaching Notes for this challenge at www.brightredpublishing.co.uk/Shop/national-5-english-course-book

Homework helper

Short as it is, this chapter helps develop themes and key characters. Examine the following quotations for the light they throw on themes and/or characters and make your own comments on what you feel each contributes.

TEXTUAL EVIDENCE	POSSIBLE COMMENT(S)
'Did I ever tell you that I once saw him ...?'	
'... like a disconsolate prisoner ...'	
'I should like to very much; but no, no, no, it is quite impossible; I dare not.'	
'... an expression of such abject terror and despair, as froze the very blood of the two gentlemen.'	
'... they turned and left the court without a word.'	
'They were both pale; and there was an answering horror in their eyes.'	

You can download Teaching Notes for this task at
www.brightredpublishing.co.uk/Shop/national-5-english-course-book

TEACHING NOTES

Commentary: 'The Last Night'

Key chapter elements:

- Wild weather
- Order overturned
- The broken key
- Poole's testimony
- Behind the red baize door
- Jekyll's new will

Wild weather

As a backdrop to this chapter, Stevenson prepares us for the turmoil in Jekyll's last hours with similarly turbulent weather: 'It was a wild, cold seasonable night of March, with a pale moon, lying on her back as though the wind had tilted her.'

Even the moon seems to have been rudely upended and 'The wind made talking difficult and flecked the blood into the face' as Poole and Utterson struggle determinedly against it. The wind 'seemed to have swept the streets unusually bare of passengers. [...] the thin trees in the garden were lashing themselves along the railing'. All nature appears in an uproar, mirroring the upheaval in the normal order at Jekyll's home.

Poole's testimony

Poole is responsible for bringing Utterson (and readers) up to date with recent activities at the doctor's. For the past week, an indeterminate voice (Jekyll's? Hyde's?) from behind the red baize door of Jekyll's cabinet has been calling for 'some sort of medicine'. When delivered, it never appears to be sufficiently pure to satisfy the voice. It's Jekyll's handwriting, but the glimpse Poole had of the creature at the cabinet door did not appear to be Jekyll: '... if that was my master, why had he a mask on his face? If it was my master, why did he cry out like a rat and run from me?'

This creature was not tall but 'more of a dwarf', in Poole's words. Although hoping for some rational explanation, Utterson is finally persuaded by Poole's suspicion that the 'masked thing like a monkey' which Poole spotted at the cabinet door is Hyde. Poole is convinced his master has been murdered. Utterson agrees to break down the door.

Order overturned

If there was disorder in the elements, there's also upheaval in the social order. For a start, Poole abandons his customary role of the dignified butler to call – in some distress – on Utterson, imploring the lawyer to investigate disturbing proceedings at Jekyll's house. Once there, Utterson finds the servants all huddled together in the public area of the house rather than in their own quarters, behaviour which he 'peevishly' remarks is 'Very irregular, very unseemly: your master would be far from pleased.'

The house-maid is whimpering hysterically and the cook, on seeing Utterson, 'ran forward as if to take him in her arms'. Poole rebukes the maid 'with a ferocity of accent that testified to his own jangled nerves'. All in all, the normal social order has been wildly upset, faced with the abnormalities coming from behind the red baize door.

Behind the red baize door

Poole, armed with an axe, and Utterson, with the kitchen poker, get ready to break down the red baize door leading to Jekyll's cabinet. They post the footman and the knife-boy at the laboratory door to stop Hyde escaping that way. All they can hear is a light tread moving to and fro, far removed from Jekyll's heavier footfall.

Poole remarks he has heard a voice weeping 'like a woman or a lost soul'. Utterson gives warning of his intention to break in, but the voice which replies is Hyde's. At this, they set about the stout door determinedly and find 'the body of a man sorely contorted and still twitching'. The face was that of Hyde, but he was dressed in clothes far too big for him, clothes of the doctor's size.

From the crushed phial in the body's hand and the strong smell of 'kernels', Utterson deduces suicide. Hyde, they see, is dead, but where's Jekyll? Given the locked and guarded laboratory door, he can't have escaped. They search fruitlessly everywhere but can't find him. The full truth of the Jekyll/Hyde relationship still eludes both men.

The broken key

There are signs at this laboratory side of the house that a struggle for identity has been going on. Poole and Utterson find the door to the street locked and the key broken 'as if a man had stamped on it'. The decency remaining in Jekyll seems to have determined that the Hyde persona, in his moments of ascendancy, should not escape to wreak his havoc on the world.

They also find 'a copy of a pious work for which Jekyll had several times expressed a great esteem'. But now it is 'annotated, in his own hand, with startling blasphemies'. But given, as we know, that there's great similarity in Jekyll and Hyde's handwriting, can we accurately identify the author of the annotations? The fact that Jekyll was seeking comfort in a pious work suggests lingering spirituality, interrupted only by the blasphemous Hyde. Jekyll has gone, but not without a final struggle between good and evil.

Jekyll's new will

On Jekyll's desk, they find a large envelope, addressed to Utterson, containing several documents. The first was a new will from which Hyde's name has been removed as the beneficiary and Utterson's substituted. Another note with the current day's date instructs Jekyll to read the letter Lanyon had previously left with the lawyer. There's a third document which is the confession of Jekyll himself, which will throw yet more light on the solving of the mystery.

True to form, Utterson instructs Poole to 'say nothing of this paper. If your master has fled or is dead, we may at least save his credit'. Jekyll's life may have been destroyed, but Utterson, again true to form, remains the steadfast guardian of reputation.

TEACHING NOTES

You can download Teaching Notes for this challenge at www.brightredpublishing.co.uk/Shop/national-5-english-course-book

Classroom challenge

Examine the following comments before trying to track down supporting textual evidence.

TEXTUAL EVIDENCE	POSSIBLE COMMENTS
	Stevenson's use of setting in this chapter helps prepare us for the turmoil evident in Jekyll's laboratory.
	Extreme events have brought about odd changes in the Jekyll household.
	Utterson, once in Jekyll's home, at first seems doubtful of Poole's explanation of events behind the red baize door.
	Jekyll's total desperation finds expression in his note to the chemist.
	There is more evidence in this chapter of Hyde's less-than-human appearance.
	Finding a note written that very day by Jekyll prompts new fears in Utterson regarding his old friend.

Homework helper

The breaking down of the door, far from resolving the mystery of Jekyll's strange behaviour, leaves Utterson and Poole with many more unanswered questions. List at least five mysteries puzzling the two men. If you notice more, add them to your list. Can you begin to suggest possible solutions?

TEACHING NOTES

You can download Teaching Notes for this task at www.brightredpublishing.co.uk/Shop/national-5-english-course-book

DON'T FORGET

The last we hear of Mr Utterson is that he's returning home to read the narratives of Dr Lanyon and Dr Jekyll. Think about what you know about Mr Utterson and what you think he might do with these documents once he's read them.

Commentary: 'Dr Lanyon's Narrative'

Key chapter elements:

- Jekyll's letter
- Lanyon's midnight visitor
- The potion: its effects on Hyde
- The potion: its effects on Lanyon

Jekyll's letter

This chapter gradually reveals why Utterson met with a closed door at Jekyll's on the 12th January. On the evening of the 9th, Lanyon received a letter from his estranged friend, now clearly in great distress. Despite their estrangement, he begs his medical friend to go to Jekyll's house that very night to retrieve a drawer from the locked 'glazed press' of his locked cabinet.

So great is the urgency, both locks are to be broken if necessary. (In this most secretive of worlds, the willingness to smash locks is testimony to Jekyll's desperation. This desperation finds further expression in the minutely detailed instructions on which drawer to select.) The drawer is to be taken to Lanyon's home and that same night, at midnight, he is to admit personally 'a man who will present himself in my name' and the drawer handed over. So critical is this undertaking that if Lanyon fails in this service, it might lead to Jekyll's death or 'the shipwreck' of his reason.

Although suspecting Jekyll may be already mad, Lanyon obligingly agrees, retrieves the drawer (while avoiding smashing the locks) and awaits his midnight visitor.

Lanyon's midnight visitor

At midnight, Lanyon found 'a small man crouching against the pillars of the portico', uneasy clearly at the presence of a nearby policeman because, after all, Hyde is a murderer on the run. Even in the persona of Hyde there is still a divide; there's 'a remarkable combination of great muscular activity and great apparent debility of constitution'.

Furthermore, Lanyon could see that 'in spite of his collected manner, he was wrestling against hysteria'. Lanyon's description is useful since his is the first from an objective, medical standpoint. But like others, he finds describing Hyde difficult: '... there was something abnormal and misbegotten in the very essence of the creature that now faced me – seizing, surprising and revolting'.

While the man's clothes are comically too large for him, Lanyon finds nothing amusing in his appearance: '... his face was so ghastly to see that I grew alarmed both for his life and reason'.

The potion: its effect on Hyde

We remember that it was Jekyll who begged Lanyon for the favour, but it's Hyde who's receiving it. The tensions which had earlier clouded the Lanyon/Jekyll friendship (with Jekyll calling Lanyon 'an ignorant, blatant pedant') emerge again in Hyde's arrogant challenge to his former critic after he has prepared the multi-coloured concoction.

He gives Lanyon the choice of letting Hyde depart with the mixture or, rather combatively, suggesting he remain to see the triumph of what he, Lanyon, had once described as 'unscientific balderdash'. Holding up the carefully prepared mixture, Hyde

spitefully taunts Lanyon: '... you who have so long been bound to the most narrow and material view, you who have denied the virtue of transcendental medicine, you who have derided your superiors – behold!' Despite saving the situation for Jekyll, we have Jekyll's darker side – Hyde – settling some old scores with his benefactor Lanyon.

Lanyon, nevertheless, agrees to remain, watching while the amazing transformation takes place: '... he reeled, staggered, clutched at the table [...] staring with infected eyes, gasping with open mouth [...] he seemed to swell – his face became suddenly black, and the feature seemed to melt and alter ...'

And then Lanyon, transfixed, has to break off as he sees appearing before him the form of Henry Jekyll.

The potion: its effect on Lanyon

As well as having a transforming effect on Hyde, the potion has an equally strong one on Lanyon. While the moment of transformation shakes Lanyon to the core, the next hour spent with the Jekyll is even more disturbing: 'What he told me in the next hour I cannot bring my mind to set on paper. I saw what I saw, I heard what I heard, and my soul sickened at it. Lanyon feels his life is shaken to the roots.'

The horror leads him to believe that his days are numbered – as indeed we know they are. If Jekyll appears to him 'like a man restored from death', Lanyon appears to us like a man newly consigned to it.

TEACHING NOTES

You can download Teaching Notes for this challenge at www.brightredpublishing.co.uk/Shop/national-5-english-course-book

Classroom challenge

From the quotations below, explain fully their significance to the characters or themes already discussed.

TEXTUAL EVIDENCE	POSSIBLE COMMENT(S)
'... although we may have differed at times on scientific questions, I cannot remember, at least on my side, any break in our affection.'	
'If his messenger could go to one place, why could he not go to another?'	
'There was a policeman not far off [...] and at the sight, I thought my visitor started and made greater haste.'	
'... his clothes [...] were enormously too large for him in every measurement ...'	
'... a new province of knowledge and new avenues to fame and power shall be laid open to you, here, in this room ...'	
'... you who have derided your superiors – behold!'	

Homework helper

Find supporting quotations to back up the following statements regarding events in this chapter.

TEXTUAL EVIDENCE	POSSIBLE COMMENT(S)
	The ingratiating tone of the Jekyll/Hyde letter to Lanyon suggests their friendship has never faltered (although we know better).
	Once in Lanyon's consulting-room, Hyde's language at one moment betrays his utter desperation to lay hands on the powders to make the potion.
	At one point, Lanyon fears for Hyde's sanity from his almost animal-like behaviour.
	Hyde's gleeful triumph over his old adversary is effectively conveyed by Stevenson's sentence structure.
	Sentence structure proves useful to Stevenson in effectively conveying the lengthy drawn-out process of the change overtaking Hyde.
	This circle of men are rather repressed in their attitude to discussing their affairs. Lanyon is even more restricted than the others in what he can reveal.

TEACHING NOTES

You can download Teaching Notes for this task at www.brightredpublishing.co.uk/Shop/national-5-english-course-book

Commentary: 'Henry Jekyll's Full Statement of the Case'

Key chapter elements:

- The doctor's dilemma
- Early days
- The Carew murder
- The doctor overtaken
- The doctor's solution
- Early warnings
- A problem in the park
- The final confrontation

The doctor's dilemma

Jekyll confesses right away that from an early age he had been 'committed to a profound duplicity of life'. Well-heeled and respectable as Jekyll might be, he is a man with a taste for vice. But while wishing to indulge 'such irregularities' as he was guilty of, he also wished 'to carry [his] head high' in society. While it's never made clear what his secret pleasures are, they're serious enough for him to wish to conceal them.

But, he claims, he was 'in no sense a hypocrite', for he was as much himself in indulging his vices as he was in behaving well. From his moral and intellectual reflections, he was drawn more and more to the idea that 'man is not truly one, but truly two'. From the nature of the life he led, he 'learned to recognize the thorough and primitive duality of man'. In other words, man is a compound of good and evil.

From an early age, he 'learned to dwell with pleasure, as a beloved daydream, on the thought of the separation of these elements'. But how was this to be achieved?

The doctor's solution

His medico-scientific background provides the answer. Of the nature of the constituent ingredients to bring about this physical separation, Jekyll is rather vague: 'I will not enter deeply into this scientific branch of my confession'.

Suffice it to say, he discovered a way to 'dethrone' his body from its normal state 'and a second form and countenance substituted, none the less natural to me because they were the expression, and bore the stamp, of lower elements in my soul'.

And so Edward Hyde was born. Tragically, however, as Jekyll confesses with hindsight 'my discoveries were incomplete' – a fact borne out by the instability of the Jekyll/Hyde identities.

Early days

By concocting and drinking down a potion created from various tinctures and salts, Jekyll, after suffering dreadful physical pains, finds himself in the persona of Edward Hyde. He instantly felt 'younger, lighter, happier in body' but also notes he had 'lost in stature'. Younger of course because he has not lived so long as Jekyll; lighter since he has not developed as much as the fully-grown man, but, of course, he has not just lost physical stature but moral stature, too.

And although 'evil was written broadly and plainly' on the face of the 'new-born' Hyde, Jekyll was pleased by what he saw in the mirror: '... when I looked upon the ugly idol in the glass, I was conscious of no repugnance, rather of a leap of welcome'. And, after quaffing down the potion again, Hyde transforms back into Jekyll.

Looking back in his final hours, Jekyll finally sees that, while Hyde was wholly evil, the 'other' was still 'the old Henry Jekyll, that incongruous compound' of good and evil. In other words, he had not finally silenced his troublesome conscience. The division was not complete.

Nevertheless, he liked the persona of Hyde so much he set him up in a house in Soho and made a will which meant he would also be financially secure. Being Hyde now made him feel like a schoolboy who strips and plunges 'into the sea of liberty'. But in his final hours, the older, wiser Jekyll realises that he fallen 'into slavery' to Hyde.

Early warnings

Delighted as he might be at the moment with Hyde and his nocturnal activities, there are warning signs that the moral Jekyll and his conscience have not been entirely obscured: 'Henry Jekyll stood at time aghast before the acts of Edward Hyde'. But he shrugs this off; Hyde, not Jekyll, is responsible.

Even the accident with the child can be dismissed as of 'no consequence'. Foolishly, he began to think he was 'beyond the reach of fate'. A much more serious warning comes when, two months before the Carew murder, the limitations of the potion are revealed: Jekyll went to bed as himself and woke up Edward Hyde. Alarmingly, the formula is already showing early signs of instability. Besides, he also began to see shortcomings in Hyde's company: 'Jekyll had more than a father's interest; Hyde had more than a son's indifference'.

Afraid he was losing hold of his 'original or better self and becoming slowly incorporated with [his] second and worse', Jekyll feels he has to choose. Despite the attractions of being Hyde, he feels he 'preferred the elderly and discontented doctor, surrounded by friends and cherishing honest hope; and bade a resolute farewell to the liberty, the comparative youth, the light step, leaping pulses and secret pleasures that [he] had enjoyed in the disguise of Hyde'.

Significantly, however, he 'neither gave up the house in Soho, nor destroyed the clothes of Edward Hyde'.

The Carew murder

For two months after his decision to turn his back on Hyde, Jekyll returned to his former ways. But soon he forgets the alarm he had earlier experienced – 'I began to be tortured with throes and longings, as of Hyde struggling after freedom' – so he goes back to the potion.

The devil which had been long caged 'came out roaring'. Hence the savagery of the murder of Danvers Carew. This act utterly changes Jekyll's status: previous sins had never seen him pursued by the law as a common murderer. Reality has caught up with him: 'the ugly face of my iniquity stared into my soul'.

At a practical level, he burns his papers in the Soho house to cover his tracks. But this is a wake-up call: Hyde had to be banished entirely or Jekyll could face 'the terrors of the scaffold: I locked the door by which I had so often gone and come, and ground the key under my heel'. Hyde was now locked away for good. Or was he?

A problem in the park

Jekyll's relief is short lived. 'It was a fine, clear January day, wet under foot where the frost had melted, but cloudless overhead; and the Regent's Park was full of winter chirruping and sweet with Spring odours.' This hint of Spring is ironic for there is to be no new life for Jekyll: 'I looked down; my clothes hung formlessly on my shrunken limbs; the hand that lay on my knee was corded and hairy. I was once more Edward Hyde'.

Yet again, the potion has proved unstable. Hyde is exposed to public view: '... and now I was the common quarry of mankind, hunted, houseless, a known murderer, thrall to the gallows'.

The doctor overtaken

What to do? His drugs were in his laboratory, but Poole would not admit a known murderer by the front door; and he himself had locked the back door and destroyed the key. Lanyon was his only hope.

Although now fully Hyde, 'of my original character, one part remained to me: I could write my own hand'; hence his letters to Lanyon and Poole with its plan for retrieving the drugs. Meanwhile, he remained concealed in a hotel in Portland Street awaiting the cover of darkness for his midnight rendezvous with Lanyon.

The final confrontation

Once back to the character of Jekyll, conscience resurrects itself in him: 'It was no longer the fear of the gallows, it was the horror of being Hyde that racked me'.

For the moment, he feels safe but the next day he feels the twinges he had felt in the park before the previous transformation into Hyde. He doubles his dose, but has to re-administer it regularly to maintain the form of Jekyll. Clearly, matters are getting out of hand. Soon, even dozing in his chair, 'it was always as Hyde that [he] awakened'.

He was now a body 'that seemed not strong enough to contain the raging energies' of the awakening Hyde. There was now a hatred between the two as they both struggled for ascendancy. Hyde played 'ape-like tricks' on Jekyll, wrote blasphemies in Jekyll's own hand on the pages of his books; he even burned his letters and the portrait of Jekyll's father.

His stock of the essential salt for the potion is by now running out. The salt which Poole obtained appeared to differ from the original. Jekyll fears the original may have been impure and the various replacements fail to match this impurity. The situation has now become hopelessly unsustainable. As Jekyll pens the last lines of his testimony, little of the potion remains to ward off the persona of Hyde. In anguished desperation, he brings 'the life of that unhappy Henry Jekyll to an end'.

But in the moment of Jekyll's death, Hyde finally obtains ascendancy and it's his body that Utterson and Poole find.

TEACHING NOTES

You can download Teaching Notes for this challenge at www.brightredpublishing.co.uk/Shop/national-5-english-course-book

Classroom challenge

Until this chapter, we've had to rely largely on Utterson for an answer to the question: what exactly is the truth about the respectable Doctor Jekyll and his strange friend Edward Hyde?

Utterson often struggles to make sense of what he's seen, or fails to interpret events correctly. But now, we get the 'full statement' of the facts, from the man himself – Dr Jekyll. Incidents and situations which had puzzled Utterson – and indeed some readers – now find their explanation from Jekyll's own testimony. From this chapter, we can now find satisfactory answers to the following questions:

1. Why did Jekyll leave a will leaving all to Hyde?
2. Why is Hyde younger and smaller than Jekyll?
3. Why does Hyde never dine at the doctor's?
4. Why is the murder of Carew carried out so savagely?
5. Why did a new life begin for Jekyll after the Carew murder?
6. Why did Jekyll slam down the window on Utterson and Enfield?
7. Why did Utterson and Poole find a broken key, with the breaks in it rust-covered?
8. Where is the body of Henry Jekyll?

Homework helper

This chapter has several quotations which help us understand both Jekyll and Hyde more fully. Finding them will help you to a deeper understanding of Jekyll, and of the complexity of their relationship. Search for the quotations from the clues in the right-hand column.

TEACHING NOTES

You can download Teaching Notes for this task at www.brightredpublishing.co.uk/Shop/national-5-english-course-book

TEXTUAL EVIDENCE	POSSIBLE COMMENT(S)
	Jekyll felt he was as much himself in his shameful nocturnal activities as he was when he pursued his medico-scientific career.
	The human personality consists of at least two sides.
	Jekyll, although knowing full well he might die in the process of separating his natures, manages to curb his fears given the attractiveness of the prospect.
	Far from being repulsed, Jekyll was delighted by his handiwork when he first looked in the laboratory's mirror.
	Thrown together, the personas of Jekyll and Hyde eventually developed a kind of family relationship, although not a happy one.
	It was not the fear of the scaffold that bothered Jekyll in his final hours but rather the horror of Hyde's persona taking him over completely.

Character studies

By working through these 'Classroom challenges' and 'Homework helpers', you have already acquired quite a body of information on the chief characters. These brief notes will help you to collate your existing information.

DON'T FORGET

Jekyll pays a terrible price for exploring the darker side of his personality. Think about your response to him. Consider reasons why you might admire his courage as well as reasons for condemning his actions.

Utterson

Utterson is our guide for the narrative, with the exception of the last two chapters. We see events through his objective, but not always insightful, eyes. Utterson is a sound recorder of facts but is less trustworthy when interpreting them. As a lawyer, his 'dusty, dreary' self lacks all elements of imagination or fancy. Given that Jekyll, the subject of his investigation, is 'too fanciful', (in Lanyon's words), it's no wonder that Utterson struggles to understand events surrounding his friend. They are part of the same social circle, but their mind-sets are quite different.

Unlike Jekyll, who is self-indulgent in the extreme, Utterson practises self-denial – liking fine wines but only drinking gin, enjoying the theatre but never going there in twenty years. It's second nature for Utterson to repress enjoyment; it's second nature for Jekyll to indulge it. Yet, for all their differences, the two opposites are friends, with Utterson becoming greatly distressed at the thought of Jekyll being blackmailed.

The need to preserve his friend's reputation motivates Utterson loyally throughout the narrative, refusing as he does to discuss any hint of blemish on it even with his best friend and relative, Enfield. Even when he suspects (wrongly) that Jekyll might have murdered Hyde, his last words to the butler Poole are, 'I would say nothing of this [...] If your master has fled or is dead, we may at least save his credit'.

There is surely some **irony** intended in his name – Utterson – since he utters very little indeed about matters of importance throughout these extraordinary events.

Classroom challenge

How well do you know the character of Utterson? Here are a few comments which you might wish to support with appropriate quotations, and a few quotations to which you may wish to add your own comments.

TEXTUAL EVIDENCE	POSSIBLE COMMENT(S)
'... lean, long, dusty, dreary, and yet somehow lovable.' (Ch 1)	
	He claims to lack interest in the fate of others yet he is kind to those in trouble. (Ch 1)
'... drank gin when he was alone, to mortify a taste for vintages.' (Ch 1)	
'"I wouldn't speak of this note, you know," said the master.' (Ch 5)	
	Even in moments of great drama, Utterson is a stickler for respecting social norms. (Ch 8)
	Almost the last words which Utterson utters in the text reflect his deep-seated belief in repressing any unnecessary comment. (Ch 8)

You can download Teaching Notes for this challenge at www.brightredpublishing.co.uk/Shop/national-5-english-course-book

TEACHING NOTES

Dr Henry Jekyll

We do not meet Dr Jekyll in person until the third chapter. By then, Stevenson has begun to familiarise us with a world in which, to a certain extent, duality is already present in both people and in places. (See 'Story of the Door'.) We are, therefore, not unduly surprised when the idea of the divided self is hinted early on in Jekyll's description: 'a large, well-made, smooth-faced man of fifty, with something of a slyish cast perhaps ...' Nevertheless, he gives 'every mark of capacity and kindness'.

Adding to his established respectability is his impressive list of academic qualifications and a circle of friends described as 'all intelligent, reputable men'. The darker side of this rich and successful man is more fully explained only in the final chapter where we learn he had 'a certain impatient gaiety of disposition' which bothered him since he liked to 'carry [his] head high, and wear a more than commonly grave countenance before the public'. In other words, he found it hard to reconcile private vice with public reputation; hence his interest in scientific research which would help divide his persona in two, with one representing his virtuous, professional self and another embodying his darker, vicious self. 'Man is,' he claims, 'not truly one, but truly two'.

After much experimenting, he succeeds in creating Edward Hyde out of his lower nature. The division, however, was not quite complete for although his lower impulses were now directed into Edward Hyde, his other half 'was still the old Henry Jekyll' who retained elements of conscience which resurrected themselves in places.

His transformational potion is meant to control changes both into and out of the character of Hyde, but as time passes, the fundamental instability of the potion becomes apparent. Increasingly stronger doses are required to keep the persona of Hyde at bay. (Ultimately, however, Jekyll's bold adventure is undermined by prosaic failure in the ingredients of his potion.) Hyde gradually becomes stronger and stronger, finally tormenting Jekyll literally to death. In the fate of the bold over-reacher Jekyll, we witness Stevenson's comment on the fatally corrosive power of evil.

Classroom challenge

The complex character of Dr Henry Jekyll is sometimes elusive to discuss. These quotations are useful starting points for piecing together a balanced picture. Consider what you might say about each one.

TEACHING NOTES

You can download Teaching Notes for this challenge at www.brightredpublishing.co.uk/Shop/national-5-english-course-book

TEXTUAL EVIDENCE	POSSIBLE COMMENT(S)
'The large handsome face of Dr Jekyll grew pale to the very lips, and there came a blackness about his eyes.' (Ch 3)	
'... the moment I choose, I can be rid of Mr Hyde.' (Ch 3)	
'... and there, close up to the warmth, sat Dr Jekyll, looking deadly sick.' (Ch 3)	
'... as my narrative will make, alas! too evident, my discoveries were incomplete.' (Ch 10)	
'I knew well that I risked death.' (Ch 10)	
'... above all, if I slept, or even dozed for a moment in my chair, it was always as Hyde that I awakened.' (Ch 10)	

Edward Hyde

Hyde is a creature of Jekyll's lower impulses, representing the beast in man. It's no surprise, therefore, that various animal-related descriptions surround him. In the Utterson meeting we hear of him 'hissing' like some kind of reptile. In the final chapter, he treats Jekyll with 'ape-like spite'. Poole describes him as crying out 'like a rat' and later as moving about 'like a monkey'. His hands are described as 'corded and hairy'. Jekyll himself admits him to be 'the animal within me'.

That he's spoken of as a young man is no surprise since he was brought to life much later than Jekyll himself. However, over the course of the novella, his powers develop to the point of colonising Jekyll's persona entirely. His stature, small to start with, never appears to change, with him appearing almost as a comical figure in the over-sized clothes of Jekyll at the hotel in Portland Street. Morally, he is a debased version of Jekyll, with Stevenson underlining this by making him, literally, a lesser man. Small or not, he's a violently cruel figure, as witnessed in the fate of Danvers Carew. We see, too, his vicious spite at work in the savage taunting of both Lanyon and Jekyll.

His appearance is also remarkable in that no one can quite articulate what it is about him that repulses people. They hint at deformity but fail to be more precise. The nature of the pure evil which Hyde embodies is perhaps the problem. Human descriptive powers, accustomed to the normal combination of good and evil, seem defeated by this extreme case of evil incarnate.

Classroom challenge

Describing Hyde proves difficult for several characters whom he encounters. Here are several quotations which might prove useful when it comes to revision. What could you say about each one?

TEXTUAL EVIDENCE	POSSIBLE COMMENT(S)
'... he gives a strong feeling of deformity, although I couldn't specify the point.' (Ch 1)	
'... at that, Mr Hyde broke out of all bounds, and clubbed him to the earth. And next moment, with ape-like fury, he was trampling his victim under foot ...' (Ch 4)	
'I was struck [...] with his remarkable combination of great muscular activity and great apparent debility of constitution ...' (Ch 9)	
'This person [...] was dressed in a fashion that would have made an ordinary person laughable; his clothes [...] were enormously too large for him in every measurement – the trousers hanging on his legs and rolled up to keep them from the ground ...' (Ch 9)	
'... you who have derided your superiors – behold!' (Ch 9)	
'... he loathed the despondency into which Jekyll was now fallen [...] his love of life is wonderful ...' (Ch 10)	

You can download Teaching Notes for this challenge at www.brightredpublishing.co.uk/Shop/national-5-english-course-book

TEACHING NOTES

Dr Hastie Lanyon

Like Jekyll, Lanyon is a medical man but one with far more traditional views of medicine and science than Jekyll. They had once been friends, but there had been a falling-out, as he tells Utterson: '... it is more than ten years since Henry Jekyll became too fanciful for me'.

The fact that he is clearly the only other person to whom Jekyll has confided details of his research suggests he is of some intellectual standing. He contrasts with Jekyll, however, in representing a much more conservative, rational view of medical science.

Stevenson leaves it to Lanyon to describe the transformation of Hyde back into Jekyll, possibly intending that, with his far from fanciful, 'no nonsense' approach to medical science, Lanyon will bring convincing credibility to this key event. Indeed, so great is his horror at the event, he feels 'shaken to the roots'. He takes to his bed and, within a short time, he's dead. While refusing to discuss with Utterson what he saw happen to Jekyll, he leaves a full description in a letter to the lawyer.

Classroom challenge

While Lanyon makes only three contributions, one from beyond the grave, his feet-on-the-ground reporting provides readers with important information at key moments.

Comment on how the following quotations contribute to our understanding of Lanyon and the events that he witnesses.

TEXTUAL EVIDENCE	POSSIBLE COMMENT(S)
'With that [...] he set forth in the direction of Cavendish Square, that citadel of medicine, where his friend, the great Dr Lanyon, had his house and received his crowding patients.' (Ch 2)	
'The geniality, as was the way of the man, was somewhat theatrical to the eye; but it reposed on genuine feeling.' (Ch 2)	
'He began to go wrong, wrong in mind [...] such unscientific balderdash ...' (Ch 2)	
'He had his death-warrant written legibly on his face.' (Ch 6)	
'I sometimes think if we knew all, we should be more glad to get away.' (Ch 6)	
'... "O God!" I screamed, and "O God!" again and again ...' (Ch 9)	

TEACHING NOTES

You can download Teaching Notes for this challenge at www.brightredpublishing.co.uk/Shop/national-5-english-course-book

Themes and motifs

It's testimony to Stevenson's craftsmanship that the themes he explores here are often so intertwined, it's sometimes difficult to separate out their several strands. However, the effort of doing so enriches the study process greatly and makes exam preparation more manageable.

Running through these themes are motifs which serve subtly to reinforce the ideas Stevenson is setting out in the novel.

Human duality or the divided self

'... man is not truly one, but truly two.'

Jekyll's drive to channel his respectable and evil sides into two separate 'selves' lies at the heart of the novel. It finds its fullest expression in the lives of Henry Jekyll and Edward Hyde. Driven by a desire to overcome the restrictions of public respectability in order to fully enjoy his darker pleasures, Jekyll targets research at finding a scientific formula to separate the conflicting aspects of his soul.

For a time, he seems successful. While Hyde leads a 'vile life' marked by cruel, violent deeds among 'strange associates', Jekyll maintains a respectable professional life in his handsome home. Over time, however, as the imperfections of his transforming potion become clearer, these two sides are found not to be truly equal. Evil gains strength from the exercise of its powers; the deluded Jekyll is finally subsumed into his darker self.

Although we do not hear Jekyll articulating his thesis of the duality of human nature until the final chapter, we may well have already arrived at a similar idea from our own observations of other characters in the novella. For there are several other instances of characters with contradictory or conflicting sides to their nature.

Classroom challenge

Close reading of the text may well have brought you to notice that many of the characters possess contradictory or conflicting aspects in their personalities. Here are a few contradictory or conflicting characteristics. Using your knowledge of the text, match these characteristics with a key character.

1. Excellent social behaviour but with an evil, hypocritical look.
2. Combines professionalism with an eye to the main chance.
3. Seems genial enough on the surface but is quick to anger.
4. Says he doesn't give a damn about people's fate but is often unfortunate men's last good influence.
5. Outwardly respectable to the point of dullness but leads a mysterious nocturnal life.

Find the teaching notes for this challenge at www.brightredpublishing.co.uk/Shop/national-5-english-course-book

TEACHING NOTES

But it's not only people who appear to manifest a divided self – places do, too.

While Jekyll's home wears 'a great air of wealth and comfort', it's directly joined to the squalid laboratory of Hyde with its 'marks of prolonged and sordid negligence'. Adding further to this duality is the street itself in which the laboratory is located; it shone out 'like a fire in a forest' in contrast to its surrounding dingy neighbourhood.

The wider city of London also presents a divided self. Enfield returning home in the first chapter witnesses an eerily deserted, but peaceful, nightscape which suddenly erupts into a nightmarish scene of violent cruelty to a child and which is followed by a near riot of angry women 'wild as harpies'.

The Soho quarter surrounding Hyde's home is grim in its squalor: fog lowers over the area's miserable homes and businesses, while 'many ragged children huddled in the doorways'. Balancing this portrait of the city is a scene in another district where the 'inhabitants were all doing well' with the shop fronts presenting 'an air of invitation, like rows of smiling saleswomen'. Similarly positive is the landscape in Regent's Park where Jekyll sits one fine, clear January day, noting that the park 'was full of winter chirruping and sweet with Spring odours'. Duality, Stevenson appears to be suggesting, is to be detected not only in man but in our wider environment.

The repressed society

This is a novel about a small circle of friends who've known each other since their earliest years. Despite or because of this close association, they're reluctant to discuss anything which might harm the reputation of anyone in their group. 'I feel very strongly about putting questions', says Enfield and Utterson agrees. While Utterson may be deeply concerned by Jekyll's connection with Hyde, he never mentions directly his deepest fear – blackmail – to his old friend.

Lanyon is similarly tight-lipped when Uttterson consults him about Jekyll. We discover later, in Lanyon's narrative, that Jekyll had clearly discussed 'transcendental medicine' with him, but all Lanyon tells Utterson is that he sees less of Jekyll because of the 'scientific balderdash' of his recent research, the nature of which he doesn't mention and which Utterson doesn't probe.

When comparing Jekyll and Hyde's handwriting, Utterson and his trusted head clerk both suspect forgery, but neither mentions the word to the other. A more serious aspect of this fraternity of silence is the fact that Utterson, while helpful in many ways to the police after the Carew murder, fails to mention Hyde's secondary abode which would, of course, lead back to Jekyll. The last we hear of Utterson is the lawyer telling Jekyll's butler after the finding of Hyde's body and the disappearance of Jekyll, 'I would say nothing of this ...' Why? Because Utterson believes that if Jekyll has fled or is dead, 'we may at least save his reputation'.

Jekyll, by the very nature of his outrageous experiment, is, of course, bound to silence if he is to maintain his reputation in society. But given the reluctance of his close friends to ask probing questions, discuss fears or explore potential embarrassments, it's little wonder he was allowed to advance so far down his catastrophic pathway.

A novel of motifs

Motifs are recurring ideas or images which help support the guiding themes of the novel in which they appear. This novella is particularly rich in motifs.

Classroom challenge

Here are a few of the more obvious motifs. Try to comment on their usefulness in this story. Can you connect them with major themes in the novel?

Doors **Locks, safes and barred windows**

Fog, weather and night. **Connecting buildings**

The beast in man **Ill-fitting clothes**

Exam-style tests

Topic Test 7

Read the extract below and then attempt the following questions.

***The Strange Case of Dr Jekyll and Mr Hyde* by Robert Louis Stevenson**

It chanced on one of these rambles that their way led them down a by street in a busy quarter of London. The street was small and what is called quiet, but it drove a thriving trade on the week-days. The inhabitants were all doing well, it seemed, and all emulously hoping to do better still, and laying out the surplus of their gains in coquetry; so that the shop fronts stood along that thoroughfare with an air of invitation, like rows of smiling saleswomen. Even on Sunday, when it veiled its more florid charms and lay comparatively empty of passage, the street shone out like a fire in a forest; and with its freshly painted shutters, well-polished brasses, and general cleanliness and gaiety of note, instantly caught and pleased the eye of the passenger.

Two doors from one corner, on the left hand going east, the line was broken by the entry of a court; and just at that point, a certain sinister block of building thrust forward its gable on the street. It was two storeys high; showed no window, nothing but a door on the lower storey and a blind forehead of discoloured wall on the upper; and bore in every feature the marks of prolonged and sordid negligence. The door, which was equipped with neither bell nor knocker, was blistered and distained. Tramps slouched into the recess and struck matches on the panels; children kept shop upon the steps; the schoolboy had tried his knife on the mouldings; and for close on a generation no one had appeared to drive away these random visitors or to repair their ravages.

Mr Enfield and the lawyer were on the other side of the by street; but when they came abreast of the entry, the former lifted up his cane and pointed.

'Did you ever remark that door?' he asked; and when his companion had replied in the affirmative, 'It is connected in my mind,' added he, 'with a very odd story.'

'Indeed!' said Mr Utterson, with a slight change of voice, 'and what was that?'

'Well it was this way,' returned Mr Enfield: 'I was coming home from some place at the end of the world, about three o'clock of a black winter morning, and my way lay through a part of town where there was literally nothing to be seen but lamps. Street after street, and all the folks asleep – street after, all lighted up as if for a procession, and all as empty as a church – till at last I got into that state of mind when a man listens and listens and begins to long for the sight of a policeman. All at once, I saw two figures: one a little man who was stumping along eastward at a good walk, and the other a girl of maybe eight or ten who was running as hard as she was able down a cross-street. Well, sir, the two ran into one another naturally enough at the corner; and then came the horrible part of the thing; for the man trampled calmly over the child's body and left her screaming on the ground. It sounds nothing to hear, but it was hellish to see. It wasn't like a man; it was like some damned Juggernaut. I gave a view halloa, took to my heels, collared my gentleman, and brought him back to where there was already quite a group about the screaming child. He was perfectly cool and made no resistance, but gave me one look, so ugly that it brought out the sweat on me like running.

1. From this extract, summarise in your own words as far as possible, the events which are revealed here. You should make **four** key points. **4**

2. Look at the first paragraph (lines 1–9). By referring to **two** examples of word choice and/or imagery, explain how the writer conveys the attractiveness of the street. **4**

3. Look at lines 24–29. With close reference to the extract, show how any **two** examples of the writer's language convey effectively the desolation of the scene as Enfield walks home. **4**

4. With close reference to this extract and to another elsewhere in the novel, show how the writer develops a major theme. **8**

Total – 20 marks

Topic Test 8

Read the extract below and then attempt the following questions.

***The Strange Case of Dr Jekyll and Mr Hyde* by Robert Louis Stevenson**

1 Poole swung the axe over his shoulder; the blow shook the building, and the red baize door leaped against the lock and hinges. A dismal screech, as of mere animal terror, rang from the cabinet. Up went the axe again, and again the panels crashed and the frame bounded; four times the blow fell; but the wood was tough and the fittings were of excellent workmanship; and it was not until the fifth that the lock burst asunder, and the wreck of the door fell inwards on the carpet.

The besiegers, appalled by their own riot and the stillness that had succeeded, stood back a little and peered in. There lay the cabinet before their eyes in the quiet lamplight, a good fire glowing and chattering on the hearth, the kettle singing its thin strain, a drawer or two open, papers neatly set forth on the business table, and nearer the fire, the things laid out for tea; the quietest room, you would have said, and, but for the glazed presses full of chemicals, the most commonplace that night in London.

Right in the midst there lay the body of a man sorely contorted and still twitching. They drew near on tiptoe, turned it on its back, and beheld the face of Edward Hyde. He was dressed in clothes far too large for him, clothes of the doctor's bigness; the cords of his face still moved with a semblance of life, but life was quite gone; and by the crushed phial in the hand and the strong smell of kernels that hung upon the air, Utterson knew that he was looking on the body of a self-destroyer.

'We have come too late,' he said sternly, 'whether to save or punish. Hyde is gone to his account; and it only remains for us to find the body of your master.'

The far greater proportion of the building was occupied by the theatre, which filled almost the whole ground storey, and was lighted from above, and by the cabinet, which formed an upper storey at one end and looked upon the court. A corridor joined the theatre to the door on the by street; and with this, the cabinet communicated separately by a second flight of stairs. There were besides a few dark closets and a spacious cellar. All these they now thoroughly examined. Each closet needed but a glance, for they were all empty and all, by the dust that fell from their doors, had stood long unopened. The cellar, indeed, was filled with crazy lumber, mostly dating from the times of the surgeon who was Jekyll's predecessor; but even as they opened the door, they were advertised of the uselessness of further search by the perfect mat of cobweb which had for years sealed up the entrance. Nowhere was there any trace of Henry Jekyll, dead or alive.

Poole stamped on the flags of the corridor. 'He must be buried here,' he said, hearkening to the sound.

'Or he may have fled,' said Utterson, and he turned to examine the door in the by street. It was locked; and lying near by on the flags, they found the key, already stained with rust.

'This does not look like use,' observed the lawyer.

'Use!' echoed Poole. 'Do you not see, sir, it is broken? much as if a man had stamped on it.'

'Ah,' continued Utterson, 'and the fractures, too, are rusty.' The two men looked at each other with a scare.

'This is beyond me, Poole,' said the lawyer. 'Let us go back to the cabinet.'

They mounted the stair in silence, and still, with an occasional awestruck glance at the dead body, proceeded more thoroughly to examine the contents of the cabinet. At one table, there were traces of chemical work, various measured heaps of some white salt being laid on glass saucers, as though for an experiment in which the unhappy man had been prevented.

'That is the same drug that I was always bringing him,' said Poole; and even as he spoke, the kettle with a startling noise boiled over.

1. Using your own words as far as possible summarise what happens in this extract. You should make at least **four** key points. **4**

2. Look at the first paragraph (lines 1–6).

a) Show how one example of the writer's use of language conveys Poole's strength in breaking down the door. **2**

b) Show how one example of the writer's use of sentence structure suggests the difficulty he encountered in breaking the door down **2**

3. Look at paragraph three (lines 15–27).

   By referring to an example of the writer's language explain how the writer effectively conveys the room's normality. **2**

4. By using your own words as far as possible, explain why searching the cupboard spaces was a pointless exercise in the search for Jekyll. **2**

5. By referring to this extract and to elsewhere in the novel, show how the theme of duality is developed. **8**

Total – 20 marks

THE ESSAY: WHAT'S INVOLVED?

INTRODUCING THE CRITICAL ESSAY

Writing a critical essay on a text you've studied in class accounts for 20 of the 70 marks in the final exam. Once again, a successful essay relies on many of the same skills you're already acquiring as you work on Reading for Understanding, Analysis and Evaluation. Your final score will be determined by:

- how well you **understand** what is going on in the text,
- how well you **understand** what the question is asking you to do,
- your ability to **analyse** how the author creates their effects, and
- your ability to **evaluate** the significance of the evidence presented.

In addition, however, your essay will need to demonstrate:

- your ability to **create a clear line of thought** from start to finish,
- your ability to **select only** the textual knowledge which is necessary to answer the question, and
- your ability to write technically competent prose.

This chapter will be your guide in helping you to perfect your skills in these areas by looking at each area step by step.

DON'T FORGET

The skills which you acquire for writing critical essays in English will also be useful when writing essays in other subjects. Understanding, analysis and evaluation form the core of presenting information successfully when an essay format is required.

What's coming up?

- Organising your preparation
- Selecting a question
- Planning a response
- Structuring your essay
- Maintaining the flow
- Perfecting presentation
- Practising for the exam
- Trying a test paper

ORGANISING YOUR PREPARATION

Knowing your text

An exam room is no place to discover you don't know your prepared texts as well as you thought you did. Yes, you'll have read the texts with your teacher in class, but that won't give you the mastery of them that's essential if you're to do well. You need to read them regularly on your own. You'll get to know the overall work best if you break down your reading sessions into manageable segments.

If you're studying a play, perhaps target an act or scene per session. If it's poetry, focus on a single poem at a sitting. If you're studying a novel, work on it a chapter or two at a time. Come the exam, you'll find that this kind of textual knowledge will boost your confidence hugely as you settle down to the paper.

DON'T FORGET

Confidence in an exam comes from **knowing you know** your texts really thoroughly. That means regular reading of them on your own.

Assembling study materials

Your exam preparation begins the day you start your course. You need to gather around you from day one the materials that are going to help you succeed.

Your texts

Even if your school supplies you with the texts, it's a good idea to acquire your own copies so that you can annotate them with your own notes. Second-hand copies of well-known texts can be bought online, sometimes for only pennies. You can then mark them up with various coloured marker pens in a way you couldn't with a school copy. For example, red for quotations underlining themes; blue for quotations illustrating character A, etc.

Your notes

When you take notes from lessons in class, avoid making them so short or cryptic that they make little sense when you read them back. It might be a good idea to go through your class notes on a weekly basis to check they still make sense. If they don't, ask advice from your teacher or someone else who was in the class. These checked notes you could then organise in text-specific files.

Your files

Keeping a loose-leaf file per text is a good idea. This way, you can build up your knowledge bank flexibly as you progress through the text. For instance, when studying a play, one section could be devoted to each of the various characters; another to plot developments, scene by scene, act by act; and another to themes. In this way, you can slip in new information as your study progresses. Novels and poems could be organised along similar lines.

By exam revision time, you'll have a powerful means of bringing together all your acquired knowledge on a text in one place. This approach can easily be adapted to a computer filing system, if this is your preferred way of working. (But be sure to back everything up!)

Your essays and discussions

When you get an essay back from your teacher, read the comments carefully and store the essay in your text-specific file. You'll have spent some time on the essay, so don't let this valuable revision aid go to waste. Think, too, of various discussions you may have had in class. You'll remember good points better if you make notes at the time.

Published commentaries

These can be helpful, but they're no substitute for the notes you've made in class. These commercial notes may take a different approach from your teacher and you may become confused between the two sources of information. Avoid at all costs 'lifting' from these study notes without acknowledging where these comments came from. Remember, the markers will probably be familiar with these commentaries, too!

Classroom challenge

Take one of the texts you are studying. How might you divide up a study file in a way that would be helpful come revision time? Devise the various sections you might create. By character, if a novel, play or short story? By scene or act, if a play? By theme?

What content will you be including in each section? Your own notes? Marked essays? Quotations from critics?

Have you, or will you have, sufficient material in the various sections to provide you with an effective revision tool? If not, how could you add substance to it?

TEACHING NOTES You can download Teaching Notes for this challenge at www.brightredpublishing.co.uk/Shop/national-5-english-course-book

SELECTING A QUESTION

Time is precious in the exam. You need to select a question promptly, but certainly not casually. Hence the need to know your texts thoroughly. Because if you know your texts in depth, you're better placed to make a rapid mental survey of them to decide which question your knowledge best equips you to answer.

How does that work?

Once you've decided you have sufficient information to settle on a particular question, begin by reading the question carefully. Underline or highlight what you think are keywords.

For instance, you may select a question like this:

> Choose a short story or novel in which setting figures prominently.
>
> Describe the contribution of the setting and then show how this feature helped your understanding of the text as a whole.

Underline the words which you think are pointing you to what the essay will be about. In this case, the words '**setting figures prominently**' suggest themselves. In the second line, you'll probably have underlined '**Describe the contribution**'. But notice there's a second part to the question:

> ... and then show how this feature helped your understanding of the text as a whole.

In exam questions at this level you must always be ready for this second part. Under pressure to write down all the details of setting which you wish to 'describe', you must not underestimate the importance of 'how this feature helped your understanding of the text as a whole'. For this is the key part of the question. By keeping it constantly at the forefront of your mind as you write, you are creating the clear line of thought which will shape your essay – and win the marker's approval.

Referring back to this second part in each paragraph will help you stay on task.

DON'T FORGET

You need to convince the examiner in the structure of your essay that you can do the same as you do in Paper 1:

- **Understand** the writer's intentions
- **Analyse** how they create effects
- **Evaluate** what is being achieved

PLANNING A RESPONSE

A plan is necessary for two people: you and the examiner. Start writing without a plan and you risk going off task and not answering the question. Consequently, you sell yourself short and don't make the most of your text knowledge. Similarly, the examiner fails to see a line of thought at work in the structure of your answer – and marks you down.

For practice, let's return to our focus question on page 140 and apply it to a short novel for which it would work well: Robert Louis Stevenson's *The Strange Case of Dr Jekyll and Mr Hyde.*

Pre-plan brainstorming

Before we plan, let's take a look at that rapid mental survey we need to make before beginning to write. We need to consider:

(i) how well a question matches up to our knowledge of this text. (Do you know enough about 'setting' to answer this one?),

(ii) the **precise** demands of our selected question, and

(iii) what our line of thought might be.

We're not quite at a plan yet, just a speedy mental process – but a vital one. It might go a little like this:

WHAT WE KNOW ABOUT SETTING	WHAT LINE OF THOUGHT MIGHT BE
• *Sordid and attractive houses in same street*	• *Stevenson believes man has two sides to nature*
• *Jekyll's handsome house linked to broken down laboratory*	• *The same split exists all around us, not just in human nature*
• *Several key events happen at night*	• *The split's not always visible and setting helps lays this out physically for the reader*
• *Do I have evidence to illustrate all this?*	• *Jekyll's maybe not unique*

A possible approach to planning

Everyone has their own way of planning an essay. Some make lists of points they wish to include, linking them to particular characters, settings or themes.

Others may prefer diagrams, or a mind-map of the kind illustrated here. Here's how our earlier brainstorming might work out as we get down to assembling more detailed material:

Point 1:
sordid and attractive mixed up in opening description

'… the street shone out in contrast to its dingy neighbours, like a fire in a forest.'

'… freshly painted shutters, well-polished brasses, and general cleanliness and gaiety of note …'

BUT *'… a certain sinister block of building thrust forward its gable on the street.'*

'… and bore in every feature the marks of prolonged and sordid negligence.'

'The door […] was blistered and distained. Tramps slouched in the recess …'

Point 2:
direct linking of Dr Jekyll's handsome home to this sordid building

'Round the corner from the by street there was a square of ancient, handsome houses, now for the most part decayed from their high estate.'

'One house wore a great air of wealth and comfort …'

Question: why does Stevenson link them? Making a point about duality? Respectable Jekyll's connection to the sordid?

Choose a short story or novel in which setting figures prominently.
Describe the contribution of the setting and then show how this feature helped your understanding of the text as a whole.

Point 3:
key events take place at night/in fog

'I was coming home from some place at the end of the world, about three o'clock of a black winter morning …' (Hyde's attack on child)

Utterson first encounters Hyde at night

Danvers Carew is murdered at night

'A great-coloured pall lowered over heaven …'

'… and the next moment the fog settled down again upon that part, as brown as umber and cut him off from his blackguardly surroundings.'

Question: why darkness and fog? Night mirrors darkness of J's intentions? Fog aids concealment, used literally and metaphorically?

DON'T FORGET

You may decide not to use all the quotations initially selected for your mind-map. The time available and their precise relevance to the question may require you to reject some. Prioritise only the ones you think are truly key. Time presses on!

Classroom challenge

Here's the kind of question you might encounter in an exam.

> Choose a poem which features an encounter or an incident.
>
> By referring to appropriate techniques, explain how the poet brings the encounter or incident to life for you.

Without necessarily going as far as answering the question fully:

- choose any poem you have read recently which features an encounter or incident
- brainstorm a) details of the encounter/incident b) techniques employed c) what your line of thought might be
- organise your thoughts into a mind-map (two or three main points may be enough)

To get you started, the models we've looked at here could be helpful.

If you can't immediately think of a suitable poem on which to practise this exercise, type "'The Moleman's Apprentice' @ Scottish Poetry Library" into your browser. This unusual poem by Jim Carruth would work well for this purpose. As indeed, would 'Death of a Naturalist' by Seamus Heaney.

Swap your results with a partner. How helpful do they think your mind-map would be for writing a successful essay?

ONLINE

Head to www.brightredbooks.net for a link to The Scottish Poetry Library website. It's a treasure trove of poems on all kinds of subjects. You can use its 'Search' box when looking for poems on specific topics.

STRUCTURING YOUR ESSAY

We've worked on a rough, overall plan for our essay on *The Strange Case of Dr Jekyll and Mr Hyde*. Now we need to transform it, step by step, into a full essay.

Introductions

Done clearly and concisely, your introduction will make a favourable impression on the marker. You don't have much time to create this impression, so:

1. In your first sentence, make clear the title of the selected text (in inverted commas) and its author. (Nothing makes a worse impression than getting the spelling of the author's name wrong. Make sure checking basics like this is part of your revision process.)
2. In that same sentence, adopt some wording which suggests that you've chosen this text because it fits the set question.

Going back to the wording of the question on our Stevenson text, we might write as an opening sentence:

A novel in which setting figures prominently is 'The Strange Case of Dr Jekyll and Mr Hyde' by Robert Louis Stevenson.

3. Briefly outline the significance/role of setting in this essay. (It gives the marker a hint as to the direction of your line of thought.)

Respectable Dr Jekyll, impatient with respectability, longs to indulge in hidden, evil desires. To do so, he invents a potion which turns him into wicked Mr Hyde, thereby living out his dark side in another self. In Jekyll, the virtuous and the evil live side by side, just as, in the novel's setting, the attractive and the ugly co-exist in the world around him.

4. Now revisit the wording of the second part of the question to assure the examiner you have not forgotten about that bit.

By frequently drawing attention to the dual nature of the setting and setting several key events at night, Stevenson uses these features to help us understand what he is saying about the divided nature of Jekyll and his progress into his darker self.

Note that, in this example, we are giving not just a reference **back** to the question but also a reference **forward** to our 'road-map' for the essay: discussion of the physical setting, followed by discussion of the impact of night-time settings.

Body paragraphs: opening statements

Our mind-map gave us some rough key points. Now we need to fashion them into the kind of statements which will be effective lead-ins to each paragraph in our essay – statements which demonstrate to the marker where our line of thought is going, and which keep us on task. A good statement sets the agenda for the paragraph.

From the points in our mind-map, we might end up with statements such as these:

Statement 1:

In the opening chapter, Stevenson goes to great trouble to establish that the area around Hyde's laboratory home presents a setting which is a curious mixture of the attractive and the dingy.

Statement 2:

There is a further contrast of environments, for we later learn that this squalid laboratory is connected to buildings in a nearby square.

Statement 3:

The setting is enriched even more by having the key moments in the story take place at night.

A checklist for statements

- A good statement sets out a focused agenda for the paragraph which follows.
- This may be a single sentence, sometimes called a topic sentence. Or, it may require two or three sentences to make the paragraph's key point.
- A good statement will always be fairly general and should not get down to specific details or quotations. Save these for the evidence section which follows the statement.

Classroom challenge

Here are four opening statements for a paragraph in which the writer attempts to describe the overall atmosphere in a poem which is set on a hot summer's day.

Bearing in mind what we've said about what a good opening statement should do, which statement do you find most effective in setting out the agenda for the paragraph to come? Give reasons for your rejection of the others.

Statement 1:

The poet describes the day by saying:

'Bubbles gargled delicately, bluebottles

Wove a strong gauze of sound around the smell'

TEACHING NOTES

You can download Teaching Notes for this challenge at www.brightredpublishing.co.uk/Shop/national-5-english-course-book

Statement 2:

The day is brought alive by the poet using really good language. You can really picture yourself being there.

Statement 3:

To suggest the peaceful scene that hot summer's day, the poet employs a range of figurative language items such as onomatopoeia, alliteration and assonance.

Statement 4:

Alliteration is used well to picture the day, with words that help you imagine how the butterflies moved around the scene.

Body paragraphs: supporting evidence

We've seen the kind of statements needed to set out a clear agenda for a convincing paragraph. These statements form the paragraph's backbone. Now we need to put flesh on the bones. In other words, we must now provide **evidence** to support these opening statements.

Evidence can take two forms: direct quotations from the text or detailed references to information in the text. A good essay will use both.

To see evidence at work, let's go back to our essay on *The Strange Case of Dr Jekyll and Mr Hyde*. One of our statements told us:

In the opening chapter, Stevenson goes to considerable effort to establish that the area around Jekyll's laboratory presents a setting which is a curious mixture of the prosperous and the dingy.

Now we need to offer evidence to support this claim of a mixture of appearances:

We find the street 'shone out in contrast to its dingy neighbourhood, like a fire in a forest'. Stevenson also notes the buildings presented 'freshly painted shutters, well-polished brasses, and general cleanliness'. But Jekyll's laboratory sticks out harshly in this attractive area. We are told that 'a certain sinister block of building thrust forward its gable on the street'. This block 'bore in every feature the marks of prolonged and sordid negligence' and its door was 'blistered and distained. Tramps slouched in the recess ...'.

DON'T FORGET

Quotations must be **woven** into the text, not merely deposited. Avoid writing: 'The building was very run down: "*the marks of [...] negligence*"'. It's much better to say: 'Stevenson tells us the building was very run down and "bore *the marks of [...] negligence*".' Integrating longer quotations into your text needs some care, so check out how to do this by going to page 154. There you'll find very detailed advice on how to do this correctly.

So, yes, we can now say we've supplied detailed evidence from the text to support our statement that the area was a mixture of shabby and smart.

Put another way, our statement has shown our **understanding** of the text; we have then produced textual evidence on which we have given an **analysis** or explanation of **how** the author has created his effects and **why** this evidence supports our point.

Body paragraphs: clinching commentary

Let's take stock for a moment: your paragraph has provided a clear statement; it has also supported that statement with detailed textual evidence. But what exactly is the reader supposed to make of this evidence? In other words, it might be sensible to unpack this evidence a little to explain to the reader how it establishes the point(s) you made back in your statement. You need to **evaluate** its significance to round off your paragraph.

Candidates sometimes panic at this point. 'What exactly **do** I think about this? What **should** I be saying?' is a common complaint. At this point, there are certain 'lead-in' phrases which can help focus your thoughts:

'From evidence such as this, we can see that ...'

'Clearly then, Stevenson is guiding us to think that ...'

'This suggests that ...'

'From this, we may understand that ...'

'Alert readers will note/conclude that ...'

Essentially, you're suggesting to readers what they are to make of all this. You're, in a sense, 'selling' your evidence to them. This is your opportunity to link the evidence to your line of thought which you set out way back in your introduction. So, our paragraph might end along the lines of:

Clearly then, Stevenson is suggesting the area around Jekyll is a curious mixture of the smart and squalid. In other words, this is a neighbourhood whose identity is not clear-cut, one where the sordid cannot be separated from the attractive. Given that Stevenson is suggesting elsewhere in the novel that man contains both the nasty and the virtuous within him, this split personality of the street helps us understand in a visual way that this split exists in society as well as in the individual. Stevenson seems to be hinting that Jekyll's divided personality may not be unique.

And there you have it: a paragraph which shows understanding, analysis and evaluation. We might call it a SEC paragraph:

You have made a **statement** setting out a point about Jekyll's surroundings (showing understanding of the text).	**S**
You have produced **evidence** to support this point (showing analysis of the means whereby you came to this understanding).	**E**
You have helped the reader with an explanation of what all this evidence is suggesting by providing a **commentary** on it (showing an evaluation of the evidence's significance).	**C**

DON'T FORGET

Statement: Say it!
Evidence: Show it!
Commentary: Sell it!

The SEC acronym is useful for helping you remember easily what needs to be in your body paragraphs. You may find that some teachers use slightly different letters. These are equally helpful for keeping you on task. You may already have encountered some of them.

SEEC	Here we have a **S**tatement, then **E**vidence, then an **E**xplanation of that evidence and, finally, your own **C**omment on the significance of all this.
PEE	Here we have your **P**oint which is then supported by **E**vidence, to which you add your own **E**xplanation of the significance of the Point and Evidence.
PEA	Here we have your **P**oint, supported by **E**vidence and then your own **A**nalysis.
SQC	Here we have a **S**tatement, followed by **Q**uotations and, finally, your **C**omment. (But remember, quotations are not enough on their own; there needs to be some analysis or explanation of their significance.)

Conclusions

Once you've covered your main points with SEC-type paragraphs, there isn't going to be much time left for a lengthy conclusion. If possible, try to round off your essay with a brief restatement of the main points that formed your line of thought throughout the essay. A good tip here is to have some synonyms up your sleeve so that your wording has some variety to it.

Make no new points here or seek to bring in quotations. You don't have time and they would only spoil the sharp focus of the rest of your essay.

If you've been referring to your line of thought in each paragraph, there's no need for an elaborate conclusion. Do not leave a great final statement of your line of thought to the conclusion: you might run out of time!

DON'T FORGET

If you've made your line of thought clear in every paragraph, your conclusion can be brief.

It is no bad idea to begin your brief conclusion with a phrase that signals the rounding off:

Standing back from the text as a whole, we see that Stevenson may be suggesting that ...

Classroom challenge

The **S**tatement/**E**vidence/**C**ommentary structure, as well as providing a persuasive body paragraph in your essay, is also a handy way of getting to grips with certain aspects of a text you may be studying. It forms, if you like, a miniature essay. Here are some general ideas to get you thinking.

Choose an incident/scene/character from a play, novel or poem which you're working on in class. First, think about the statement you want to make about it/them; then find the supporting evidence for the statement; and , finally, think about the points you're going to make in your commentary.

To check the contents of statements, evidence and commentaries, have a look at the advice provided earlier in this section.

Here are some questions to get you started.

1. What makes character X in your play/novel/poem a likeable person?
2. Suggest what setting contributes to the atmosphere at a particular point in your play/novel/poem.
3. How does one episode in your novel or one scene in your play illustrate a major theme in the work?

Swap your answer with a partner. How convincing was your paragraph?

Homework helper

Now you've tried out in class the **S**tatement/**E**vidence/**C**ommentary method of focusing on one targeted area of your text, try one of the following questions at home. It's an excellent way to revise a set text. Choose a title and write a SEC paragraph on it as a revision aid.

1. How does the writer arouse our interest in the opening scene of the play you are studying?
2. Why is character X in conflict with one other character in the novel/play?
3. Suggest why a particular scene/episode in the text you are studying is important.

Classroom challenge

Now that you've studied the construction of essays in some detail, you'll be beginning to recognise the kind of language you might find useful in each section. Here are six extracts from essay introductions, body paragraphs and conclusions to help you get even more familiar with the type of language which might help you to write convincing essays.

Say from which section of the essay you believe the extract to come.

If you decide a certain extract is from the body paragraph, say if it is from the statement, evidence or commentary section.

1. A novel in which there is an unreliable narrator is *'The Confessions of a Justified Sinner'* by James Hogg.
2. He describes the air around him as being full of lark song which rose 'on long thin strings of singing'. The heat haze is to him 'the shimmer of angels', so wonderful is its subtle movement.
3. From comments such as these, it is clear Hale has changed from the person he was when we first met him. Where, we wonder, is the man who believed that ...

1. Symbolism is yet another technique which Donovan uses to arouse our sympathy for the old lady.
2. Looking at the play as a whole, we see that evil is only partly triumphant.
3. To understand her isolation fully, we need to examine why her relations with her husband, her family and the wider community became so troubled.

TEACHING NOTES You can download Teaching Notes for this challenge at www.brightredpublishing.co.uk/Shop/national-5-english-course-book

MAINTAINING THE FLOW

The most successful critical essays follow a clear line of thought from start to finish. To achieve this, you cannot simply round up a few ideas, loosely related to the question, and call it an essay. There must be a guiding idea or shaping principle, established in the introduction, which unites the ideas you present in the various paragraphs. And these paragraphs, too, need to flow seamlessly, one to the next. Readers should not be pulled abruptly from one idea or one paragraph to the next and be expected to see a link between them somehow.

There are several signalling words, phrases and techniques which can help you to achieve flow. Let's look at the most common and useful signalling words:

LISTING (WHEN YOU NUMBER STAGES IN YOUR ARGUMENT)		
'First(ly), ...'	'Furthermore, ...'	'Finally, ...'
'To begin with, ...'	'Secondly, ...' 'In addition, ...' 'What is more, ...'	'In conclusion, ...'
Note: 'first and foremost' and 'first and most important(ly)' mark the beginning of a **descending** order. 'above all' and 'last, but not least' mark the end of an **ascending** order.		
TRANSITION (WHEN YOU GUIDE YOUR READER ONTO A NEW POINT)		
'Now, ...' 'As far as ... is concerned, ...' 'Turning to ...' 'Regarding the question of ...' 'As for ...'		
Note: 'Incidentally, ...' indicates a brief digression from your main topic		
CONTRAST (WHEN YOU EMPHASISE THAT THE UPCOMING COMMENT IS QUITE DIFFERENT FROM THE POINT YOU'VE JUST MADE)		
'On the one hand, ... On the other hand, however, ...' 'By way of contrast, ...' 'Conversely, ...' 'Whereas ...' 'While ...' 'XXXX, on the contrary, is ...'		
CONCESSION (WHEN YOU ALLOW THAT WHAT YOU'RE ABOUT TO SAY MAY BE SURPRISING, GIVEN WHAT YOU'VE JUST SAID)		
'However, ...' 'Even though ...' 'Nevertheless, ...' 'Nonetheless, ...' 'Yet, however much we ...' 'XXXX notwithstanding ...' 'In spite of ..., we ...' 'For all this, however, ...'		

Refer to this table when the time comes to structure your essay paragraphs.

It's also effective to signal transitions in your line of thought in the final or opening sentences of your paragraphs.

Remember, the skills you develop to maintain a 'reader-friendly' flow will help you not only in your Critical Essay but in your Folio essays, too. In fact, learning how to maintain the flow from sentence to sentence and paragraph to paragraph will help you in **all** those subjects which require extended writing.

From introduction to first paragraph

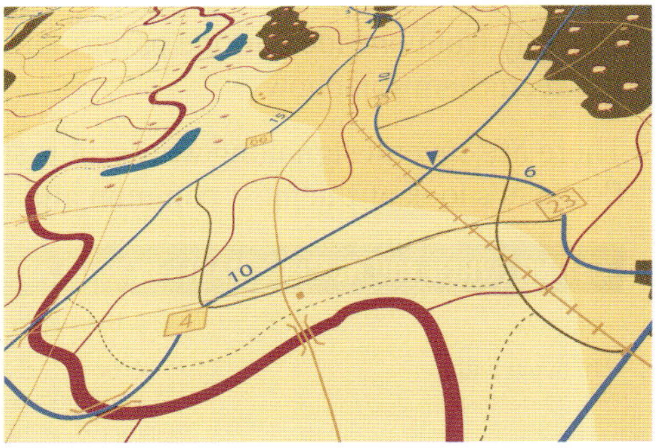

A sensible idea in your introduction is to indicate in its last lines the areas you will be covering in your essay – creating a 'road-map'. This helps give your essay that shaping idea or line of thought mentioned above. So, for example, in an essay about 'Loast', your introduction might end with the words:

Donovan arouses sympathy for the protagonist through her handling of Miss O'Halloran's social isolation, the use of symbolism and the second-person narrative.

Make sure you pick up your chosen topics in the order you mention them here, beginning the first SEC paragraph after the introduction with phrases such as:

Examining first Miss O'Halloran's social isolation, we notice that ...

Isolated socially, Miss O'Halloran has only ...

The social isolation of Miss O'Halloran is insisted on by Donovan throughout the short story.

DON'T FORGET

If you take care with the smooth flow of one paragraph into the next, you'll be helping keep your line of thought on track.

From one body paragraph to the next

Once you've completed your discussion of your first point, your task is to ease the reader from this paragraph onto your next point smoothly. In the example we're using here, you must lead the reader **from** your paragraph about Miss O'Halloran's 'social isolation' **to** your next paragraph, which should discuss the 'symbolism' in the story, the second area you mentioned in your road-map. This can be done effectively by using statements like these:

The sympathy aroused by the old lady's social isolation is further intensified by Donovan's use of symbolism.

Equally effective in arousing our sympathy for Miss O'Halloran is the way Donovan uses symbolism.

Symbolism is the second technique by which Donovan invokes our sympathy for her protagonist.

Note that all these sentences, as well as making good linking sentences, would also make useful opening statements which you could develop successfully to create a convincing SEC paragraph.

Successful flow is helped by making a brief reference – direct or indirect – to the subject of your previous paragraph in the first sentence of your new one.

Once completed, this paragraph needs to be linked to the next one in the way you have done for this one. And so on.

Indicating a conclusion

Your essay's flow is neatly rounded off by signalling the final stage is approaching with a 'summing-up' phrase, followed by a reminder of what was said in the introduction.

Seen overall, this is a short story in which the author successfully employs the techniques of ... to bring us close to the misery of ...

Standing back, we note that, throughout the tale, the techniques mentioned in the introduction have succeeded in ...

Summing up, we have seen the three techniques of ... have been successfully employed to arouse our sympathy for a character who ...

Not only is a conclusion indicated by an opening phrase of the type employed here, but the examiner is reminded of your loyalty to the points you raised in your introduction. In this way, your essay is rounded off briefly, but in a thoroughly satisfactory manner.

DON'T FORGET

Creating a strong introduction is crucial if you want to produce a successful critical essay. However, a smooth flow from paragraph to paragraph is equally important because it helps the reader understand that there's continuity in your thought – and readability in your paragraphs.

Classroom challenge

Before testing out these shaping techniques on a brand-new essay, try this experiment. Take an essay which you have already written and check it out for the following points:

CHECKLIST	TICK
1. Does your introduction have some indication of the line of thought your essay will follow?	
2. Are there any techniques at work in the body of the essay to ease the reader from one paragraph into the next?	

Were you able to tick both boxes? Even if you have ticked the boxes, are there any ways in which introduction and paragraphs could be improved?

You don't need to re-write the essay; simply work on rewriting those parts that needed some attention. Now swap your original essay and rewritten sections with a partner. Has enough been done to make the new text more reader-friendly? Has your partner any suggestions to make?

You're now in an increasingly better position to create a successful critical essay. But there's always room to polish your performance to ensure optimum marks. Let's see how.

PERFECTING PRESENTATION

Longer quotations

There's more than one way to introduce a long quotation into your paragraph.

Sometimes you will pave the way for a quotation by first **describing** it. In this case, it's best practice to use a colon (:), drop a line, indent slightly and begin the quotation using inverted commas. This gives us:

> *Her clear-sighted sadness is seen in the words:*
>
> *'I have betrayed a great man and his like will never be seen again.'*

Sometimes your sentence will not describe the quotation, but simply **introduce** it. In this case, the colon would only interrupt the natural flow of the words. So, instead, it would be better to write:

> *Her clear-sighted sadness is seen when comments that she has*
>
> *'betrayed a great man and his like will never be seen again.'*

Longer quotations should have room to breathe; so, drop a line (with or without a colon), indent slightly and add quotation marks. Drop another line before continuing your own text.

Shorter quotations

A good essay will have a mixture of longer and shorter quotations. Shorter ones can be just as effective as longer ones. If the longer quotation escapes you in full, you can use the remembered parts to great effect.

For instance, if you wanted to use the following quotation:

'the street shone out in contrast to its dingy neighbourhood, like a fire in a forest.'

but you couldn't quite remember it in full, you could use the remembered phrases to good effect and paraphrase the rest.

> *The street is described as making a sharp contrast to its 'dingy neighbourhood' and standing out 'like a fire in a forest'.*

DON'T FORGET

If you can't remember the exact wording of the extract you wish to quote in your essay, a series of short quotations will serve you just as well – if not better! But remember to 'weave' them smoothly into your text.

ONLINE

For a more detailed review of how to use quotations correctly in your essay, head to www.brightredbooks.net

As long as you weave the short quotations seamlessly into your own text, this kind of paraphrase-plus-quotation style will prove more effective than a longer, misquoted extract. It may also pinpoint more sharply the exact point you wish to make.

Giving a context

There is a danger of assuming readers understand more than they do. No quotation, however well chosen, will make its desired effect unless you give it a brief **context**. In other words, indicate briefly not just who said it but why, and under what circumstances it was said.

If, for instance, you had been reading *Macbeth* and wanted to comment on King Duncan's generous nature, you might want to mention his kindness to a wounded messenger, but be careful how you do it.

> *Duncan shows he has a great generosity of nature:*
>
> *'Go get him surgeons.'*

✗

> *Duncan has a great generosity of nature. Seeing a badly-wounded messenger collapse, he orders him to be taken care of:*
>
> *'Go get him surgeons.'*

✓

A context does not need to be long; it simply needs to lead readers into the quotation in a way that helps them make sense of the point you're making.

Making your lead-in work for you

Make sure your lead-in to the quotation doesn't simply repeat the content of the quotation. For example, in this description about *Buddha Da* by Anne Donovan, a bad lead-in would be:

> *Jimmy tells his wife he is going on a journey but he is not sure where he is going:*
>
> *'Ah'm on a journey but ah don't know where ah'm gaun.'*

A better lead-in might be:

> *Jimmy comes across to his wife – and to readers – as rather vague about his plans for taking his study of Buddhism forward:*
>
> *'Ah'm on a journey but ah don't know where ah'm gaun.'*

In other words, a thoughtful lead-in does more than simply help the reader to understand the quotation's context; it can also underline your ability to evaluate its significance.

How does that work?

Now we've looked at all the bits and pieces that go into writing a critical essay, let's see what it looks like when we put it all together. Read through the following essay, noting the various 'landmarks', and see if it helps model your next critical essay.

Remember, there's no one approach to answering a question for a critical essay; this is only one suggested line of thought.

Note how the underlined phrases pick up wording from question.

Choose a short story or novel in which setting figures prominently.

Describe the contribution of the setting and then show how this feature helped your understanding of the text as a whole.

Final two sentences of the introduction suggest line of thought to be followed and the order in which evidence will be examined – and a reference back to the wording of the question.

A novel in which setting figures prominently is *The Strange Case of Dr Jekyll and Mr Hyde* by Robert Louis Stevenson. Respectable Dr Jekyll, impatient with respectability, longs to indulge in hidden, evil desires. To do so, he invents a potion which turns him into wicked Mr Hyde, thereby living out his dark side in another self. In Jekyll, the virtuous and the evil live side by side, just as in the novel's setting the attractive and the ugly co-exist in the world around him. By frequently drawing attention to the dual nature of the setting and setting several key events at night, Stevenson uses these features to help us understand what he is saying about the divided nature of Jekyll and his progress into his darker self.

Statement for SEC1

In the opening chapter Stevenson goes to great trouble to establish that the area around Hyde's laboratory home is a curious mixture of the prosperous and the dingy. We find that:

Start of Evidence for SEC1

> 'the street shone out in contrast to its dingy neighbourhood, like a fire in a forest.'

It is presented as a particularly attractive, welcoming street since the shop fronts had 'an air of invitation' and seemed 'like rows of smiling saleswomen'. There are also 'freshly painted shutters, well-polished brasses, and general cleanliness' to be noted. But Hyde's laboratory spoils this attractive setting, for its 'sinister block' thrust itself into the street, suggesting 'prolonged and sordid negligence' with a 'blistered and distained doorway' around which 'tramps' slouched.

Start of Comment for SEC1

Clearly then, Stevenson is suggesting the area around Jekyll is a curious mixture of the smart and the squalid. Side by side with the sparkling shops is Hyde's grubby building which seriously detracts from an otherwise attractive street. Indeed, its thrusting gable introduces a sinister and faintly menacing air to its environment. In only one street, we have evidence of both good housekeeping and complete neglect. In other words, this is a neighbourhood whose identity is not clear-cut, one where the sordid cannot be separated from the attractive. Given that Stevenson is suggesting elsewhere in the novel that man contains both the nasty and the virtuous within him, this split personality of the street helps us understand in a visual way that this split exists in society as well as in the individual. Stevenson may be hinting – long before we meet Jekyll himself – that Jekyll's divided personality is perhaps not unique.

Line of thought highlighted

Statement for SEC2

But there is yet a further contrasting split of environments, for we later learn that this squalid laboratory building is connected to buildings in a nearby square. We learn that:

> 'Round the corner from the by street there was a square of ancient, handsome houses, now for the most part decayed from their high estate . . .'

Start of Evidence for SEC2

This decayed environment, however, is brightened by:

> 'One house [which] wore a great air of wealth and comfort ...'

This, it turns out, is the rather splendid home of Dr Jekyll. Stevenson is directing attention to the fact that there is a duality of identity in these very closely related environments; grubbiness rubs shoulders with the smart and attractive. This use of physical setting is key to our understanding of Stevenson's intentions here, for in this novella he is exploring Jekyll's claim that:

Commentary for SEC2

> '... man is not truly one, but truly two.'

Jekyll believes that man has two sides to his nature: the decent, God-fearing respectable side which his day-time life of Dr Jekyll represents and the other, more sordid, side of human nature – the side drawn to the evil and corruption in which his night-time persona, Hyde, revels. Just as sharply contrasting environments can exist side by side in towns and streets, so, too, may contrasting sides of human nature co-exist in the same being. Jekyll, it is being discreetly hinted, is perhaps not unique; duality exists all around us, not just in human personalities but in society, too, as these contrasting but connected physical environments suggest.

Line of thought revisited

This split is given focus in one further way. While Jekyll's respectable medical life takes place by day, his activities as Hyde happen at night, underlining again a different kind of divided setting. Key moments in the story take place at night. Enfield's first encounter with Hyde takes place in darkness at:

Statement for SEC3

> 'about three o'clock of a black winter morning'.

Start of Evidence for SEC3

The narrator, Utterson, makes his first contact with Hyde at night, and one of Hyde's most vicious crimes – the murder of the MP Danvers Carew – also takes place at night. Jekyll's death and final transformation into Hyde takes place after midnight.

In a tale which explores the defeat of goodness in Jekyll's nature by his evil side, the setting of darkness is only fitting. Both goodness and evil originally lived side by side in Jekyll, but the goodness is gradually overtaken by the dark. Just as day gives way to night, so too does goodness here gives way to evil. Darkness is, in the end, a useful setting for underlining the darkly tragic direction Jekyll's life increasingly takes.

Start of Commentary of SEC3

Line of thought revisited

Standing back from the text as a whole, we see that setting has been useful in helping understand it. We see that Stevenson has used contrasting townscapes to suggest that, just as it is difficult to separate the attractive and grimmer aspects of society, so it is with Jekyll – who may not be so different from the rest of us. And, as this is a tale which explores the darker side of human nature, it is only appropriate that evil frequently has darkness as its backdrop.

Conclusion (if time permits)

PRACTISING FOR THE EXAM

We have looked at various **structural** ways of presenting your knowledge successfully in critical essays. But, remember, your grade will also depend on the **technical competence** of your expression. That means that, while you're trying to answer the question as convincingly as you can, you need to think of the detail of your expression, too.

DON'T FORGET

Your technical competence is a factor in your final grade. Make sure it doesn't let your essay down!

You can't afford to have your soundly argued essay undermined by weak critical vocabulary, poor spelling or punctuation. So here are a few ways to eliminate some of the weaknesses you may have in these areas. Parts of this section will also be useful when you come to write your Folio pieces.

Improving critical vocabulary

It is self-defeating to hide behind tired words like 'good', 'bad', or 'brilliant' to describe characters and situations in your essays simply because you're nervous about attempting more ambitious terms. A convincing critical essay also requires a convincing critical vocabulary. But how do you go about acquiring one?

- Your preparatory reading for the RUAE paper will help here. Published authors and journalists in quality newspapers are a rich source of sophisticated critical vocabulary. List new words you come across and check their meaning in a dictionary. These could be useful for **all** your N5 reading and writing tasks. Experiment with them as often as you can.
- Check out your teacher's vocabulary. Your teacher will have used quite sophisticated critical vocabulary in class. Jot down new words in your notes and, in your own time, check in a dictionary their precise meaning – and spelling.
- Make text-specific lists. As part of your study file, why not take a page to list main characters in your studied text(s)? Beside each one, list the keywords which apply to them or which keep recurring to describe their changing fortunes. For instance:

Martin	adolescent, gregarious, conceited, disfigured, mischievous, physique, unprejudiced, self-conscious, admirable
Natalie	ambitious, callous, commercially minded, narcissistic, independent, self-obsessed

As well as creating a list of keywords for key characters, you may also wish to create a similar grid or list of vocabulary you hear being regularly applied to a particular play, novel or poem; or, indeed, its theme or our response to it – 'problematic', 'elusive', 'evocative', 'ambiguous', 'poignant', 'subjective', etc.

Go over your lists regularly, adding new discoveries whenever you make them.

Classroom challenge

To get you started on developing your vocabulary for critical essays, here are a few adjectives that might prove useful.

The definitions of the words are all here but have been deliberately mixed up. Pair the word on the left with its correct definition. Use a dictionary to help if you need one. But see how far you get on your own first.

Simply knowing the meaning of a critical term is only part of the story; even more important is your ability to use the word appropriately in its context. Now you know what these words mean, try to work out which context is appropriate for each of the adjectives above.

ADJECTIVE	DEFINITION
a) adamant	1. Bringing strong images or feelings to mind
b) ambivalent	2. Spread throughout
c) evocative	3. Unable/difficult to choose between two viewpoints
d) halting	4. Small/not obvious but significant/important
e) pervasive	5. Tending to remind you of something else
f) poignant	6. Closely related to the subject under discussion
g) recurrent	7. Creating a keen sense of sadness or regret
h) relevant	8. Occurring often or repeatedly
i) reminiscent	9. Slow, hesitant, faltering
j) subtle	10. Refusing to be persuaded or to change your mind

i) With fog invading all parts of the city, Dickens creates a _________ atmosphere of gloom in the first chapter.

ii) With its light, bouncing rhythms, the poem is ____________ of many of those we first encountered in nursery rhymes.

iii) It is heartbreakingly ____________ that the woman who once used words so effectively is now no longer able to find even the basic ones for daily life.

iv) When planning an essay it is vital to select only that which is wholly ___________ to the demands of the question which you have chosen to answer.

v) After consulting his conscience at great length, Macbeth seems ____________ that he will go no further in thoughts of killing the king.

vi) The poem ends with many of the same lines as those with which it began, but now there have been ________ changes in the poet's choice of adjectives.

vii) Throughout each act of the play there is a ______________ image of clothes which do not fit.

viii) With its clever use of onomatopoeia, alliteration and assonance, the opening lines of the poem are ___________ of the atmosphere of a hot summer's day.

ix) With its ___________ rhythms and series of self-doubting questions, the poem is successful in conjuring up for us the poet's insecurity.

x) Seeing both his occasionally bloodthirsty side as well as his high moral sense, we may be forgiven for feeling ____________ towards him.

You can download Teaching Notes for this challenge at www.brightredpublishing.co.uk/Shop/national-5-english-course-book

TEACHING NOTES

Applying spelling strategies

It's one thing to acquire a sound critical vocabulary, but you also need to know how to spell these useful new terms. We all have words which keep catching us out when it comes to spelling them. The exam room, however, is no place to discover you can't remember how to spell, for example, 'embarrassed' or 'prejudiced', useful common words for many texts.

This is where your vocabulary lists described on the previous pages will again come in useful. Using a similar approach, collect together keywords for important characters in your study text(s) – words which may pose potential spelling pitfalls for **you**. For instance:

Macbeth	courageous, zealous, desirous, contemplative, tyrant, tyrannical, callous, regicide
Lady Macbeth	deceitful, ambitious, manipulative, aggressive, conscience, immoral

- Take a character at a time. Cover up your keywords then write down what you think is the correct spelling of each one. Do this regularly and start well before exam time. (You'll have other things on your mind come the final revision stage!)
- Swap with a partner. Someone who's using the same text-specific approach to solving spelling challenges may well have a different list. Test each other on your individual list. Check if there are certain words on your partner's list which you might benefit from learning, too.

DON'T FORGET

Devise a strategy for learning how to spell keywords for your text(s) well before the exam.

Classroom challenge

Sorting out spelling and punctuation

Here are some sentences of the kind associated with critical essays. In each one there may be one or more spelling **and/or** punctuation mistake(s). See how well you do.

a) The plays two main characters while living together in the same house lead very separate/seperate lives.

b) There is definitely/definately an absence/absense of any embarrassment/embarassment when Abigail one of the plays cheif/chief characters is challenged about this.

c) Lady Macbeth described later as his fiendlike queen looses/loses no time in seizing/siezing the opportunity/oportunity to plan the murder.

d) Although this significant conversation occurs/ocurrs early in the novel Natalie later dissappears/disappears/disapears from it entirely.

e) Nora a source of much of the plays humour/humor retreats into a world of interior decoration.

f) There is a me in this poem presumably Morgan himself.

g) When 'Macbeth' says He's here in double trust we see that his conscience/consciens is beggining/beginning to trouble him.

h) Clare whose name is a corruption of the French word for 'light' is always associated/associeted with sparkle and colour.

i) Duncan is a character who while being seriously flawed is often refered/referred to positively.

j) It is necesary/necessary in a critical essay to answer the question and wholely/wholly unecessary/unnecessary to re-tell the plot.

TEACHING NOTES

You can download Teaching Notes for this challenge at www.brightredpublishing.co.uk/Shop/national-5-english-course-book

Classroom challenge

Laying out quotations

Here are some analysis sections from student paragraphs. The content is sensible but the quotations have been poorly integrated into the text. Their cramped appearance on the page makes life difficult for the marker – not a sensible idea in an exam.

If you need to check how to lay out quotations in a paragraph, look back at the 'Perfecting presentation' section on page 154.

Re-write each paragraph, setting out the quotations as you think they should appear.

a) Anne Marie sees her father as someone with an irresponsible streak. 'Ma da's a nutter. Radio rental. He'd dae anything for a laugh so he wid.' In their household he is well-known for taking up projects and then dropping them. 'Wanst it wis building a gairden shed, anither time it wis strippin an auld sideboard. And of course he'd start it and then get fed up and no finish.' So when this 'nutter' takes an interest in Buddhism, Anne Marie sees it as no different from any of his other passing fads.

(*Buddha Da* by Anne Donovan)

b) The poet sees the day as 'peculiar to this piece of the planet' where 'larks rose on long thin strings of singing'. So beautiful are the air currents that he sees their movement as the 'shimmer' of angels. Glorying in their movement , he feels The grasses / Shivered with presences, and sunlight / stayed like a halo on hair and heather and hills. Delighted by all this beauty the sunstruck madman as he calls himself foolishly comments on it to a grumpy passer-by.

('Scotland' by Alastair Reid)

c) McSeveney presents downie covers as 'big animals' who 'sleep a lot of the time,/ barely stirring as they snooze endlessly/loafing around on beds.' When, however, their owner comes to change them, suddenly you have 'six by three/ of feathery incorporeality kicking and screaming/ in your hands.' She is quite brutal with them, choosing to 'wrestle' them to the ground, finding that only 'Pushing their head into the bag/keeps them quiet.' This, she feels, is the only thing to ensure peace and quiet from them. 'They give up after that./Pinioned in floral print polycotton/they lie back down and sleep.'

('Changing a Downie Cover' by Angela McSeveney)

TEACHING NOTES

You can download Teaching Notes for this challenge at www.brightredpublishing.co.uk/Shop/national-5-english-course-book

Classroom challenge

Composing an effective introduction

A successful introduction immediately sends a clear message to the marker: I have planned my essay and my knowledge is thorough. To help you focus on the elements of a persuasive introduction, here is one with the various sections mixed up. Write out the introduction in what you think is the most convincing order. Even if you have not studied this play, you will find the exercise accessible due to the several structural clues.

Choose a play in which there is a flawed character for whom you feel sympathy.

By referring to appropriate techniques, show how the flaw(s) are revealed and explain how our sympathy is, nevertheless, maintained.

Finally, Shakespeare surrounds him with images of growth and fertility which set him apart from the Macbeths, further adding to his sympathetic portrayal.

King Duncan, whom Macbeth murders to win the crown of Scotland, is a character who reveals flaws, yet he is one whom the playwright presents sympathetically.

A play in which a flawed but sympathetic character appears is Macbeth by William Shakespeare.

Duncan's flawed nature is established early on when we see the limitations in his kingship sharply revealed at international, national and personal levels.

Our sympathy, however, is maintained by his generosity of spirit to all around him and the affection with which he is surrounded.

You can download Teaching Notes for this challenge at www.brightredpublishing.co.uk/Shop/national-5-english-course-book

TEACHING NOTES

TRYING A TEST PAPER

You have seen some of the various moves and steps that go into creating a successful critical essay. You've also seen the importance of improving your technical competence in producing these essays. Now, the time has come for you to try writing some essays based on sample titles. Here are a number of subjects of the kind you may encounter in the exam.

Note the text box at the head of each section. It's there to jog your memory about the various aspects of the text you might well consider. Use it!

DRAMA

Answers to questions on Drama should refer to the text and to relevant features such as characterisation, key scene(s), structure, climax, theme, plot, conflict, setting ...

1. Choose a play in which there is a flawed character for whom you feel sympathy.

   By referring to appropriate techniques, show how the flaw(s) are revealed and explain how our sympathy is maintained.

2. Choose a play in which an important theme is made clear.

   By referring to the techniques which make this clear, show how the playwright makes this theme clear to the audience.

PROSE

Answers to Prose questions should refer to the text and to relevant features such as characterisation, setting, language, key incident(s), climax, turning point, plot, structure, narrative techniques, theme, ideas, description ...

3. Choose a novel **or** short story in which the writer creates a character who is isolated or lonely.

   By referring to appropriate techniques, show how the author makes this isolation or loneliness clear and say why you find this portrait convincing.

4. Choose a novel **or** short story which explores a theme of importance to young people.

   By referring to appropriate techniques, show how this theme is made clear to the reader.

POETRY

Answers to questions on Poetry should refer to the text and to relevant features such as word choice, tone, imagery, structure, content, rhythm, rhyme, theme, sound, ideas ...

5. Choose a poem whose subject **or** setting **or** speaker is powerful in appeal to you.

   Briefly describe the poem and say how the poet's skills made this appeal powerful.

6. Choose a poem written in free verse.

   Explain how the poet made the subject interesting for you.

FILM AND TELEVISION DRAMA

Answers to questions on Film and Television Drama should refer to the text and to relevant features such as use of camera, key sequence, characterisation, mise en scène, editing, setting, music/sound, special effects, plot, dialogue ...

7. Choose a film or television drama* which represents aspects of the supernatural.

   Explain how the director made its representations thrilling for you.

8. Choose a film or television drama* which transports you to a setting with which you are unfamiliar.

   By referring to appropriate techniques, explain why you found the setting credible.

   * 'television drama' includes a single play, a series or a serial.

LANGUAGE

Answers to questions on Language should refer to the text and to relevant features such as register, accent, dialect, slang, jargon, vocabulary, tone, abbreviation ...

9. Choose an advertisement which is aimed at teenagers or young people.

   By referring to specific techniques, explain how successful you found the advertisement.

10. Consider the spoken language of your locality **or** of a region you know well.

    By referring to selected examples, explain the advantages and/or disadvantages it offers its speakers.

Always put the question number which you have selected to answer in the margin.

DON'T FORGET

What you now know

There is an accumulation of factors at work when an examiner decides to award top marks. These are some of the key things which should be studied well in advance of entering the exam room.

- ✔ You need to demonstrate a thorough knowledge of your texts. That means reading them not just in class, but regularly on your own as well.
- ✔ You must select **only** the information from your text knowledge which answers the specific question in front of you. Examiners don't want to know everything your teacher has taught you.
- ✔ You must be alert to all sections of the question and apportion your time accordingly.
- ✔ You need a plan to help you structure a coherent essay which is more than a loose collection of good points. There should be a line of thought apparent which the examiner can follow easily as one paragraph flows smoothly into the next.
- ✔ Each paragraph should be carefully structured to ensure that your claims are borne out by evidence and that you unpack this evidence for the reader. In other words, you make a **S**tatement, back it up with **E**vidence and then give a **C**ommentary on it before moving on to the next paragraph (**SEC**).
- ✔ A soundly structured introduction will help you stay on task and a 'road-map' in the introduction's last sentence will help examiners find their way round your arguments. A brief conclusion reminds them of your key points.
- ✔ Lay out your longer quotations as clearly as you can to differentiate your text from the author's. Don't be nervous about dropping a line to mark the start of longer quotations. (A colon just before you do so also makes your quotation stand out a little more clearly.) In shorter quotations, always check that you have put quotation marks before **and** after your quotation.
- ✔ Make sure your quotations make sense. That means checking that you have given each one a context, however brief.
- ✔ Technical competence is important. Ensure your spelling and punctuation do not let down the overall quality of your essay.

GETTING IT TOGETHER

MAXIMISING YOUR PERFORMANCE

The Folio is an ideal showcase for your writing skills if you feel exams don't bring out the best in you. This is where you can really bring up your grade without any exam-room pressure. But to do this, your choice of folio pieces must be considered very carefully. Think back over the kind of writing you have excelled in. Don't be in a hurry to decide on a topic or genre. Study the tips below and practise the activities before making your final choice. It's not just any piece of writing; it's the most important piece you've tackled so far in your school career. And it's worth 30% of your final assessment.

To help you achieve your best writing performance, we're offering you some straightforward ways to maximise your skills in a variety of the most popular genres. This will ensure you end up with a folio that does you full justice.

What's coming up?

- Pre-writing tips
- Choices available
- Making your choice
- Creative writing: Fiction/Personal/Reflective
- Discursive writing: Persuasive/Argumentative
- Ways of working: Folio management

PRE-WRITING TIPS

Read around

The surest way to improve your writing style is to expose yourself to quality writing of all kinds: novels, short stories, biographies, travel writing, quality journalism are just a few genres to explore. By all means, read for the pleasure they offer, but now is the time to read quality texts with an added purpose: **to see what you can learn from professional writers.**

The gripping start to a story, the bringing to life of a character or setting, dialogue that crackles with realism: all these can profitably be studied for the improvement of your creative, personal and reflective writing. The engagingly witty opening to an informative article, the usefulness of illustrative examples, the seamless transition from one paragraph to another: these are all aspects of quality journalism you can absorb to add conviction to your argumentative or persuasive texts.

There's no shortage of models out there to study. Adopt a few ideas from the professionals, adapt them to suit your purpose – and you'll quickly see how your writing will progress!

Classroom challenge

Check out some quality journalism online by visiting some major broadsheet websites, such as http://www.scotsman.com/, http://www.heraldscotland.com/ and http://www.guardian.co.uk/.

Bring to class an article from the lifestyle, travel, culture, or opinion sections of a quality paper. Say how, in your opinion, the writer is likely to make their readers continue to read on. Point out at least three techniques which made this piece memorable – arresting opening sentence, unusual word choice, striking metaphor, humorous tone? Or perhaps you've noticed one of the many other techniques which journalists use to enliven their prose.

Keep these techniques in mind when you come to consider an essay of your own. (You may find effective use of language in other sections of the newspaper; not every newspaper uses the same headings for non-news articles.)

Think about what you already know

Another way to 'up' your standards – one that's been right under your nose for some time – is to think about all the technical features you've been noting as you analyse Reading for Understanding, Analysis and Evaluation texts. How about bringing some of them into your own writing? You're used to explaining the impact of minor sentences, inversion, metaphors, word choice, parallel structures, etc., so why not make all this hard-won information work for you in another context?

DON'T FORGET

Copying is plagiarism. But adopting ideas or techniques from writers who impress you – adapting their approach to your task in hand – is, in fact, how many professional writers learn their trade!

We'll spend some time looking at this approach but, before you even switch on the computer, it'd be wise to spend some time thinking over these practical considerations.

What you need to consider before writing

Does it really interest me?

Don't even think about committing yourself to paper until you're sure what you're writing about is something that truly interests you. Whether it's a short story about a friendship that went wrong, or an analysis of the future of renewable energy sources, spend plenty of time considering whether the core idea **really** interests you.

Are you willing to spend many hours on this idea or topic? If in doubt, the chances are it's the wrong choice. It will save a lot of time and effort in the long run if you do some hard thinking **before** you start.

Do I know about it?

Write from your existing knowledge base or about a topic you want to get to know about. If you don't know about deserted tropical islands, it's clearly not the setting for your short story – unless you want to do some serious research. Discursive writing will always need research. Do you know how to get the most reliable, up-to-date information? And are you interested enough in the topic to **want** to set about getting it?

Do I have a plan?

Before even drafting a word, plan your ideas in rough. Use whatever method works for you: a mind-map, a list of possibilities, a page of random brainstorming thoughts. Mull them all over, eventually discarding the non-starters before trying to organise the remaining ones into some rough outline of paragraph content and sequence.

Have I considered my audience?

You're not yet a professional writer writing exclusively to please yourself. Yes, of course you should enjoy your own writing, but remember you're also writing to impress examiners in a public exam. Try to keep that in mind at all times. Crisp, clear prose which hangs together well, and which offers a rich reading experience, is what they are looking for. Indulge them.

Have I considered my purpose?

What are you setting out to do? Entertain? Persuade? Analyse? Whatever your aim, you must always be examining your language to see if it's fulfilling the purpose you think it is. It's easy to set out on a persuasive tack, then discover later on that your language has become simply factual and informative. A creative essay can easily become just a catalogue of events without imaginative use of figurative language. Keep checking that you're using the language appropriate for the task you've set yourself.

Is my plan working?

Yes, we all need a plan to get started, but as your text progresses, are you noticing weaknesses or possibilities you didn't at first consider? Relax. It's a good sign, showing that you're beginning to think like a professional writer. Don't be scared to move paragraphs about, delete sentences, add phrases, discard a word to find a better one or whatever seems necessary. With information technology this becomes relatively easy.

Is this the best I can do?

Don't get so lost in your story or analysis that you forget to check the basics. Before handing in any draft, make sure you proofread it to check the grammar, spelling, punctuation and vocabulary. Don't be caught out with basics like **its/it's, their/there, to/too**, etc.

WHAT DO I HAVE TO WRITE?

You are expected to write two folio pieces of up to 1000 words each. These will account for 30% of your final grade. For people who're not always at their best in exams, this is a chance to make a major difference to your grade. With folio work, you have time to consider what you want to write, time to write it and, most important of all, time to edit it carefully to ensure that these two pieces show your writing skills at their very best.

What are my choices?

One of your two pieces will be drawn from the genres identified in Group A, the other from Group B. The group possibilities are as follows:

Group A: Creative

- A personal essay/reflective essay
- A piece of prose fiction (for example, short story, episode from a novel)
- A poem or set of thematically linked poems
- A dramatic script (for example, scene, monologue, sketch)

Group B: Discursive

- A piece of transactional writing
- A persuasive essay
- An argumentative essay
- A report for a specified purpose

Before making any decisions about your choices, let's look at some popular genres in each group to see what they involve. This way, you'll have a better idea about which ones best match your skills.

Group A: Creative

PROSE FICTION	PERSONAL/REFLECTIVE
If you're someone who's always enjoyed writing short stories or episodes from a novel, this is a really pleasurable choice. If you're not sure if this is something you enjoy, a folio piece for an important exam probably isn't the best place to find out.	Nobody can write better about you, your life and your reflections than **you**. You already have all the information to hand, it's just a question of digging deep to bring the experience alive for others.
Opportunities	*Opportunities*
Within the word limit, you're free to create your own world: atmospheric settings, characters who become convincingly alive, dialogue that fully reflects the characters and their lifestyles. Their fates are all in your hands. You must be prepared to explore all the possibilities of figurative language in the way of a professional writer.	In personal or reflective writing, you need to offer readers the same rich reading experience as you would in a short story. The difference is that in personal writing you're not creating an imaginary event or experience but considering one which you've lived through yourself. In reflective writing, you are considering aspects of the world around you which has captured your attention or imagination.
Considerations	*Considerations*
A successful piece of short fiction needs a strong sense of structure; it can't just ramble on. You'll find the word limit imposes restrictions on any unnecessary material. Here, a plan is essential before you begin. Feel free to alter it, but never lose sight of the overall shape. Limit your characters if they're to be described fully. Remember that contrasting characters will spark conflict which is great for moving stories on.	Whether it's a personal or a reflective essay, make sure the topic has sufficient depth to sustain your interest – and your reader's – for a whole essay. As in a short story, your language should draw on many of the techniques you've been studying in your RUAE work: sentence structure, word choice, repetition, etc. are just some of the ways you can enliven your text.

ONLINE

For some advice about writing short stories head to www.brightredbooks.net

Group B: Discursive

ARGUMENTATIVE AND PERSUASIVE WRITING	
Here you have an opportunity to demonstrate your grasp of issues which affect us all. Learning how to research a topic, how to organise your findings convincingly and how to present them with authority, will be invaluable not only in this exam but in other subjects, too – and in your life beyond school or college.	
ARGUMENTATIVE WRITING	**PERSUASIVE WRITING**
Opportunities In this genre, you lay out, factually and neutrally, two sides of a topic in a logically organised structure. You may already know of a topic which you would enjoy examining in more detail. If not, quality journalism will alert you to the 'hot' topics of the day. The essential thing is to enjoy researching and sharing your results in prose which reads fluently and carries real conviction.	*Opportunities* Here, you take a topic that you feel strongly about and present your case as persuasively as possible. Unlike the argumentative essay, the persuasive essay is far from neutral in its analysis and language. To succeed here, you need to examine the many techniques of persuasion which we will discuss in detail later.
Considerations An objective tone is of key importance in argumentative writing. Remember, too, the best discursive writing needs research to convince, but facts and expert opinion are only a starting point; you need to organise your own clear line of argument throughout.	*Considerations* Persuasive writing requires you to adopt an outgoing, involved approach, appealing strongly to your reader's emotions. While you must acknowledge that others may not always agree with you, sheer verbal enthusiasm in making a strong pitch for your own viewpoint is essential for success.

DON'T FORGET

Don't finally commit yourself to any essay choice until you're sure you know enough about the topic or are really keen to learn or write about it.

DON'T FORGET

Start to try out ideas and plans well before the deadline; be prepared to accept that your first thoughts might not be your best ones. Successful folio writing is about being willing to draft and re-draft several times before you even think of presenting a first version to your teacher.

Reflect carefully before choosing

Notice that we've not looked at all the genres you might explore in your Folio. Remember, however, that the writing of poetry and plays is a highly specialised art. Perhaps you've experience writing in these genres and have had your work noticed by experts in these fields. If this is the case, then these might be choices worth considering. However, for most candidates, the possibilities we've looked at in more detail are probably the most accessible. They offer choices with which you'll perhaps feel most comfortable, as well as the surest chances of success.

GROUP A

CREATIVE WRITING

Writing prose fiction

Short story or episode from a novel? An intriguing choice, but whichever you choose remember that **character** and **setting** are as important as **plot** in both. Characters that don't come alive – who simply remain names on a page or fail to engage the reader's interest – and narratives that take place in a vacuum create little in the way of atmosphere to catch the reader's attention. Remember, you can write up to a maximum of only 1000 words. This means you have to set certain boundaries on your narrative. Keep this right at the front of your mind during the planning stage.

Reading for inspiration

Writing well means reading widely. Reading as many short stories as you can will give you lots of ideas. You may already have looked at some in class. Here are six more. They not only set a high standard for what's possible in this genre but suggest highly imaginative ways of approaching **the three pillars of successful short-story writing – character, setting and plot.**

- 'Pigeons at Daybreak' by Anita Desai from *Games at Twilight and Other Stories*
- 'The Lottery' by Shirley Jackson (available to read online)
- 'Girl' by Jamaica Kincaid from *At the Bottom of the River*
- 'The Artist' by Patricia Highsmith from *Little Tales of Misogyny*
- 'The Black Cap' by Katherine Mansefield from *The Stories of Katherine Mansefield*
- 'I could see the smallest things' by Raymond Carver from *The Stories of Raymond Carver*

Alternatively, try looking out for the *Oxford Book of Scottish Short Stories* or the *Oxford Book of Short Stories* in your library. These are both rich mines of short-story writing from which you can learn a lot.

Classroom challenge

In groups or individually, choose a short story which has impressed you. Briefly introduce your story to the class. Say what made the story interesting for you. You could use the questions below to get you started, or you may have points of your own to make about how the author achieves their aim of involving the reader.

MAIN CHARACTER	SETTING	PLOT	LANGUAGE
How has the author made the character interesting/likeable?	How important is the setting to the story? Would it lose anything if set in another time/place?	What triggers the action? How does the situation differ at the end from what it was at the start?	What features of the writer's language impressed you? Metaphors? Sentence structure? Dialogue? Word choice? Some other feature?

So how do you go about planning your own prose fiction?

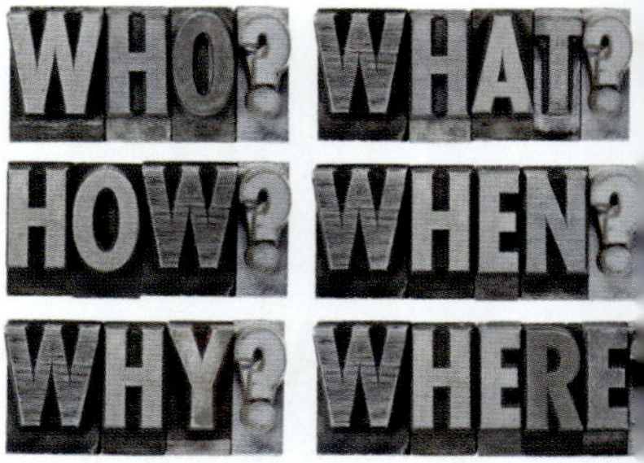

One way is to set yourself a number of '**wh**-' tasks which you can tackle in any order you wish, depending on how you like to compose fiction. Do you prefer beginning with characters, setting or plot? Here are some starting points for all three.

Who?	• Your word limit means it's a good idea to restrict your characters to a number you can describe adequately. Don't introduce characters who play little part in the final outcome. Two, three or four might be a sensible cast list. • Contrasting characters often lead to conflict, which moves a story along very nicely. For example, try contrasting youth and age, rich and poor, sensible and rash, shy and outspoken or good-natured and quick-tempered. • Jot down facts about each character before you start. Not just appearance, but personality traits, nervous habits, likes, dislikes, hobbies, interests, tastes in music, people, food, etc. Don't blurt these all out at once but weave them from time to time into your narrative. Passing references to such features bring characters alive.
Where?	• Setting is a key factor in a good short story. A detailed, realistic setting is a grand start to a fiction piece. But don't do it well in the first paragraphs and then forget all about it. Keep it going with brief references to it as the story progresses. • To write well about setting you need to know it intimately. Write from your knowledge, either first hand or from research. • Given your word limit, restrict changing the setting too often. You'll use up too many words. • Think of films you've enjoyed where the setting transported you somewhere that felt totally real. Your narrative should do the same.
What?	• Again, your word limit reduces the kind of story you can handle here. Epic adventures are out. • To be successful, a good short narrative need not be about dramatic events; a minor incident carefully observed and imaginatively related is more likely to suit the required length of your text. • Time sequences of hours, days or weeks are probably more practical than years or decades as your time frame.
When?	• The present causes less trouble, but if you have an interest in earlier periods, some basic research might furnish a credibly different setting, while a fertile imagination could provide the detail necessary to convince in a sci-fi tale. • Remember that setting encompasses not only a place and period but the seasons, weather and time of day as well. These can be manipulated tellingly to bring atmospheric colour to your fiction. Use them to reflect changing moods and attitudes of your characters in their situations. For example, perhaps spring/green shoots indicate hope, evening/mist a threat.
Why?	• Credibility is something you need to be alert to. So why something happens needs to be addressed carefully. • The far-fetched can weaken even the most carefully realised settings and characters. Keep the plot within the bounds of the believable.
How?	• As important as the 'wh-' questions is **how** the story is to be told. Is the narrator to be 'I'? This will bring you close to the speaker and their thoughts. Or are you going to use the third-person narrator: he or she? This will let you observe everyone and allow you into everyone's thought processes. • And how is the plot to advance? In normal time sequence or by a dramatic flash-forward or flash-back? The latter two will get you off to a flying start before you go back and fill in the details. Many successful films use this technique.

We'll come back to these points in the following pages with suggestions for approaches of your own.

ONLINE

Use the guide to the elements of a short story at www.brightredbooks.net for extra help getting started.

Creating characters

Characters who come to life on the page need individual personalities to make them credible to your readers. This comes from detailed observation of all aspects of character and appearance.

This can be approached in a number of ways.

APPROACH	WHAT THIS INVOLVES	CONSIDERATIONS
Interpreting personality	The narrator or a character in the story 'interprets' one of the characters. This can sometimes be useful in telling us details about a character's appearance, circumstances or personality.	Readers like to meet characters in action themselves. Too much interpretation may limit the characters' opportunities to come alive in their own right.
Profiling identity	Draw up identity checklists, one for each of your main characters. Try to contrast them as much as possible. Give details of their physical appearance, psychological make-up, social skills, personal history. This helps firm up in your own mind what such people might get up to.	For some people, this might seem too pre-meditated. Sometimes characters develop characteristics as the story progresses. But homing in on one of these features when your story falters might be a useful way to overcome writer's block.
Showing not telling	Film directors often introduce characters with a single action. These actions – kindly, cruel, impatient, etc. – are useful for establishing immediately and economically a character's personality.	This is perhaps one of the more reliable ways of bringing characters alive. Often, too, it will be an action that triggers a crisis in the story line.
Speaking volumes	A character's way of talking says a great deal about personality. Try to give your characters contrasting ways of speaking and you'll be well on the way to differentiating them.	Speech patterns are useful for underlining other existing contrasts in personalities.
Mixing and morphing	Take some of your own personal characteristics and mix them up with those of someone you know well – morph the two personalities. OR take a character you know well from a work of fiction you've studied and send them off into a scenario from your own experience.	This can result in highly convincing characters since the personalities which emerge are based on carefully observed data from various sources, real or fictional. It can also be a lot of fun!

Profiling identity

In a short story, only a limited number of characters is possible.

Here's a template to help you start thinking about a principal pair. The headings are only suggestions. Feel free to replace them with your own.

		FIRST CHARACTER	CONTRASTING CHARACTER
EXTERNAL	Name/nickname		
	Age		
	Appearance – give at least 4 adjectives		
	How do they feel about appearance? Proud of it? Hides weaknesses?		

INTERNAL	Happy/unhappy by nature?		
	Are they clear-sighted about personality strengths and/or weaknesses?		
SOCIAL/CULTURAL	How are relationships with family/ friends/ teachers?		
	How intelligent/educated are they?		
	How well-adjusted to present life circumstances?		
	Musical/sporting interests?		
LANDMARKS	Greatest achievement to date?		
	Worst moment so far?		

How to use your profiling grid

Your grid, whatever its headings, should contain a fair amount of detailed observation about the two characters. It would be a huge mistake, however, to imagine you have to include **all** this information in your story.

How does that work?

Use only as much of your personality profile as you need at any given moment. The profile is primarily to allow you to close your eyes and imagine these characters as living, breathing people right in front of you. Dip into the profile as and when you feel you need to in order to advance your narrative.

Try not to shout information at reader. For example:

> Sandra loved Jessie J's first album.

Allow it to slip almost unnoticed into the narrative:

> 'Sighing, she slipped "Who You Are" into its plastic box. He hadn't phoned. Again. Well, Jessie J, you know all about men like this, she thought.'

Use the profile to get over writer's block. Should you get stuck about what to write next, go to the grid. Look down the list. Is there anything there that you might refer to at this moment to get the narrative moving again?

Suppose the block started when two characters meet up for the first time? How would the exchange start? Well, if stuck, why not try this:

> Her image seemed blurred. Was she looking at him or not? He pretended to look unconcerned. Hi, he said, staring glassily into her vague general direction.

This reference might help you get started again if you had indicated to the reader earlier that the character was short-sighted and desperate to conceal the fact. (Block now overcome because 'she' is now obliged to say something to 'him'.)

Contrasting characters often find themselves in conflict. And conflict is great for advancing a narrative.

DON'T FORGET

Showing not telling

Certain brief actions can say as much as many words of character description. Here is John Steinbeck in *Of Mice and Men* introducing a violent character:

> His eyes passed over the new men and he stopped. He glanced coldly at George and Lennie. His arms gradually bent at the elbows and his hands closed into fists. He stiffened and went into a slight crouch.

From this character's body movements, only minutes into arriving in the story, we know we're dealing with an aggressive, possibly violent person.

Classroom challenge

Look at the following list of characteristics. Choose one of the adjectives. Invent a brief action (or series of actions) to illustrate how someone demonstrating this characteristic might arrive in a story of yours.

- Write (like Steinbeck here) a maximum of four sentences
- Do not use the actual word in the grid
- Read your sentences to the class
- Did they recognise the characteristic you were aiming for?

frightened	cruel	determined	kind	impatient	laid-back

Remember, your description should **not** contain the word you have selected from the grid.

Homework helper

Go back now and choose one more adjective from the grid. Illustrate it in the same way as you did in the previous exercise, taking care not to use the actual word in your four sentences. Read it aloud to the class. Did they recognise the adjective you were trying to illustrate?

Speaking volumes

If actions can help create characters, so too can a person's speech habits. The type of dialogue you give your characters can spare you a lot of wordy description. Characters can come alive not just by what they say, but how they say it. Let's put that to the test.

Classroom challenge

Here your knowledge of sentence structure should help you greatly. Below, on the left, you will see a variety of speech habits at work in dialogue.

- Match the dialogue extract with the correct descriptive adjectives in the right column.
- List which aspects of sentence structure helped you pair the dialogue with the correct descriptive adjective.

I did put the kitchen lights off, didn't I? Or did I? Did you see me do it, Stuart? Jenny, help me here. Did I or didn't I go into the kitchen before we left? Or am I just imagining I did?	dynamic
Let me see ... You wrote on the ... Hm ... Last month sometime. You said you were living somewhere beside ... Let me see ... Manchester, was it? No, no, that's not right ... Liverpool. Yes, that was it, I think. Well, somewhere like that anyway ...	anxious
OK, OK. Point taken. But go easy on her. She's, you know, kind of touchy. Play your cards right and she'll be as nice as nine-pence. No laying down the law. No way. She can change in a jiffy. Not a pretty sight. Be warned now, bro.	aggressive
Right, first things first, lady and gentleman. We need answers and we need them fast. You, Barry, could you please ask Accounts for last month's figures. Sheila, there's a useful article on trends in yesterday's *Times*. See if you can find it, please? Let's meet back here at three. Have your thinking caps on!	boring
No, not later, now! Read my lips! You are not going out. You are going up to your room. You are going to work. And you are going to pass that damn exam. Get on with it! Move! Up the stairs!	vague
So I said to Amy – she's my first wife's daughter, my step-daughter so to speak, but a great lassie at times – 'Amy,' I said, 'When was the last time you had a meal like that? She, I have to say, has her moments and is sometimes not the most polite of people, so much so that, at times, she can be, how shall I put it – a right madam, not to say a cheeky wee besom.	chatty

TEACHING NOTES

You can download Teaching Notes for this challenge at www.brightredpublishing.co.uk/Shop/national-5-english-course-book

DON'T FORGET

When thinking about contrast in your characters' interactions, don't overlook the usefulness of pairing a Scots-speaking character with one using Standard English.

Homework helper

a) Now that you've had time to think about the usefulness of contrasting ways of talking, try writing around 300 words of dialogue between two characters over a situation in which they're not seeing eye-to-eye. Maybe thinking about some headings from your profile identity grid could help get you started? Remember, this is simply an exercise in dialogue writing, but what you learn here might be useful in an actual story.

OR

b) Invent a character of your own whose sentence structure/vocabulary reflects their personality as they introduce themselves to the reader. For example, 'Me? I'm ...' You could consider the personality types in the previous Classroom challenge, or invent your own. Whoever you decide on, make sure their personality comes across through your control of sentence structure/vocabulary. Write around 150 words. Read your character introduction to the class. Did they spot the personality you were aiming at?

Setting the scene

When you have a good idea for a story, it's tempting to want to get down to the action right away. You know, of course, that you need to mention a setting somewhere near the start: a kitchen, a street, a shop, a classroom or some such place. But a story with only a token setting and no fully developed sense of setting suggests a situational vacuum which will rob the reader of the chance to **experience** what it's truly like to be in this invented world of yours.

If you mention a setting in the opening paragraphs and then forget about it, you're seriously short-changing your reader. Why? Because effective use of setting requires you to remember three important facts:

1. Setting is about more than place
2. Setting helps to advance the story
3. Setting needs to be regularly revisited

Setting is about more than place

You can improve the quality of your story by enriching the context in which your characters find themselves. A good setting will often have several elements to it:

TIME OF DAY	Just as words have connotations, so, too, do times of day. Morning can be associated with a new beginning or fresh hope. Evening may suggest the end of things in some way or, perhaps, romance. Night can be threatening. There are various possibilities to be had from working with your own associations of these times of day. One idea might be to have your story move through them to underline various points in your characters' moods or situations.
SEASON	Again, seasons tend to carry connotations with them: spring – hope; summer – ripeness, harvest; autumn – the hint of an ending; winter – cold and death of the year. Of course, you might want to turn these connotations completely on their head to create contrasts, for example, sadness in spring when everything else feels full of life.
WEATHER	Weather is a powerful way of supporting the atmosphere you're creating around your characters. For instance, when something is starting to go wrong in a good relationship, maybe there's a rumble of distant summer thunder. What might lashing rain suggest about the emotional situation of characters? If your characters were subjected to unrelenting sun, how might this underline their feelings? And a harsh, cutting wind – how might this affect their mental state?
OBJECTS	Something as simple as a vase of flowers can add greatly to your story-telling. Fresh flowers; a few petals scattered on a table top; withered blooms in a dry vase – all these can signal landmark moments in an evolving narrative. If someone is regularly visiting someone in hospital and each visit sees an increasing array of hospital equipment around a patient's bed, how does that affect the emotional impact of your story? Suppose, too, that there was less equipment on each visit? How does that advance the story?

In other words, thoughtful use of setting can not only establish a sense of place but give us a valuable sense of the character's mood, attitude or situation. And by so doing, it can also help advance the story.

Setting helps to advance the story

Let's see how the American writer Michael Chabon makes setting work for him.

> *It was a mile and seven tenths from the campus to my house on Denniston. All the houses I passed were dark, with cars arranged in their driveways as neatly as duck decoys on a mantelpiece. I limped right down the middle of certain streets, and stood for an entire minute in the centre of a desolate intersection as the lights changed around me and the traffic signals swung from their cables in the wind. I walked endlessly through an uncharitable and sobering rain. The pain in my ankle grew worse the longer I walked and the soberer I got.*
>
> Adapted from *Wonder Boys*, Harper Perennial, London, 2006

The dark houses, the 'desolate intersection', the wind and the rain do much more than describe a place: they help us understand the gloomy mood of the narrator, too. The setting also helps advance the narrative, for we wonder now how the narrator came to be injured and why he's apparently drunk. We wonder, too, what will happen to him when he eventually does get home.

So, in one paragraph of well-crafted setting, the writer has done more than describe a place; he has given us insight into a character and his situation. He has also got us wondering where the plot will go next.

DON'T FORGET

Figurative language – represented by metaphors, similes, personification – as well as devices such as onomatopoeia, alliteration and assonance can all do much to bring life to your descriptions of setting. Think also about how your sense of hearing, smell and touch could make your setting memorable.

By introducing elements of time of day, season, weather and external objects into your narrative, you can underline most effectively characters' states of mind and/or fortunes at any given point. Night can offer opportunities for dark thoughts and darker deeds; spring can suggest hope when the setting matches a character's mood. The changing state of a garden can hint at swings of fortune in the life of the people who tend it: have a couple divorced? Has someone fallen gravely ill? Has there been a switch of focus in the gardener's life?

Setting needs to be regularly revisited

You can help underpin the structure of your story – something much prized by examiners – by revisiting elements of your setting at various key points in your narrative.

By altering setting details as you go along, you can subtly signal certain changes of mood and/or circumstances of your characters. Fresh flowers wither; harsh rain goes off; warm sun clouds over; smart clothes grow shabby – these changes can be made to parallel landmark changes in characters' lives. Noting these changes in passing will add a powerful dimension to the unfolding of your narrative and the portrayal of your characters.

Classroom challenge

Think about the start of a short story in which a character either:

plunges into a sun-drenched swimming pool

OR

settles down, homeless, in a shop doorway for the night.

As well as describing the setting itself, your narrative should usefully prepare the reader for the character's feelings and response to this environment. Write up to 150 words.

Homework helper

Here are some opening lines from three possible short stories. Continue each extract by noting the weather and setting which characters might notice from their respective windows. Will the weather and setting match, or be in conflict with, the character's mood? Try to make a connection of some kind between setting and mood. Add around four or five sentences to each extract.

a) It was about three o'clock when Paul woke up in the back seat of the Mondeo. 'Are we near the sea yet?' he asked, refreshed from his long nap. The sun was warm on the back of his neck. His mother looked back and ruffled his hair. 'See for yourself, sleepy-head!'

b) How could he? she thought. Really, how could he? This was the limit. Angrily, she ripped up Mike's letter. Dozens of paper scraps fluttered over the carpet like directionless butterflies. Choking on her sobs, she turned to the window.

c) It was getting on for five. Where was the surgeon? He had said he would be back with the results of the tests in five minutes. That was more than half an hour ago. Mrs Wilkinson struggled up from her chair by the window to look out at the late October afternoon.

ONLINE

Head to www.brightredbooks.net and dip into the article 'Evoke a sense of place' by Judy Darley. She sums up much of what we've been talking about and reminds us how setting has enriched writing through the ages - from Charles Dickens to Monica Ali. Particularly interesting is what she says about how setting helps Tolkien conjure up the Shire in *The Hobbit* and the contrasting darkness of Mordor. She offers many other useful pointers for creating a successful setting.

Planning a narrative

You've spent some time thinking about how to create believable characters and convincing settings. But if your well-rounded characters wander aimlessly around in your well-realised setting, you'll soon lose your reader. Readers need to be kept wondering about what happens next.

Now, what happens next does not need to be a tale of death, destruction or natural disaster. Given you have only up to 1000 words to write, your narrative cannot be too complex or 'clever' either. Successful short stories often arise from very simple events; you may have noticed this in the short stories you've already read. Here's the opening of a very successful short story by Ian Crichton Smith:

> *I tell you what it is. I sit here night after night and he sits there night after night. In that chair opposite me. The two of us. I'm eighty years old and he's eighty-four. And that's what we do, we sit and think.*
>
> 'Napoleon and I' in *Selected Stories*, Carcanet Press, 1990

The tensions which arise from the everyday interaction of this simple couple are handled by the writer in a way which involves and intrigues the reader as much as any Hollywood drama.

What makes a good plot?

There are probably as many short-story plots as there are short stories. You may already have picked up ideas from the inventiveness of the authors whose stories you've already read. But if you're still struggling to shape up your ideas, here's a useful structure for a short story which you'll often find in guides to writing short stories.

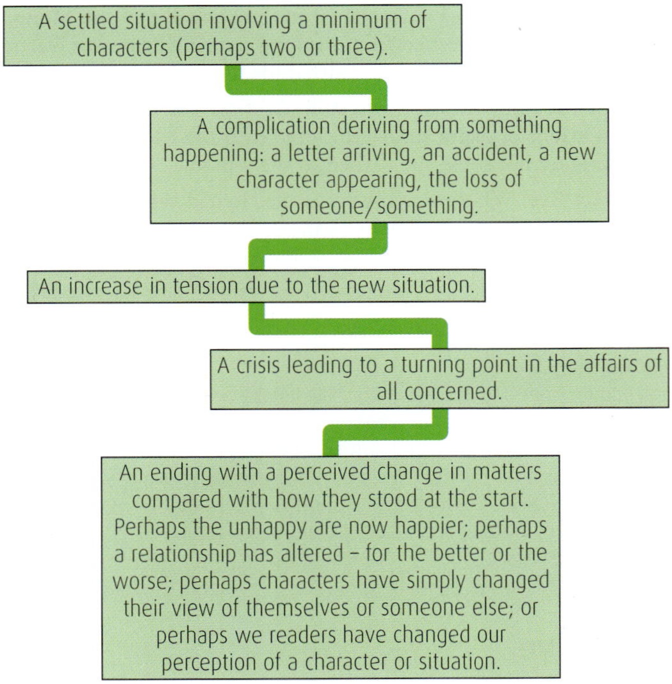

Of course, you can probably think of many good short stories which use only some of these features or perhaps none at all. But if you're stuck for a structure, this might be a useful starting point.

Finding a voice

So now that you have your characters, setting and ideas for your story, how are you going to tell it? Or rather, **who** is going to tell it? There are probably three basic methods for establishing a narrative:

	ADVANTAGES	CONSIDERATIONS	EXAMPLE(S)
The 'first-person' narrative	By using 'I', you're inviting readers into the thought processes of the character. You're establishing a close relationship with your readers, by getting them to view events through your eyes and experience them through your senses.	This method does not allow you to keep tabs on the actions of other characters when they're not present in a scene with you. And what are **they** thinking? We can only judge by their actions and comments, but do we know what **really** lies behind their reactions?	*I rose once again to look out of the window. Where were they? Damn it! I had invited them for six and it was now nearly seven.*
The 'third-person' narrative (subjective form)	A certain character is our guide here to what's happening in the story. The story is told from their point of view. Like the 'I' version, this leads you into the thoughts of the character and a bond can be forged between them and the reader.	Again, how about other characters in this story? What are **they** thinking? We have, once more, limited access to the full story behind events.	*Lucy rose once again to look out of the window, angry as to why they hadn't shown up yet. She felt really irritated. She had invited them for six and now it was nearly seven.*
The 'third person' narrative (objective form)	This is often called the 'I-am-a-camera' approach, with the writer observing and simply recording all that is to be seen.	We need constantly to be alert to what's going on internally with characters. We can only judge inner feelings from external signals.	*Lucy rose once again to look out of the window. Her eyes narrowed as she scanned the street outside. She sat down again, drumming her fingers impatiently on the arm of her chair. Every minute or so, her eyes darted between her watch and the mantelpiece clock.*

If you find yourself in doubt as to which approach suits your story best, why not try all three for the opening paragraphs? Is there one which works better than another for you?

DON'T FORGET

Classroom challenge

Here is a possible scenario for a short story:

> A boy/girl has always wanted to be a musician/sportsperson. His/her parents have always wanted him/her to be a lawyer. They have always ignored any hints about his/her plans for the future. Brilliant exam results have now just been received. The boy/girl decides the moment has come to make it clear he/she will never be a lawyer.

You need to decide which narrative stance you are choosing to describe the experience of the boy/girl? First-person, third-person (subjective or objective version)?

Write the opening paragraph. Don't forget to establish a setting.

Homework helper

Now, using the same information above, try opening this short story from the point of view of a parent. Again, decide which narrative stance you are choosing to describe the experience of the parent? First-person, third-person (subjective or objective version)?

Write the opening paragraph and then continue the narrative as far as time allows.

Don't forget to establish a setting.

Where do I begin?

Once you have decided on characters, setting, plot and narrative stance, you need to think about where in your story you are to begin. Here are three basic possibilities:

	IMPLICATIONS
Chronological order	When in doubt about explaining something, you're often told to 'begin at the beginning'. It's also the most straightforward way of imposing a narrative structure on your story. But you need to be sure to bring your setting and characters crisply to life very quickly if you're to keep your readers on board. Overly long descriptions of either character or setting risk losing readers. Hence the need to establish characters and setting with some of the time-saving techniques we've suggested earlier. Don't overlook these in your desire to get on with the narrative. It's a question of striking a balance between plot versus characters/setting.
Flashforward	This is a technique popular with many film-makers. The story begins at a crisis moment in the plot, with many details and references not quite clear to readers at once: a lap-top is thrown violently to the ground; a phone is slammed down; or an expensive bunch of flowers goes flying out of a window. But the drama and intrigue are sufficient for readers to want to keep reading. What's essential here is that, once you've created this dramatic opening, you go back in the following paragraphs to explain carefully what wasn't clear to begin with. Remember, a confused reader gets irritated and stops reading!
Flash to finish	This, too, is a fairly common device in story-telling on the big screen. The story begins at the end of events: people leaving a party clearly unhappy, a child emerging from hospital, a couple disembarking from a life-boat. Like the flashforward technique, there will probably be many details and references which don't at this point make much sense to readers. But if these details and references are sufficiently interesting in what they reveal about the event, the characters involved and the setting itself, readers will be gripped and wonder about how these events came to happen. They'll want to read on. But, once again, details referred to here must be tidied up in the following paragraphs. Failure to do so will confuse and irritate readers.

Classroom challenge

Here's an opening paragraph to a narrative where the writer has flashed forward to the very end of the story.

Write what you think the next paragraph(s) might be. Remember, here you're going to have to go back to the start of the story, where something/someone may have started to come between Nick and his dad.

Try to pick up all the clues to character and setting offered here as you go back to create your own story, for example, Nick's relations with his father, home, cat.

Avoiding the step that always creaked, Nick crept down the stairs, stopping every so often to check if all was still quiet in his dad's bedroom. Not a sound. Like a grey shadow, the cat brushed lightly against his jeans, hopeful as ever of something to eat, even at this ungodly hour. 'Oh, Soph, not now. Go away. Shoo. Go!' he hissed. The cat regarded him indignantly, then preceded him down the last few steps to the hallway, tail waving like a furry banner. Despite the tension of the moment, Nick had to smile. He would miss all this. Looking around for the last time at the familiar objects he had known for nearly twenty years, he slipped the rucksack onto his back. This was it. He was off.

DON'T FORGET

Once you've completed a story, check the final paragraph with the first one. Will readers see a connection? In other words, have you created a structure that leads the reader smoothly from start to finish?

PERSONAL WRITING

The debt to creative writing

Much of what you've learned about creative writing can be carried over into personal writing. Use the same skills you used in creative writing:

- Characters and setting have to be carefully observed and presented.
- Thought needs to be given as to how your narrative is to unfold: chronologically, by means of a flashforward or a flash-to-finish. (In other words, you need a plan.)
- Metaphors, similes, alliteration and other devices should be there to enrich the reader's pleasure, just as in a short story.
- Your opening needs to 'hook' readers to encourage them to keep reading, and.
- Events don't need to be earth shattering – no matter how ordinary your experience, it's the way you explore it and how you respond to it, which needs to be considered.

So, before setting out on a personal essay, it wouldn't do any harm to run over again what you've learned in the section about short-story writing.

The usefulness of hindsight

A personal narrative with plenty of well-observed detail, rich in the writing techniques familiar to you from your RUAE work, will always appeal strongly to examiners.

If you're considering writing about some event/experience from earlier in your life, an interesting angle to add might be hindsight. You may wish to offer two perspectives: what you felt at the time and what you feel now with the benefit of hindsight. How has your judgment of these events – and of your reaction to them – changed?

Looking back now, I see that I was being ... Since then I have become much more ...

Admittedly, I was being ... But I was only ten at the time. Then, I felt that ... Now, I see that ...

With the advantage of hindsight, I now see that ...

This is a chance to add a thoughtful, reflective dimension to your narrative, presenting yourself as someone who has not only **lived** through these events and experiences but **thought** through them as well. Something to bear in mind, perhaps.

Finding a topic

There are so many angles to your life that the problem might be knowing which to choose. Places, people, relationships, activities and jobs are just some of the possible starting points.

The visit

Here's how travel writer Ina Caro rounds off her description of a holiday travelling all over France. Her last night was at the Paris theatre, the Opéra Garnier. Note, what makes the writing interesting is not simply her descriptions but her personal response to everything she's seeing and experiencing. We learn about her as well as the theatre itself.

The Opéra Garnier is truly a palace of dreams, a colourful gem sparkling in a gray Paris. That afternoon, as we walked up the wide staircase composed of thirty-three varieties of different coloured marbles, I tried to imagine it filled with women whose 19th-century ball gowns were so wide that they were compared to fully rigged ships. When we entered the theatre, I looked at the ceiling designed by Marc Chagall, which was definitely not 19th-century, but somehow it worked. Seated in the centre of the theatre, I looked at the boxes on either side, which were arranged so that the audience could more easily see one another, and tried to imagine them filled with 19th-century occupants, the men in formal black and white, the women in gowns of silk threaded with gold metallic strands and crystal beads. Our seats were fabulous and Mozart's music was sublime. Sitting there in this glorious palace built in a city filled with palaces, my mind drifted back to the soaring cathedrals, the moated fortresses and opulent castles I had visited, and I could think of no better way to end my magical journey through time.

Paris to the Past, Norton, 2011

You don't need to visit landmark locations to write a good personal essay. You could obtain similar results by discussing some building or place, historic or otherwise in your own home town – and your response to it. The most important thing is to bring the experience alive for the reader: your mood that day; the people you went with and their reactions; how you travelled; how the weather did or did not match your mood; your reactions to what you saw; and what you took away from the visit. Remember, too, not every visit is a success, for while we may set out to enjoy ourselves, disappointments can happen. Exploring that angle might also be profitable.

The person

We're all influenced to a greater or lesser extent by people we've encountered – sometimes relations, sometimes friends, neighbours, teachers, or employers. Consider how you first met them; what your initial reaction was; how the relationship developed; what you learned from them; and how they influenced you and your way of looking at the world.

The relationship

Our life is a complex network of relationships with friends and relations. As we grow and develop, these relationships can often change. People you were once close to can become almost strangers; people you didn't immediately like have become close friends. What brought about these changes? Who is it that has changed: you or them? Have you been surprised by the reactions of someone you thought you knew? How did you respond? Bring the character and settings alive just as you would in a creative piece.

The activity

As you grow up you are exposed – willingly or unwillingly – to a variety of activities, often, but not always, by parents. Piano lessons, riding lessons, swimming lessons, scouting/guiding, air cadets, hang-gliding, abseiling (to name just a few) are all productive areas to explore. Whatever the activity, describe your first contact, your expectations and the subsequent impact on you. While the activity may have been successful, it may also have been less than fulfilling. If the latter, you might well get an amusing essay out of the experience. Again, well-realised characters and a convincing setting will be the key to success.

The job

If you're old enough to have a part-time job out of school or college, your experiences could be entertaining for readers. Was there a particular reason to make money? Was finding the job easy? How did the interview(s) go? What was your first day like? How did you react to your new colleagues? Any awkward moments? What has working taught you? Bring your place of work alive with attention to setting and the people you have met.

ONLINE

Read the article about how many of the best college applications come from everyday experiences expressed in personal writing. '*The New York Times*: Some of the more mundane moments in life make great essays' at www.brightredbooks.net

The importance of detail

Although stemming from real-life experience, your personal essay has to be as rewarding to read as a short story. Don't be tempted to generalise about locations or people; giving carefully observed detail is what helps transform your personal experience into one of universal interest, no matter how 'everyday' the event or encounter.

Here is how a writer remembers his experience at a swimming gala. Note that this is a very ordinary event but the writer's attention to detail brings it alive.

> On the day a fine crowd was banked high alongside the pool, full of summer enthusiasm and summer colour. There were dozens of boys in the under fifteen races, but only myself and one other youth in the over fifteen event. He was eighteen, muscled, bronzed and lithe, and I stood beside him on the edge of the bath, skinny, with my costume hanging around my middle like a droopy loin cloth.
>
> Adapted from *This Time Next Week* by Leslie Thomas, Constable, 1991

Disaster strikes almost immediately and, again, it's the detail that intrigues the reader:

> We bent on the starting edge, the pistol cracked, we dived, and my trunks came down, all in a matter of seconds. It might seem funny now, but then it was a moment of awful horror and shame, with everyone screaming with laughter as though I were the clown of the show. Somehow I pulled my trunks up around my bum and crying tears of anger and rage at my own stupidity I set out after my rival who was nearly home. He beat me by thirty yards out of fifty, and I staggered from the bath, glad that my face was wet anyway so they wouldn't see I was crying.

An essential part in the success of the piece is the combination of factual record and personal response to the situation.

Classroom challenge

Here are some extracts from personal writing. Some realise a setting and/or characterisation well. Some do not. Some have imaginative use of sentence structure and word choice. Some do not.

a) Decide which ones sound convincing. Which features contributed to their success?

b) Analyse what you think are the weaknesses of the less persuasive ones. What suggestions would you make to improve the presentation of the writer's information?

1. When I heard the alarm, I got up, opened the curtains and looked out. Then I put on my clothes and went downstairs and had my breakfast. Then I took the dog out for a walk down the street. Since it was about 8.30, I thought it was time to get back so I would not be late for school.

2. It's always the same: I sit down at the Hewlett-Packard laptop my dad bought me for my birthday (at great expense, he likes to tell me!), switch on, go to Documents, open up my Folio folder and right click for a new document. Obligingly, that nice white rectangle appears as if by magic. And then – nothing! Absolutely nothing. I think they call it writer's block. I call it worse things than that. Speak about frustration!

3. All night, the storm spat and battered at my window. Relentless, it seemed. Much like the thoughts that swirled round my head as I lay awake. This could not be happening. I had to be at my best for Murrayfield. Finally, I managed to fall into an uneasy sleep around three. So my mood was not of the best when my jeering alarm clock jolted me awake at seven. Bleary-eyed, I struggled into my clothes. Judgment day was here.

4. In the car my brother and I played 'I spy' until we got to the ferry. Once on the boat, we discovered we had to share a cabin. It was not very big and there was no window. There was Wi-Fi, though, so we stayed up and played games on his iPad until late.

You can download Teaching Notes for this challenge at www.brightredpublishing.co.uk/Shop/national-5-english-course-book

TEACHING NOTES

REFLECTIVE WRITING

The line between personal writing and reflective writing is a fine one. Both are concerned with you, your life and your reactions to it. In reflective writing, however, the focus is more on what goes on in your head than what you do in your life. Your life experience is important, of course, but only so far as it sets you off thinking about some aspect of the world as you see it.

Areas for reflection

A good idea for a reflective essay often springs from some feature of daily life that's drawn your attention. It could be something that you feel strongly about, whether positively or negatively. It might be something which intrigues you, puzzles you, amuses you, or irritates you – why are there so many cooking programmes on television; why do British actors do so well in Hollywood; why is a gym-fit body so prized; why are British people so bad at speaking foreign languages?

There is often a strong speculative element involved, as the above topics might suggest. Typically, the topic will be broken down into various angles as you examine and explore possible answers to share with your reader.

The nature of reflection

What might be some of the **features of an interesting reflective essay**? Here are some suggestions:

Anecdote/Observation	To get your reader interested in your reflections, you need to make clear how this topic came to your attention in the first place and why you think it's significant. This can often be triggered by an event or incident – but be careful not to let this happening dominate your essay. Here's a writer's opening to a reflective essay about his response to abstract art. The opening paragraph needs to be a 'hook' to attract your reader's interest. Work on it as carefully as you would on the start of a short story. *On a recent trip to London, I was lured into the Tate Modern by my culture-vulture sister. Wandering around these huge caverns showcasing the canvases of the great and good of modern time set me to thinking about what I really felt towards what I was looking at. Now, don't get me wrong here, I like art, but I got to wondering why it is that ....*
Character presentation	The pronoun 'I' will be important here since it's your reflections and reactions that take centre stage in this essay. The presentation of yourself must be as carefully considered as that of any character in a short story. For people to be interested in and convinced by your reflections, you need to present yourself as someone balanced in your thinking and open to the ideas and reactions of others. Their views and your reactions to them are also fruitful areas to explore as your essay advances. *Now take my sister. She has quite the opposite view, finding Mondrian a painter who really ...*
Language choices	Here, too, is another way in which your character will emerge. Remember that it's more attractive to talk **to** and not **at** the reader. Informal tone often works in this kind of essay, as though you were exchanging your thoughts with a friend. (See page 37 for features of informal tone.) Metaphors and similes will also help enrich the texture of your views, just as they would in a short story.
Process	Although you're sharing your thoughts with your reader, these cannot be presented as a loose collection of ideas; you need some kind of structure to shape your thought process. Your engagement with the topic might pass through several moods over the course of the piece. • The overall tone might be **confiding** as you take people into your private thoughts about modern art. • It may become **indignant** as you consider some aspect which you find unacceptable (for example, the colossal monetary value of certain pictures). • It may then move into **concerned** as you consider how many hospitals and schools could be built for this money. • It might be **amused** at the pompous ways some people talk about art on television. By the end of the essay, your reflections may have passed through several of these moods. Make sure you signal changes of direction clearly to ensure the overall structural unity of your reflections.

How does that work?

Let's take a possible question to see how we might break it down for an essay. Not all topics might suit this approach, but it might be a useful starting point which you could possibly adapt to suit your own subject. The essential thing is to find the angles that you feel would be interesting to explore and to share with others.

Why do talent shows enjoy such popularity on television?

Topic introduced	Give a context/reason for your selection of this topic.	*Switch on your television at peak viewing-time any time during the winter months and you're almost sure to come across a talent show of some kind at the weekends. On BBC, you might discover ... On ITV, ...*
Writer's overall stance outlined	Make clear your viewpoint on the phenomenon you're starting to explore.	*Let me make my viewpoint quite clear. To me it seems healthy that society and the media are open to new talent. At times, the talent revealed is quite extraordinary ... Take the discovery of Susan Boyle ...*
Reflection aroused by topic	Flag up your concerns.	*This constant search for new blood, however, raises a number of questions. Is it because television companies ...? But is it not cruel to raise hopes in people who ...? And is this exposure eventually likely to ...?*
Broader focus	How do others see this?	*Whatever my own doubts, on Monday mornings the chat invariably ... Some relish the no-hopers ... which always seems to me to be ... Others fancy themselves as real talent scouts, picking out whoever seems ... There's no disputing their ...*
Specific comment	Consider independent commentators.	*My mother, usually the most kindly of people, cannot stand ... Perhaps the most scathing criticism comes from ... Television critics take it all very seriously, however, ...*
More comment	Consider involved participants.	*The queues of hopefuls waiting for hours for auditions never seem to ... When interviewed, one actually said, '...' For one wannabe, the process was simply ...*
Summing up of view and final reflections	Pull various strands together.	*So what does this tell us about our society? Perhaps it is hopeful in that ... But does it suggest that television companies are so ... that ... How long can this phenomenon enjoy ...? As for me, come Saturday night you'll find me ....*

DON'T FORGET

Remember, it's the exploration of the topic which is important. You're not out to make the case for one side or the other, or to persuade people to take a certain point of view. Your role is to open up aspects of a topic that people may not have considered before and to share your thoughts with the reader.

Classroom challenge

In groups, work out an approach you might take to these topics, answering the questions posed in the bullet points. Share your results with the class. Did even more angles/aspects come to light in the class discussion? Add the more interesting comments to your notes.

- How will you introduce this topic? Anecdote? Quotation? Personal observation?
- Which aspects/angles will you explore in your chosen topic?

Why are gyms so popular?
What makes a successful holiday?
The attraction of soap-operas
Why I'll never be a slave to money

Homework helper

Now, with the benefit of your notes, write the introduction to a reflective title which you have selected from the grid in the Classroom challenge. Remember, this introduction needs to 'hook' the reader from the first sentence.

DON'T FORGET

A serious point can be made with a light touch. Humour in a reflective essay can often make an important point as effectively as factual information can.

GROUP A ACTIVITIES

1. Setting

Read the following descriptions of setting. For each location, work out which of the descriptions is the most effective and why. Some of them will obviously be better or worse, but some will be less clear cut!

A graveyard at night

There were grave stones all around him. Mist curled around the stones. Everything was dark. He couldn't see how to get out of the graveyard.

With a start he recognised the shapes looming out of the mist. Gravestones. He must have blundered into the graveyard in the darkness. Dimly he could make out the twisted old trees that marked the boundary. He knew that beyond those trees lay the church, and past the church, the village. But he could see no light from the houses, only the trees, the gravestones, and darkness.

The black iron gate swung slowly open with a tortured squeal of its ancient, rusted hinges. In the darkness, a sable-feathered raven croaked foully and an owl hooted mysteriously. In front of him he could see row upon row of dark gravestones – some fallen over – that looked like crooked teeth in a hideous, grinning skull. A chill mist curled around his feet like evil snakes, and he shivered in fear.

An office

There were sixteen cubicles in the office. Standing up, he could see over the dividers into the semi-private spaces of his co-workers: Maureen with her dog pictures; Matt with his Lego; Sarah with her football stuff – Chelsea mad, that one; and Steve, nothing personal there, just the phone, the computer and the notepad, all aligned perfectly on his sterile desk.

There were sixteen cubicles in the office. Standing up, he could see over the dividers into the near-identical spaces of his co-workers: Maureen, at her desk, with her phone, computer, notepad; Matt, at his desk, with his phone, computer, notepad; Sarah; Steve; Bill; Mark; Carole – all sitting in cubicles with a desk, phone, computer, notepad. All sitting in perfect replicas of his own cubicle. Sighing, he sat down at his desk, picked up the phone and stared blankly at his own reflection in the computer screen.

The room had sixteen cubicles. All of them contained a desk with a phone, a computer and a notepad. Here and there the workers had tried to add some personality – some Lego, pictures etc. – but they were mostly identical.

A park

Green. Everywhere. All around him, on every side: green. Rich, vibrant green of the grass, stretching away to the horizon, undulating slightly like the sea. Clusters of bushes, shrubs – rhododendrons, maybe? – were darker green islands on the sea. And in the distance the land: the towering shapes of trees, darker still, trunks lost in the gloom of their own shadow, only the shades and hues of their leaves visible. He breathed it all in, feeling alive, forgetting all the stress of the city, leaving the noise and the steel and the concrete behind.

The park was about 100 metres on each side. It was square, the edges marked out by black iron railings and there was a gate in the middle of each of the four sides. From each gate a path led straight into the middle, where there was a stone fountain and some benches. Each of the four quarters of the park was different. One had a playpark for little kids, with swings, a roundabout and those little wooden animals on thick springs you see in parks. Another had a wooden fort for bigger kids to clamber over. The third had some flowers, roses, daffodils and the like, and some more benches. The final quarter was grass, and some kids were playing football.

It was a summer's day: hot, clear blue skies. So of course the Meadows was heaving. A group of lads were playing some kind of rugby, though it seemed the rules, and even the teams, were in a state of constant flux. Next to them some younger kids played football. The pitches seemed to overlap, but nobody cared, they just played around each other. The faint sounds of bongo drums drifted over their heads, mingling with the laughter of some students who were sprawled underneath the trees. A toddler was chasing a dog, while an office worker on their lunch break watched on, laughing.

2. Character

Read the following descriptions of three different characters. For each character, work out which description is the most effective and why. Some may be objectively better or worse, while others may be more or less suitable to different styles of writing.

Character 1 – An angry parent

Mum walked in, clearly angry. She yelled at me to go upstairs to my room, and wouldn't listen when I tried to ask why. She was too upset with me to listen.

I could hear mum's footsteps thumping down the hall, before the door swung open violently. Her face was flushed, and her forehead was creased. Before I could say anything she let out a torrent of anger, her words battering me relentlessly. Knowing there was no reasoning with her, I retreated upstairs, even as I wondered what I could have done to make her so angry.

'Where are you?'

Mum's voice drowned out the sound of the TV as she threw open the door violently.

'I …' was all I managed to get out, before she cut me off.

'You little … do you have any idea what you've done?'

As her voice grew louder I backed away, raising my arms, hands open, like I'd seen people do on TV shows. It didn't work, though. She kept coming, kept yelling.

'Get upstairs! Now!'

Character 2 – A confused elderly neighbour

'Is that you Billy?'

She reached out her hand, and I could see the soft, criss-crossed lines on her skin, the pale brown spots on the back of her frail, birdlike wrists. Her fingers shook slightly as I reached out, and squeezed them gently.

'No, Mrs Magee, it's me, Sonia. From next door?'

She relaxed, then, a peaceful smile crossing her face. Her eyes flitted across my face, but they didn't seem to see me.

'You're a good boy, Billy. A good lad.'

I reached my arm around her shoulders, hunched and tight with age, and gently led her back through the door, into her cluttered front room with all the pictures on the wall.

Mrs Magee was standing in the street, in her nighty, even though it was the afternoon. She didn't look like she noticed how cold it was. It was like her mind was somewhere else.

'Is that you Billy?'

'No, Mrs Magee, it's me, Sonia. From next door?'

She seemed to relax and smiled at me, as I led her back into her cluttered front room.

Mrs Magee was having another one of her 'turns', as mum put it. She was dithering about in her garden – well, the three-square feet of concrete outside her front door, if you can call that a garden – one hand worrying at her bottom lip, the other curled tight around her waist. Her milky blue eyes were flitting around, but it was clear she wasn't seeing anything clearly. The cold January wind whipped the hem of her nighty around her ankles; I could see the goosebumps on her pale legs, but she didn't seem to notice, or care.

All I wanted to do, was to go home. I knew that I could walk past, make no eye contact, and pretend I'd seen nothing. But she looked so cold. So frail. I couldn't ignore that.

It only took a few minutes to escort her in, get her settled with a blanket and a cup of tea, then disentangle myself. A few minutes that, under the circumstances, I could scarce afford.

Character 3 – A successful businesswoman

I looked at myself in the mirror. Sharp suit. Versace. Black. Make-up precise, expensive, but subtle. I reached up to adjust my hair, tucking stray strands away, drawing it back into a pony tail that was severe, serious. With a practised flick of the wrist I tied off the tail, straightened my jacket and smiled. My teeth were white, even. My lipstick was red, clean. But the smile never touched my eyes.

She walked into the room like she owned it, which, in a sense, she did. She smiled as she shook my hand – firm, dry palm – but the smile never touched her eyes. She was all business, just like her reputation. Not a hair was out of place, not a crease on her black designer suit. It was like she was a machine, built in a factory somewhere. He shivered slightly, and fought to keep the panic down. He needed this deal, and it all hinged on her.

Everything about her screamed success. Her suit was clearly expensive, hair immaculate, nails manicured daily. She had a stillness to her that could be unnerving. No tics, no twitches. No tells. She'd be a great poker player, not that she'd ever play a game so crass. No, risk taking and bluffing weren't her style. She didn't gamble. She won.

TEACHING NOTES

You can download Teaching Notes for activities 1 and 2 at www.brightredpublishing.co.uk/Shop/national-5-english-course-book

GROUP B

DISCURSIVE WRITING

An overview

In this group, you have a choice between writing an argumentative essay or a persuasive one. So, what are the differences?

- **A persuasive essay** is one in which you attempt to win over the reader to your view on a controversial topic. Here there will be researched data to support your viewpoint, but it will not be balanced as in an argumentative essay. Contrary viewpoints may be entertained but only to be dismissed. Here the language will be unashamedly emotive as it seeks reader approval.

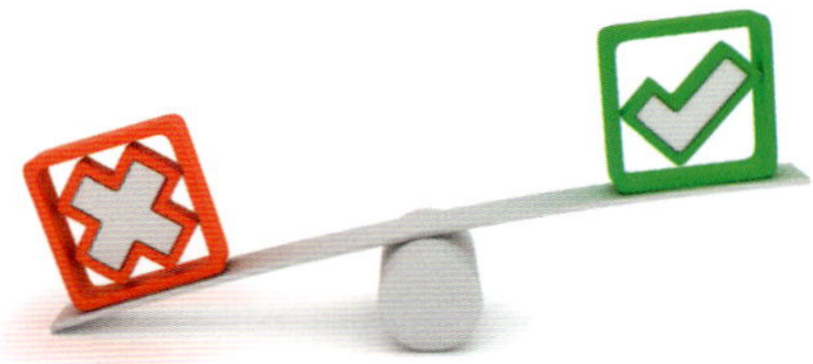

- **An argumentative essay** is one in which you explore and evaluate opposing viewpoints on a controversial topic in formal and neutral language, calling on objective data before offering any final opinion of your own.

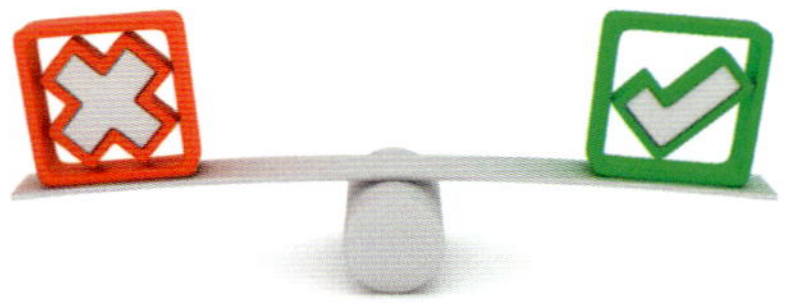

How does that work?

So how does that look in practice? Let's see how an introduction to an essay on the issue of Closed-Circuit TV (CCTV) might appear in its persuasive form and in its argumentative form.

PERSUASIVE	ARGUMENTATIVE
The curse of Closed-Circuit TV	CCTV: big benefit or Big Brother?
Next time you're in your local shopping mall, look up at some of the multiple CCTV cameras dotted around. Ever wonder where they first started? Well, those surveillance cameras that now allegedly 'guard' Super Dry, Next and Claire's Accessories first saw the light of day guarding Hitler's 1942 V-2 rocket launch site. From this ill-omened start, they have swarmed remorselessly all over Europe. Today, Britain, once Europe's bastion of freedom, now has more spy cameras than any other European country. For years, they have ridden rough-shod over the individual privacy of law-abiding citizens; they have cost Britain nigh a staggering billion pounds these last four years; and, according to a recent report by UK police chiefs, they have helped solve only 3% of the nation's crimes. Surely, it's high time to roll back this most intrusive, costly and inefficient feature of our ever-growing nanny state?	In this age of terrorism, there are few areas of major cities which are not under the surveillance of thousands of CCTV cameras. They transmit images to a central control to monitor security in places where security might be an issue. For some, it is a comfort that suspicious behaviour does not go unnoticed, thereby limiting potential attacks of all kinds. Among civil liberties groups, however, there is grave suspicion that this surveillance could be abused by unscrupulous governments to spy on their citizens in the way prophesied by George Orwell in his novel *1984*. A balanced view requires us to examine how, in an increasingly violent world, CCTV cameras can help keep us safe and, at the same time, to study the validity of claims regarding potential abuse of surveillance material.

Classroom challenge

To help you be clear right away about how your language needs to differ in the two discursive genres, here are some more extracts from persuasive and argumentative essays. Remember, persuasive writing is unashamedly emotive in its appeal; argumentative writing tends to favour more neutral, formal language. We shall look at the types of language each genre employs in much more detail shortly. But, for the moment, try to see the broad differences.

- In which column would you place each extract?
- List the features of language which helped you decide.

Tip: Going back to look at 'Tone' in the RUAE section of this guide might help you here (see page 37). Look also at our two model introductions above.

	PERSUASIVE	ARGUMENTATIVE
1. A closer inspection of the figures suggests that long-term obesity is no longer a problem exclusively for the Americans but currently extends to several European countries as well.		
2. Imagine what it must be like for these poor children: alone, cold and with no friendly adult in sight.		
3. To its detractors, the gap year is frequently viewed as an unproductive use of time; to its supporters, it's seen as an investment in life experience which will render study more meaningful in the longer term.		
4. What kind of world are we creating? What view of humanity are we encouraging in our young people? And how will history judge our feeble efforts at tackling this and other natural disasters?		
5. Surely, this is an approach that desperately needs investigation, not just for cash-strapped students like us but for the rest of the struggling university sector, too?		
6. This is an approach which, while it appeared novel at the time of publication, is now seen simply as routine in most Human Resources departments.		
7. No, the time is long past for letters to the papers and street protests. What we need now – and desperately, folks – is for action by our leaders, action that will rid us of this scourge once and for all.		
8. According to Professor Janine Davidson, writing in the August 2016 issue of *English Teaching for Tomorrow*, the attainment gap between teen-age boys and girls could shortly narrow as a result of government initiatives.		

TEACHING NOTES

You can download Teaching Notes for this challenge at www.brightredpublishing.co.uk/Shop/national-5-english-course-book

Argumentative and persuasive: family likenesses

Although we have seen significant differences in their approach to language, the two genres share certain elements. Whichever approach you decide on, your completed essay must offer the reader just as much satisfaction as any piece of fiction or reflective writing. So how is this sense of satisfaction achieved? Let's answer this by asking some of the questions your reader might be asking of both an argumentative and a persuasive essay.

Why is this subject worthy of attention?

In your introduction to an essay of either genre you must establish enough background information to convince the reader the topic is sufficiently important and compelling to be worth reading about.

How reliable is the research?

Your sources should be acknowledged at the end of your essay. So, how well will your list read? Nutritional 'facts' from the website of a fast-food manufacturer could hardly be taken to be evidence of sound research. Website information might be useful as a starting point for topics which have only recently touched our consciousness. So far, these may not have been dealt with in book form, but more traditional topics will have been explored in peer-reviewed publications. These latter are usually the most reliable and authoritative.

Quality journals and newspapers employ acknowledged experts and pollsters whose accuracy and readability can usually be counted on. These, of course, can be viewed online, mostly free of charge. A list of sources balanced between the paper-based and the electronic impresses.

How up-to-date is the information?

In this multi-media age of 24-hour news gathering, there's no excuse for out-dated statistics and information. Check publication dates of books, journals and newspapers and posting dates of websites before beginning note-taking.

Has plagiarism been avoided?

Research means note-taking and, while engaged in this, ensure that you do not 'lift' unacknowledged stretches of text. Lifting text from websites or publications is simply theft and experienced examiners have a sixth sense for detecting it. Often, this 'lifting' may have been accidental, but you must be aware of the danger. (We shall return to this topic in more detail later.)

DON'T FORGET

Avoid setting out to write an argumentative essay and then slipping into personal views along the way, thus destroying your claim to objectivity. It would be similarly foolish for the writer of a persuasive essay to end up simply presenting information rather than seeking to persuade.

Shared features

Having looked at some broad likenesses, let's look more closely at some more detailed features which the two genres share. These could profitably be introduced into your essay, whether persuasive or argumentative.

FEATURE	AIM
Anecdotes/illustrative examples	To assist reader understanding
Analogies (comparing one situation with another)	To suggest parallels aiding understanding
Quoting/criticising/rebutting experts	To show familiarity with the topic
Citing polls/surveys	To show familiarity with research
Mentioning and replying to opposing views	To demonstrate discussion skills
Indicating consequences	To show awareness of the implications of views expressed

The need for evidence

ONLINE

If your topic reflects current issues and debates, the chances are that published texts may not yet have caught up with them fully. Quality journals, magazines and newspapers can help here. Using a search engine, type in your topic or issue followed by the name of a quality online publication to see what's available. *The Independent, The Guardian, The Herald,* and *The Scotsman* are all good places to start.

Just as you need evidence in your critical essay, so, too, do you need it in discursive writing. Whether you decide on an argumentative essay or a persuasive one, you need evidence to support your case. In a critical essay, this took the form of close reference to the text or a quotation. Here, it's the backing of what we call authority. By this, we mean the opinion of an acknowledged expert in their field, the results of a respected poll or a reference to a published study or report.

In every instance, you need to make clear who your authority is, and where and when the evidence appeared. Without authority, you're attempting to make out a case simply from your own subjective opinions. These, while no doubt interesting, will not carry the weight that expert opinion will. Having some expert evidence on both sides will immeasurably strengthen your arguments.

But beware of overusing this; it's only there to support **your** carefully argued case. It's not a substitute for it.

DON'T FORGET

You'll never be penalised for opinions which may run counter to those of the examiner. You're being assessed on the strength of your case, not on the nature of your beliefs.

A note on note-taking

Time is precious in your N5 year. But looking for evidence in articles to support your case in a persuasive or argumentative essay can be time-consuming. So, you need to be as efficient as you can be when taking notes. You need to learn how to read texts speedily, extracting only essential information and notes. So how do you do this?

Here are a few tips for reading both electronic and paper-based texts efficiently:

- Read the title. You can usually tell right away if the article is going to be relevant to your topic.
- If it seems to match your needs, read the first paragraph. Still relevant?
- Then, check out any subheadings. One of them could lead you to precisely the information you're searching for.
- Read the first sentence of each remaining paragraph to see if there are other points which might be useful.
- Read the final paragraph to see what the writer has to say in their summing up.

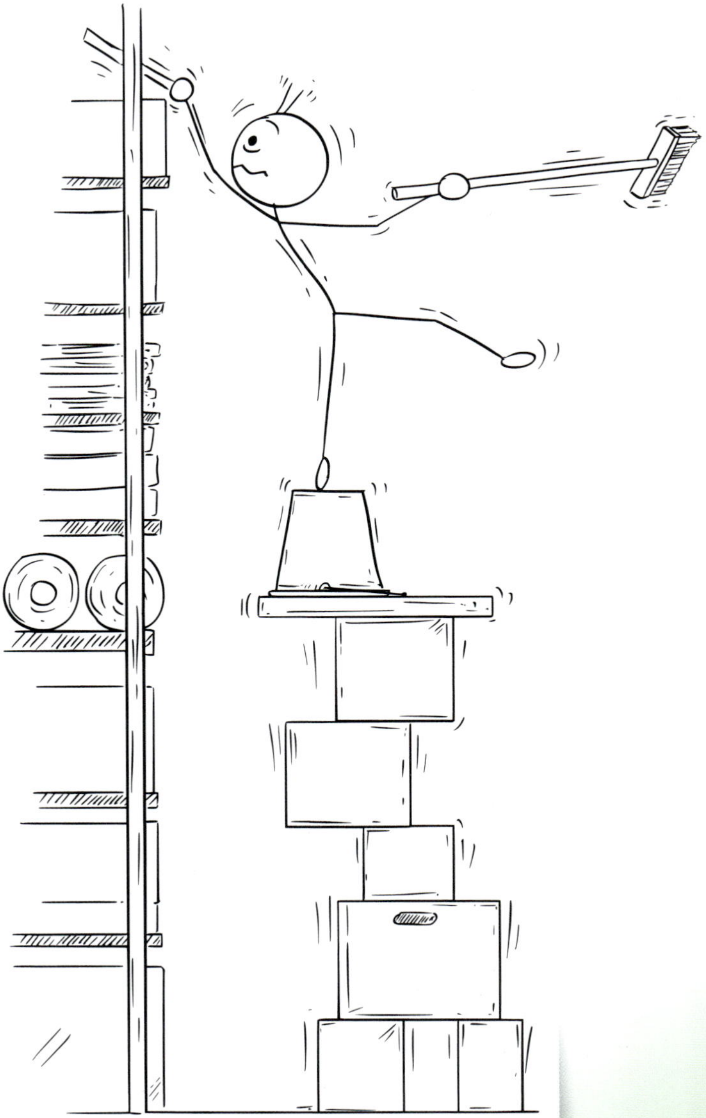

When it comes to writing down your notes, use your common sense:

- Be selective. Write down only key points: *exports rose 13%, first quarter 2016, first time an increase since 2011.* Too many points will challenge you as much as too few.
- You don't need to write your notes in sentences. But make sure they aren't too brief either, otherwise you won't be able to make sense of them later.
- Note down where and when this information was given out, for example: *August edition Pig Breeders Quarterly.* Note also who said it and their position: *Cassie Scott, Professor of Biology, University of Reading, Craig Aitchison, CEO United Wire, etc.* This will save you time looking for the information again when you come to write the essay itself.
- Relevant information needs to be paraphrased into your own words if you wish to use the writer's ideas. You must not 'lift' information. You need to acknowledge the source of this information, even when you've paraphrased it.
- Should you wish to use actual quotations from a text, you need to set the selected text in inverted commas and acknowledge the source and the author fully. (To safeguard the flow of your paragraph, you merely need to give the name of the person quoted in the text and then give the source in your list of sources at the end of the essay.) Failure to acknowledge your cited author counts as plagiarism and will count heavily against you. Use a coloured marker pen to highlight actual quotations when you make your notes. This will help you avoid accidentally 'lifting' other people's ideas and seeming to pass them off as your own.

Classroom challenge

Expert opinion can be introduced into your essay in a variety of ways without risking plagiarism itself. Here are some student texts which use the same basic information. More than one of them, however, is guilty of plagiarism.

- Which texts plagiarise?
- How did the other texts avoid plagiarism?

All of these students wished to quote information from a book on Kirkcudbright-based artists by Haig Gordon. Here's the extract they wished to use:

> For about one hundred years, roughly from 1880 to 1980, the ancient Royal Burgh of Kikcudbright in Galloway was widely renowned as an artists' colony, often described as the St Ives of Scotland. The town retains a certain afterglow of aestheticism and is now marked as a tourist destination under the title of 'The Artists' Town'. Essentially, however, Kirkcudbright's reputation rests upon its past.
>
> Haig Gordon, *Tales of the Kirkcudbright Artists*, Galloway Publishing, 2006

Tip: keep in mind what you learned about paraphrasing (putting into your own words) in the 'understanding' questions in the RUAE paper. This should help you avoid unintentional plagiarising.

Student A

In his study of Kirkcudbright artists, Haig Gordon comments that the town is often seen as 'the St Ives of Scotland', though today it is more of a destination popular with tourists.

Student B

The town's claim to fame, according to Haig Gordon in his study of Kirkcudbright artists, spans approximately a century from the late 19th to the late 20th century. Although its glory days are long past, it retains a certain afterglow of aestheticism which we can see today as we wander about it.

Student C

Haig Gordon admits that nowadays Kirkcudbright is known as 'The Artists' Town' but this fame relies on its past history. There are, he suggests, certain reminders of its artistic past, but today, to all intents and purposes, it is a tourist town.

Student D

Roughly from 1880 to 1980, Kirkcudbright was widely renowned as 'an artists' colony' often described as the St Ives of Scotland. Today it is more a tourist destination under the title of 'The Artists' Town'.

If you're concerned about having perhaps plagiarised accidentally, there's a link to a plagiarism checker at www.brightredbooks.net – simply upload a draft of your discursive essay and run the check. This should put your mind at rest.

Be aware that proper names, book titles, etc. may be flagged up as 'borrowed', but this is only natural and cannot be avoided. Quotations may also turn up as 'plagiarised'; this can be put right by ensuring that the guilty words are put into inverted commas and their source correctly acknowledged.

TEACHING NOTES

You can download Teaching Notes for this challenge at www.brightredpublishing.co.uk/Shop/national-5-english-course-book

PERSUASIVE WRITING

This is a form of writing which responds well to strong opinions. However, these opinions need to be credibly supported by researched data, otherwise your essay will sound like an empty rant.

There are plenty of models out there for you to study. First, try looking in the 'Opinion', 'Comment' or 'Leader' pages of a quality newspaper. Or listen to a politician making a speech in parliament. Here you'll find plenty of tips for writing (and speaking) persuasively. You'll notice that authority is often cited but skilfully manipulated to back up personal points of view. So, what should you consider including? Let's take a look at some possibilities.

The language of persuasion: getting the reader onside

Pronouns are useful

Generous use of personal pronouns such as 'we', 'us' and 'you' are a useful tool in successful persuasive writing. They immediately suggest that 'we' are on the same side to start with, a team already:

We are surely alike in thinking that when we ...

You, like me, surely feel that whenever we see ...

Informal commands

Bonding with the reader is further reinforced when we use informal commands frequently:

Imagine how much better our world would be if ...

Just think what an improvement it would be if ...

Emotive language

Every opportunity is taken to work on readers' emotions. Descriptions can be emotionally loaded rather than left simply factual:

'bureaucrats'	→	*'hard-hearted bureaucrats'*
'parents'	→	*'seriously concerned parents'*
'children'	→	*'gravely undernourished children'*

The aim here is to arouse strong feelings in the reader: feelings of sympathy or support for those unjustly treated; anger or criticism for those responsible. If you cite famous or celebrity figures, you're free to attach emotive phrases to their names:

... Charles Dickens, that great champion of the exploited underdog, ...

Rhetorical questions

These are questions which the reader is not expected to answer directly; their purpose is merely to elicit the reader's support and agreement:

What are we to think of a government that treats its pensioners this way?

Not a lot, is what we are expected to concur silently. Sometimes, writers and speakers will go a bit further and answer their own questions for effect:

I'll tell you what we think: we think they are a mean-spirited, heartless bunch!

Used occasionally, particularly after a description packed with emotive word choice, rhetorical questions are particularly effective in stressing shared values between writer and reader. Used too often, they tend to sound rather hollow. Ration their use!

Attitude markers

After some particularly informative yet emotive reporting, attitude markers can be useful in guiding reader response to the writer's viewpoint:

Clearly, then, ... So obviously, ... Surely, ... Fortunately, ...

are just a few examples. Use them to win readers over to the point of view you're proposing that they adopt for themselves.

Parallel structures

Recurring patterns in phrases make for a memorable way to present a persuasive message:

> ***We welcome the frankness*** *of her efforts to ...*
> ***We admire the honesty*** *of her admission that ...*
> ***We share the generosity*** *of her spirit in ...*

Here, the 'we' + verb + 'the' + noun + 'of her' + noun formula creates a pleasing pattern that the reader can partially predict and certainly remember.

Repetition

Parallel structures use repetition for their effect, but repetition does not always need to be so elaborate:

> *We* ***cannot*** *understand her attitude ... The public simply* ***cannot*** *believe in someone who ... Most companies* ***cannot*** *support certain of her initiatives which ...*

Here it's merely the repetition of a single word which reaches out to us, but its very repetition can create a powerful (here, negative) effect in our response to a person or topic.

Rising rhetorical triads (or tricolons)

These are rather fancy terms for something which you are probably quite familiar with from watching television or reading newspapers. They are closely related to the parallel structures and repetition we've already looked at. These are tripartite statements or phrases which typically appear in the final section of an article or speech, with each element gaining in power as the writer seeks to build up the text towards a ringing climax:

> *Let us hope that this will lead to ... Let us hope this will also lead to ... And let us hope that, above all, this will lead to a world in which ...*

DON'T FORGET

The novelist Joseph Conrad once remarked:
'He who wants to persuade should put his trust not in the right argument, but in the right word. The power of sound has always been greater than the power of sense.'
Keep Conrad's advice in mind throughout your persuasive writing!

DON'T FORGET

Think in threes! In persuasive writing, three is a magic number. Parallel structure and rising rhetorical triads (tricolons) give you a fine opportunity to exploit this. Three-part phrases seem to stick in the mind and have a pleasing ring to them. Invent them! Write them! Exploit them!

How does that work?

In the following quote, you instantly see the power of threes at work. It's part of Barack Obama's speech marking the 50th Anniversary of Martin Luther King's Washington address on civil rights. Note the use of parallel structures, ascending in power as the paragraph advances. Keep the power of these tricolons in mind when you come to work persuasively on your readers. Note, too, the parallel structures again in 'washing somebody else's laundry' and 'shining somebody else's shoes.'

Because they marched, the civil rights law was passed. **Because they marched**, the voting rights law was signed. **Because they marched**, doors of opportunity and education swung open so their daughters and sons could finally imagine a life for themselves beyond washing somebody else's laundry or shining somebody else's shoes.

ONLINE

For more inspiration on persuasive techniques at work, check out the *Telegraph's* list of the 'Top 25 political speeches of all time' at www.brightredbooks.net

Classroom challenge

Go back to look again at the introduction to a persuasive essay on page 195, the one on CCTV.

With the above analysis of the language of persuasion in mind, list the techniques which the writer used to win readers over to his point of view in this introduction.

TEACHING NOTES

You can download Teaching Notes for this challenge at www.brightredpublishing.co.uk/Shop/national-5-english-course-book

Homework helper

Here's an example of a young writer trying to find his feet in persuasive writing. It is, however, more factual than persuasive. Using as many features of the language of persuasion as you think would be successful, rewrite the information in a form which is more directly persuasive.

Work which exploits child labour should be discouraged. The International Labour Organisation is agreed on that. It says that it deprives children of their childhood, their potential and their dignity. Not only that, it is not good for their physical and mental well-being. Child labour is something which gets in the way of their schooling, sometimes by interfering with it or stopping them going to school at all or making them leave school too soon. Maybe even worse, it makes them try to combine schooling with long hours and heavy work. It should be ended right now.

Re-read our list of persuasive features. Try to make as emotive an appeal as you can out of the facts, working towards a truly emotional climax. The words here need only be a starting point.

Classroom challenge

Work in pairs. Examine your partner's text on child labour. As well as giving a mark out of five, comment on the features employed. Do you have suggestions on how to improve the text?

FEATURES	MARK OUT OF 5	COMMENT
Use of pronouns		
Commands		
Rhetorical questions		
Emotive language		
Other persuasive features. Name them.		

Ordering your arguments

In a persuasive essay, you're setting out to persuade readers of the rightness of your case. This frees you from the need to balance your arguments as you would in an argumentative essay and from having to present your case in neutral language. Here you are at liberty to use persuasive language techniques of the kind we've just been discussing.

You must be careful, however, to marshal your arguments just as carefully as in an argumentative essay, although somewhat differently. To win over readers, it's wise to establish yourself as a sensible, reasonable person. And sensible, reasonable people are always aware that their opinion is not the only one around. How, then, do you deal with possibly contrary viewpoints when you set out your own persuasive case?

As in an argumentative essay, it might be wise to deal with them early on so that your increasingly powerful arguments push them aside in your reader's memory.

This might be a possible solution:

- Make your viewpoint abundantly clear in your introduction.
- Acknowledge perhaps a conflicting opinion but refute it in a reasonable, logical way. (It's always a good idea to show respect to contrary views.)
- Launch your first persuasive paragraph.
- Continue with similarly persuasive paragraphs, saving your strongest argument until last.
- Finish strong with your conclusion.

Getting your essay started

You need to quickly establish yourself as an informed commentator with a firmly committed point of view. Let's look at how we might organise that introduction to create the best possible effect. Let's go back to the topic of CCTV. Remember, this is only a suggested template; you may find your topic requires a different treatment.

How does that work?

The Curse of Closed-Circuit TV *Next time you're in your local shopping mall, look up at some of the multiple CCTV cameras dotted around. Ever wonder where they first started? Well, those surveillance cameras that now allegedly 'guard' Super Dry, Next and Clare's Accessories first saw light of day guarding Hitler's 1942 V-2 rocket launch site. From this ill-omened start, they have swarmed remorselessly all over Europe. Today, Britain, once Europe's bastion of freedom, now has more spy cameras than any other European country. For decades, they have ridden rough-shod over the individual privacy of law-abiding citizens; they have cost Britain nigh a staggering billion pounds these last four years; and, according to a recent report by UK police chiefs, they have helped solve only 3% of the nation's crimes. Surely, it's high time to roll back this most intrusive, costly and inefficient feature of our ever-growing nanny state.*	• Note that the title is unashamedly biased against CCTV • The first two sentences 'hook' the reader with and informal command and rhetorical question. • Sentences 3–6 outline the background and significance of the topic. • Sentence 7 lists the writer's three objections. • Sentence 8 is launched with an attitude marker and the writer's stance outlined in a clear call to action. Note, he keeps to the order outlined in sentence 7, signalling the order in which he is going to sequence the essay.

Classroom challenge

So far, the views on CCTV cited have been rather negative. Now, with a partner or as a group, write the **introduction** to a persuasive essay which is unashamedly **for** CCTV and its benefits. Remember to include a persuasive title. Here are some pro-CCTV points you may wish to raise in your introduction. Feel free to add researched information of your own. Try to write about 100–120 words. Remember to keep up the persuasive tone.

A 2009 Cambridge University report found CCTV cameras reduced crime in car parks by 51% and 23% on public transport.	Used to safeguard banks, airports, convenience stores, factories, schools, casinos, military installations.
First use in Britain was in King's Lynn, Norfolk in 1987. Nowadays, they cover most town centres and shopping precincts.	CCTV helps detect and convict offenders. Also useful in tracking terror suspects.

Work in pairs. Examine your partner's introduction to a persuasive essay on CCTV. As well as giving a mark out of five, comment on the features employed. Do you have suggestions on how to improve the text?

FEATURES	MARK OUT OF 5	COMMENT
Use of interesting 'hook' to launch intro?		
Significance/background/context of topic outlined?		
Writer's stance on topic made clear?		
Use of persuasive features? Which ones?		
Hint of a 'road-map' for rest of essay?		

Structuring the persuasive paragraph

A convincing body paragraph in a persuasive essay can benefit from what we learned about body paragraphs in critical essays: a strong Statement (S) composed of one or more sentences to open the paragraph, followed by detailed Evidence (E), the significance of which is more unpacked for us in a Commentary (C) of our own. Here are elements of a persuasive paragraph about CCTV with that familiar SEC structure.

How does that work?

For some time now, those resisting the growing intrusion in our daily lives have been pointing to some alarming CCTV statistics. The magazine CCTV Image reported recently that the number of local government and private CCTV cameras operating in 2011 was around an alarming 1.85 million. These are the most reliable figures currently available, extrapolated from a report by no less an authority than the Cheshire Constabulary. Going by other figures in this same damning report, there is one camera for every 32 of us. And worse still, the Cheshire Constabulary reckons that each one of us is seen by 70 cameras a day. Now these are troubling numbers indeed. And they date back several years. Heaven alone knows what they have now spiralled up to! The fact that the average person cannot go about their business without being spied on 70 times a day is truly shocking. How can we call ourselves a civilized nation when we employ techniques usually associated with Stalin's KGB or East Germany's Stasi?

- First sentence is our Statement.
- Sentences 2–5 form our Evidence section. Note that the writer, although citing evidence, is far from neutral as he cites it. His persuasively hostile stance can be detected in phrases such as 'an alarming 1.85 million', 'no less an authority than', 'damning report', 'worse still'.
- Sentences 6–10 provide a Commentary on the evidence (although the writer has already started commenting negatively in sentences 2–5). Note the Commentary sums up the 'damming report' with a ringing rhetorical question.

DON'T FORGET

A weak argument at the end of a persuasive essay will lessen the impact of your persuasive efforts earlier. Make sure your final paragraph builds to a stirring climax. Unleash the full force of persuasive devices here!

ARGUMENTATIVE WRITING

In making up your mind whether to write an argumentative essay or a persuasive one, you need to think about the kind of person you are. Do you like enthusiastically championing a viewpoint of your own? If this is the case, perhaps a persuasive essay would suit you best. Or do you prefer to take a cool, balanced view of a current 'hot' topic and to give a measured survey of both sides? If so, then you might enjoy the challenges of argumentative writing.

Organising an introduction

In argumentative writing, as in its persuasive counterpart, the opening paragraph is particularly important for establishing your credentials as a trustworthy investigator of the topic. It needs to suggest you're reliably informed, clear-sighted in your appraisal of the opposing viewpoints and well-organised in your presentation of material.

Let's see how an introduction for this kind of essay might work by looking more closely at our earlier introduction to an argumentative essay on CCTV.

How you organise these elements in your own essay will probably depend on the topic and your approach, but the important thing is to make the stance of the two sides clear and establish the significance of the subject.

CCTV: big benefit or Big Brother?	• The title itself balances both viewpoints. Note the order in which they appear.
In this age of terrorism, there are few areas of cities which are not under the surveillance of CCTV cameras.	• Significance of topic established in first sentence.
They transmit images to a central control to monitor security in places where security might be an issue.	• Topic defined in second sentence.
For some, it is a comfort that suspicious behaviour does not go unnoticed, thereby limiting potential attacks of all kinds.	• Sentence three outlines one side of the argument – the positive.
Among civil liberties groups, however, there is grave suspicion that this surveillance could be abused by unscrupulous governments to spy on their citizens in the way prophesied by George Orwell in his novel 1984.	• Sentence four outlines the other side – the negative.
A balanced view requires us to examine how, in an increasingly violent world, CCTV cameras can help keep us safe and, at the same time, to study the validity of claims regarding potential abuse of surveillance material.	• Sentence five suggests how essay will develop by a) looking at benefits and b) examining darker side.

The language of argument

In an argumentative essay, you're **not** out to win over readers as you are in a persuasive essay. Your approach is rather more cool-headed, avoiding emotive vocabulary and persuasive devices.

Where the persuasive essay is often informal and colloquial, the argumentative one is neutral in its choice of language. Where the persuasive essay is **subjective** in its approach to the topic (in other words, it's the very personal views of the writer which are being presented), the argumentative essay is **objective** in its attitude to the topic (that is, information is examined in purely factual terms with no personal slant colouring its presentation).

So how does neutral, formal tone show itself in writing?

Vocabulary choice

Words and expressions you might use when talking to your friends are not really appropriate if you're targeting formal tone in an argumentative essay.

Sentence structure

Formal tone avoids minor or one-word sentences of the kind you might use in persuasive writing. Sentences might tend to be longer here and be composed of several subordinate clauses. For example – 'This is a subject **which**, **while** it may be of concern to older people, is not of primary interest to teenagers **whose** concerns are more travel-focused.'

Pronoun usage

Be wary when using pronouns. Of course, you may need to use them, but use them sparingly, particularly 'I' and 'you' which immediately introduce a very personal note. ('I', of course, will be needed if and when you come to give a final verdict in the conclusion of your argumentative essay.) 'We' can be useful when discussing the public perception of something – 'Over the years, we have become accustomed to ...' But use of the third-person narrative reinforces formality of tone more firmly – 'the public has become accustomed to ...'.

Informal commands – 'Imagine how ... consider for a moment ...' – might best be avoided since they lead you into a 'you' situation. For example, 'imagine how you would feel ...' and 'consider for a moment what you might ...' are phrases more appropriate for a persuasive essay than an argumentative one.

Abbreviations

Formal writing avoids abbreviations such as 'it's', 'there's', 'that's' and 'doesn't'. They add a chattiness which this more detached form of writing seeks to avoid.

Punctuation

When writing formally, be wary of exclamation marks. They suggest the anger, excitement or surprise that you might find in persuasive writing. Rhetorical questions also suggest personal involvement. Your appeal here is to the head, not the heart. But in putting forward a reasoned case you may find colons and semi-colons a useful addition to full stops and commas.

Classroom challenge

In this extract, the writer is using an informal, chatty style to discuss underage drinking. Rewrite the paragraph in a more formal, objective style using some of the guidelines we've suggested. There's no one correct answer here; what matters is presenting the topic in more neutral and detached language.

> So if politicians really want to do something about stopping some teenagers drinking themselves senseless, they need to tell supermarkets where they get off. It's no good giving pubs a bad time about underage drinking if, once chucked out, the same guys can get their big brother to nip into a supermarket for their favourite tipple. And get it a whole lot cheaper! Until pubs and supermarkets are both singing the same tune and upping prices so it hurts, the politicians are strictly up the creek without a paddle on this one.

Ordering you arguments

A convincing argumentative essay should flow, with no sudden or unexplained change of direction to jar or puzzle readers. Sensible ordering of ideas and thoughtful linking will strengthen your case-making skills in the eyes of the marker. But how will you ensure this seamless flow of ideas and text?

A first step would be to examine your evidence to decide where your final verdict falls. Are you for or against the idea under discussion? Suppose you had decided you were **for** CCTV as discussed earlier; you might usefully consider the following order of presentation:

- An introduction which sets out both sides but places the positive second.
- Following paragraphs deal with the negative side of CCTV.
- Leading to paragraphs examining CCTV's benefits.
- A summative conclusion making clear where you stand on CCTV – in other words, in favour of it.

Why this particular order?

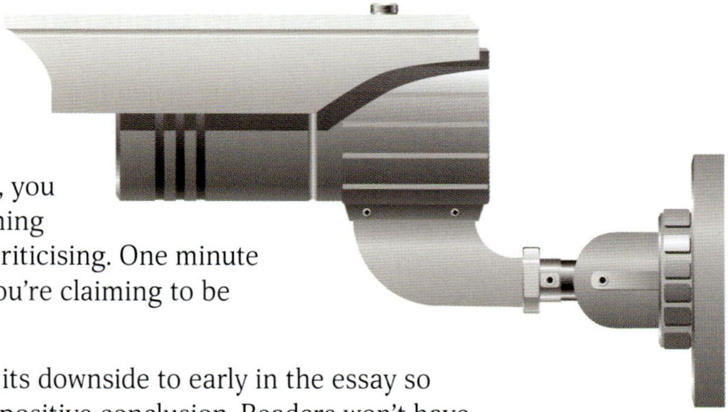

Well, suppose you were in favour of CCTV but left discussing its downside until the second part of your essay. Consider, then, the effect on your readers if, in the very next, concluding paragraph, you abruptly announced you were in favour of something which, a few lines before, you had been expertly criticising. One minute you're pointing out the flaws of CCTV; the next you're claiming to be in favour of it.

If you're in favour of a topic, banish discussion of its downside to early in the essay so that your positive case seamlessly precedes your positive conclusion. Readers won't have forgotten your negative points, but the positive ones will be fresher in their minds. Your approval of these positive arguments will appear more understandable and logical.

The reverse also holds good: if you're against an issue, acknowledge its benefits first and then discuss its shortcomings so that your conclusion follows on naturally from a discussion of these shortcomings.

Withholding a personal verdict

If you decide to withhold a final opinion of your own, be careful how you do so. This is a perfectly legitimate position to take up, but make sure you give a reason: current lack of credible evidence, rapidly changing situation, or perhaps a final verdict depends on individual political/social/cultural views. Try to give reasons for your rejection of settling for one side or the other, otherwise you might appear to be simply a ditherer!

Reflecting your thoughtfulness

Discursive writing requires you to present yourself as a thoughtful, informed commentator. In your essay, you should be putting forward a well-considered case which reflects this thoughtfulness. (Even in the most enthusiastic of persuasive essays!)

Avoid sweeping statements in argumentative writing; very few situations in life are strictly black or white. Try to avoid claims such as 'This proves conclusively that ...'. or 'This definitely shows that ...' The auxiliary verbs such as 'may', 'might' and 'could' are your friends, as are adjectives such as 'possible', 'probable', 'conceivable' and 'likely' when it comes to making claims. Introductory phrases along the lines of the following are helpful when fine-tuning your claims:

'This tends to suggest that ...'
'It has been suggested that ...'
'This could be seen as evidence ...'
'It is probable that ...'
'According to some observers ...'
'On available data it could be argued that ...'
'It could be argued that ...'
'There are those who consider ...'

These are just a few phrases which help qualify claims you might wish to make in argumentative writing. You can probably think of lots more.

Classroom challenge

Look at these sweeping generalisations below, then qualify them in as many ways as you can to make them intellectually defensible statements. Try to find at least three qualifying phrases for each one. Vary them as much as you can.

Continuous assessment is better than examinations to determine a student's ability.
Leicester City's success was a mere twist of fate.
Wind farms are not cost-effective.
American cars are inferior to European ones.
CCTV simply drives crime to camera-free areas.
Geologists believe we are now living in the Anthropocene age.

Giving sources for discursive writing

Earlier in this section, we mentioned the importance of giving your sources for this kind of writing. These can be as informal as a discussion with your friends or family or a straw poll taken in your year group. However, to be fully credible, your list might usefully suggest your research went a bit further than that to include both library and online research. Be sure to list your online/library sources clearly in a way that could allow others to check out the same information.

Bear in mind that if you're thinking about going on to college or university, learning how to set out your sources in one of the accepted formats might be a useful skill. There are several recognised ways of setting out sources; coming up is one example of best practice. This is known as APA style (American Psychological Association) and is commonly used in British academic institutions. You might find it helpful in later years to understand how it works.

Referencing books

To reference books in the APA style:

Start with author's name: surname first, then initial. (Followed by the year of publication in brackets) *then comes the title in italics*. Then the city of publication: and, finally, the publisher.

A complete book reference should appear like this:

King, R. (2000) *Brunelleschi's Dome*. London: Penguin.

Referencing newspapers and magazine articles

To reference articles from newspapers or magazines:

Start with author's name: surname first, then initial. (Followed by the publication date in brackets.) Next include the title of the article itself. *Then the name of the publication should come in italics*. And, finally, the page reference.

A complete article reference should appear like this:

Goring, R. (2003, January 4) She's Talking Our Language Now. *The Herald*. p.14.

Electronically sourced material

To reference electronically sourced material:

Name of author (if available) and title of article/publication as you would for a print publication. In place of city of publication and name of publisher, put the web address and the date when the article was posted (if available) and, also, the date when you accessed it.

ONLINE

For more information on listing web addresses, head to www.brightredbooks.net

DON'T FORGET

All references should be arranged in alphabetical order – this should be by the first letter of the author's surname or by the name of the website if there's no author listed!

GROUP B ACTIVITIES

1. Introductions

The following paragraphs are six introductions to discursive essays. Three are argumentative, three are persuasive: can you identify which is which? You may want to refer back to the earlier sections of this chapter to remind yourself of the differences.

The introductions are of varying quality. Can you identify which are more effective, and explain why?

For extra practice, why not rewrite the weaker introductions to improve their quality, or to change the argumentative introductions into persuasive introductions, and vice versa?

The world is in crisis. Billions of humans, across the globe, are addicted to a poison that is slowly killing them. A multi-billion-dollar business that thrives on exploiting the weaknesses in human nature for profit. But what is this dangerous drug? It isn't heroin or cocaine. It's not nicotine or alcohol, or social media either. No, the drug that's tearing us apart is sugar.

Immigration. A sensitive subject, to say the least. Setting aside the polarising rhetoric of the Brexit campaigns though, the impact of immigration on Britain remains significant. On the one hand, we need immigration: an aging population means an increase in pension pay outs and a decrease in taxpayers funding those pensions. On the other hand, social services like housing, schools and the NHS are facing unprecedented financial stresses, and that pressure needs to be relieved. This is such an important issue, that we cannot allow partisan demagogues and party politics to dominate the discussion: what role does immigration play in Britain's future?

Indyref. Brexit. The public has spoken, twice. The public have voiced their opinions, clearly. Twice. And the public have got it wrong. Twice. It is clear, looking at the aftermath of the two referendums that have dominated politics since 2014, that the public can't be trusted with important decisions. How could anyone with two brain cells to rub together have trusted 'the vow' that the Unionist parties offered at the 11th hour? Was anyone really gullible enough to believe that a millionaire banker, Nigel Farage, was really a 'man of the people'? Seriously? There's only one clear conclusion to draw from this: the public can't be trusted, we need to ban referendums.

When I read that a family in Italy risked losing their child for daring to raise them vegan, I nearly choked on my soy-milk and cornflakes. How can raising a child to value all life be wrong? How can teaching our children to empathise with animals be 'child abuse'? How can the idea that we should spare animals unnecessary suffering and death be so controversial? It's absurd. Clearly raising a thinking, feeling creature in order to slaughter it and consume its flesh is immoral. Clearly raping an animal, forcibly impregnating it, then dragging its offspring away is indefensible. The truth, uncomfortable as it may be, is clear: raising our children as anything but vegan is child abuse.

Reading is important. Everyone knows this, even people who don't read. Studies show that what you read when you're at school will determine your university education, your career trajectory, your income when you're an adult. No-one wants to appear illiterate or poorly educated. So why don't more people read? What are schools doing wrong? Could it be the choice of texts? Is Pip's journey in *Great Expectations* really relevant to a modern teenager? Are his struggles with social class, money, and love the same as today's issues with Instagram, cyberbullying and Pokémon Go? Is *Hamlet* a fascinating deconstruction of a beautiful mind, revealing fundamental truths about human nature, procrastination, grief and madness? Or is it a boring bunch of gobbledegook about a bonkers Dane? Or both, maybe? It is important that the literature we teach in schools is of a good quality, yes, but it is also important that it excites the imagination, the way *Harry Potter* and *The Hunger Games* do. Has classic literature had its day in schools? Is it time for something more modern?

2016 was jam-packed with bad news. Bowie's death. Brexit. Trump. Worst of all, though? *Bake Off* is moving to Channel 4. The horror! OK, so the hyperbolic reaction to this news was over the top, but it raised an important question about the future of the BBC; how much of its budget should be spent on maintaining proven successes, like *The Great British Bake Off*, or *Strictly Come Dancing*? Should those be allowed to move to a commercial channel, while the BBC focused on more, new, cheaper shows? In a world with Netflix and Amazon Prime Video, with satellite and cable TV, with the internet at our fingertips, on TVs, consoles, tablets and even in our pockets, on our phones ... just what is the BBC for?

2. Line of argument

Five paragraphs have been removed from this article by Elena Orde from *The Independent* newspaper.

Read the article and work out which of the five paragraphs (A to E) fits in which gap (1 to 5). Think about how the paragraph would relate to the paragraph that came before and try to identify words and phrases that link forwards and backwards. It's important that your own discursive writing is similarly 'woven' together carefully in a logical order.

Vegan diets for children aren't abusive – raising a child to eat meat is actually more extreme

You may have seen recent news stories about a malnourished child who was removed from his parents. A sad case, of course, but given that malnutrition affects over 3 million people in the UK, why has this particular story made international headlines? Because the child was vegan.

1

Let's debunk the health claims first. Vegan diets can be suitable for anyone, of any age. That's the position of the British Dietetic Association, the qualified experts. Vegan or otherwise, all parents should take care to ensure that their children get the right nutrition. But, given that babies and children can get everything they need and more from a vegan diet, why does the concept provoke such judgement, fear and anger?

We raise children to love animals, to care for and protect them. From talking cows and chickens in picture-books, to TV shows like *Peppa Pig*, to pretty much every Disney film, animals take centre stage, and children are encouraged to empathise with them.

2

Children are then conditioned to see meat as food, and to forget it was once part of a living, breathing animal. Most parents wouldn't dream of telling their kids how animals are killed, presumably because the truth is considered inappropriate to explain to young children. But if the truth is too disturbing, surely we should stop funding it, rather than help to keep it hidden.

3

Vegans are often penalised for 'forcing' their child to eat like them. But it's unreasonable to expect a vegan parent to give their children chicken nuggets and cheese toasties just because this is what most people do. All parents make decisions on behalf of their children – left to their own devices, kids would wear toilet paper and eat glitter.

4

Of course, any child can choose to change their diet when they're old enough. People raising vegan children simply want this to be a choice informed by facts and compassion rather than habit. Instead of teaching children to love cats and dogs, and eat cows and pigs, vegans teach their children to care for and value the lives of all animals – a far more consistent viewpoint.

5

A

When children are simultaneously fed meat and other products taken from animals, this sends a very confusing message. Children are often upset when they find out that the meat on their plate comes from the animals they have been taught to love. Who can blame them? By that age, children already understand that animals can feel pain and distress, have desires and emotions and don't want to die – just like them.

B

Vegan diets are often described as being controversial or extreme. But if we know we can live healthy, happy lives without killing animals, what now seems the most controversial and extreme choice?

C

In the wake of this news, chat show *The Wright Stuff* posed the question, 'Is it abuse to put children on a vegan diet?' while the *Telegraph* asked 'Can vegans ever be good parents?' You can spot the media bias a mile off.

D

It's important for children to understand about nutrition and to know where their food comes from. But 'tales from the slaughterhouse' tends to not make the cut for bedtime reading. A school trip to an orchard sounds far better than one to an abattoir.

E

A vegan parent will have chosen their lifestyle for all kinds of reasons: be it love for animals, concern about the environment, or a desire to improve their own health. Why wouldn't they want to share all of these benefits with the people most important to them?

TEACHING NOTES

You can download Teaching Notes for these activities at www.brightredpublishing.co.uk/Shop/national-5-english-course-book

WAYS OF WORKING

MANAGING YOUR FOLIO

Writing can be a fairly lonely business. The need for concentration tends to make us want to shut ourselves away to get on with the task. Of course, you'll maybe have discussed your choice of Folio pieces with a friend or two and will have shown a plan to your teacher. But, once your plan has been approved, you'll probably have set about your first draft in some quiet corner of the library or at home, perhaps showing the piece to somebody you know just before handing in the draft.

Now, friends being friends, and – catching sight of your neatly typed manuscript – they will probably make polite noises. But what do they **really** think? If they can see that your work is already far advanced, they probably won't tell you in any great critical detail. So, can we really call this peer-reviewing? It's more like going through the motions.

Find a Folio friend!

A better method of working might be to find a 'Folio friend' **right at the beginning** of the Folio planning process; somebody whose judgement you respect and who knows you and your work fairly well, somebody you see and talk to regularly.

Involve them right from the beginning of the process, not just at the end.

As you discuss possibilities, check with the relevant section of this Study Guide to see how it could help you with the various genres. Previewing your intentions is as important as reviewing your outcomes. Perhaps even more so.

DON'T FORGET

Previewing your intentions is as important as reviewing your outcomes.

Start with basics

Discuss together which genres for the Folio you are each contemplating. Go through this Study Guide, looking at the kinds of writing which attract you and in which you've maybe already shown some ability. How difficult do you think you're going to find an argumentative essay at this level? If you went for that option, what might you choose to write about?

Maybe you like the idea of personal reflective writing. Maybe you should revisit this territory. Bounce ideas off each other. List potential genres and discuss together the pros and cons of each one. Spend considerable time at this stage before ever thinking of a specific title or topic, before planning or drafting a single word. Time well spent here will probably save you a lot of time later on.

Research topics together

So maybe you've decided on an argumentative essay and prose fiction. Let's look at them, one by one. What controversial topic are you interested in exploring? Discuss together what's involved in gathering evidence. How difficult or easy might this be given the topic?

Is there any possibility that you could research a topic together, with your friend deciding on a persuasive essay and you an argumentative essay? By pooling your research, you would both become subject 'specialists', with your essays benefiting from the added depth and breadth of joint research?

Use this book's discursive section to help you try out some approaches to these kinds of writing. Does this kind of writing feel the right choice for you? What do you think? What does your partner think? Consult. Discuss. It's good to air your views, feelings and – yes – doubts at this early stage.

If you're considering a short story, a similar approach holds good. Is there an idea at the back of your mind? What does your partner make of it? A bit far-fetched? Too complicated for the word limit? Test out your ideas against the suggested processes in the prose section of this book.

Triangulate advice

Teachers also have their roles to play in this process. Once you've discussed your general intentions with your partner and teacher, the time has probably come to shape up a plan for your teacher's inspection. Once you have the feedback, you're in the healthy position of having a triple perspective on the plan.

Consult regularly

Don't be in any hurry to complete the first draft. Your plan will have broken down the essay into several sections. Consult with your partner at each stage of creating these sections. If you were working on an argumentative essay, the process might go like this:

- **Introduction**. After having checked what this book has to say about introductions, does your partner feel your introduction is appropriate? Are there parts missing? Is the opening sentence too dull?

- **Body paragraphs.** In a discursive essay, are they sufficient to explore fully your topic? How strong are the opening statements in each section? How convincing is the evidence you're producing? Does your commentary on the evidence do the evidence full justice?
- **Conclusion.** Check again with this book to see if your conclusion matches up with what an examiner might expect. Does your partner agree with how you have rounded off your discussion of this topic? Are there any lingering weaknesses in their opinion?

Whatever genres you choose to explore for the Folio, adopt a similar approach with your chosen partner for each of your two pieces. Finally, remember that the examiners are looking for work that reveals appropriate:

- content,
- structure, and
- expression,
- technical accuracy.

Make sure at this stage that each of these four criteria is being given sufficient attention. You'll find that the interchange of ideas with your partner on all these points will strengthen not only your work but your self-confidence, too, as you proceed to the completion of the Folio.

Continue the process

After your teacher has seen and made suggestions on how the draft might be improved, talk over the proposed changes with your partner. Re-draft the areas that need adjusting.

DON'T FORGET

Use email to keep in touch with your partner. This way, changes and improvements can be implemented more quickly and don't need to wait for a face-to-face encounter.

ONLINE

Check out 'SQA Study Guides' at www.brightredbooks.net for further useful information on how to manage your time.

PROOFREADING YOUR FOLIO

In the long process of preparing your drafts, you'll likely have made numerous changes: perhaps a missing sentence was added, perhaps you inserted a quotation from a leading authority, or maybe you changed the order of certain paragraphs. This is all for the good. This is how a serious writing process should happen.

But there are hazards, too. As a result of all these improvements, irritating glitches may have crept in while you were concentrating on drafting the major changes. Minor they may seem, but nevertheless they count against you in terms of technical accuracy. And more than a few interesting Folios fail each year on the grounds of technical inaccuracies. So, how do we avoid or eliminate them?

Leave time

Don't leave finalising your 'polished' draft to the last minute. If you allow yourself sufficient time, you can put your essay aside for some time before the due date and come back to it fresh for a final read-through. You will be astonished how many slip-ups you'll notice straight away, slip-ups which totally escaped your notice in the white heat of drafting.

Read aloud

Here's where your Folio friend can come in useful again. Reading a text through silently to yourself to check for errors can be unreliable. We tend to 'read' what we **think** we see, rather than what's actually on the page. Reading it aloud – preferably in the presence of your Folio friend – will be a safeguard against this very human failing.

Furthermore, hearing sentences read aloud can often help detect clumsy expressions or sentences which either go on too long or don't quite make sense.

Check linkage

A good essay, whether it be discursive, personal, reflective or creative, needs to maintain a smooth flow from beginning to end. The introduction must flow into body paragraphs and they, in turn, must run smoothly into each other before merging satisfyingly into your conclusion. Reading aloud will also help here. That clumsy, unprepared-for change of topic will immediately be obvious to the ear when read aloud, although it may have slipped by unnoticed on countless silent readings. There are the basics to demonstrate sequence such as:

'Firstly, ...' 'Furthermore, ...' 'In addition, ...' 'What is more, ...' 'Finally, ...'

These show simple progression from one topic to another. But you may wish to use connectives of transition to move your reader from one topic to the next:

'Now, while it is true to say that ...'

'As far as ... is concerned, ...'

'Turning to ...'

'Regarding the question of ...'

And if you want to introduce a brief aside to your reader there is always '*Incidentally, ...*'

If you wish to change direction from a preceding comment you have various choices:

'On the other hand, however, ...'

'By way of contrast, there is ...'

'Conversely, ...'

Spell check

Yes, you've got a spell-checker on your computer, but there's only so much it can spot. It'll help you out with the more difficult words but it won't help you when you accidentally type 'bit' when you mean 'but'. Even in university dissertations, examiners constantly complain of finding the following very basic errors. Don't spoil fine work with confusing elementary items like these:

- were/we're/where
- too/to/two
- its/it's
- who's/whose
- they're/their/there
- lose/loose

Better still, go over **now** all the words you know you've been getting wrong in your essays for years. Get them right once and for all! You know which ones I mean!

Check punctuation

From your preparation for RUAE, you should have a sound knowledge of how punctuation works in creating certain effects. Make sure you apply this knowledge to your own writing. Be particularly careful with direct speech in short stories or personal/reflective writing:

WRONG: 'Well, I suppose you've talked to Jean', she sighed.

CORRECT: 'Well, I suppose you've talked to Jean,' she sighed.

Above all, avoid the comma splice: the joining together of two independent statements incorrectly with the use of only a comma.

WRONG: It was a fine spring morning, Hamish decided to go for a walk by the shore.

CORRECT: It was a fine spring morning. Hamish decided to go for a walk by the shore.

CORRECT: It being a fine spring morning, Hamish decided to go for a walk by the shore.

CORRECT: Since it was a fine morning, Hamish decided to go for a walk by the shore.

A comma will not do the connecting! Either use a full stop to acknowledge that these are two independent clauses or statements, or use connecting mechanisms such as the above. If in doubt, consult your teacher.

Check agreement

In longer sentences, where the subject may have become separated from the rest of the sentence – including the verb – make sure you've not started with a singular subject and ended up with a plural verb, or vice versa.

DON'T FORGET

You've had plenty of time to prepare your Folio pieces. So, imagine the poor impression you'll give the marker if you leave spelling mistakes and typos in your final version.

ONLINE

For more resources on proofreading, click the 'BBC Skillswise: Editing and Proofreading' link at www.brightredbooks.net

LISTENING AND TALKING

THE IMPORTANCE OF LISTENING AND TALKING

So far, we've covered critical reading and critical writing skills. Now it's time to look at skills for listening and talking (in groups and in solo mode).

These are not only skills you'll need for this course; they are two of the greatest skills you can acquire for your career beyond school.

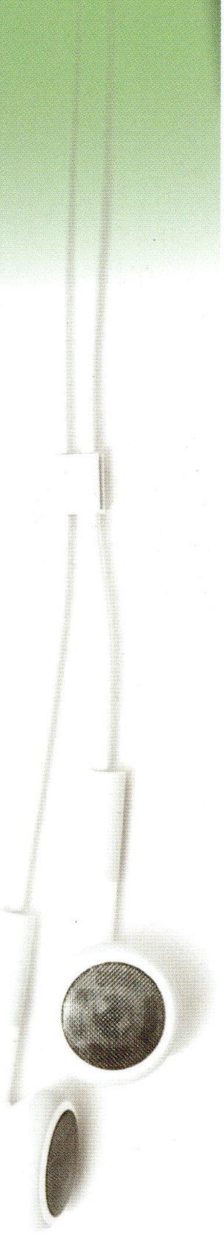

Whether you want to work in the world of commerce, public service, academia, science, medicine or media, you'll discover you spend a great deal of your time attending meetings of one kind or another. Being able to function effectively in this environment will be a great career plus. So, studying how best to develop skills for talking and listening in group discussions, or how to present your own ideas effectively, is time very well spent. Let's look first at effective listening and how to acquire effective listening techniques.

ONLINE

Check out the article about how important listening skills are in business at www.brightredbooks.net

BEING AN EFFECTIVE LISTENER

If we're honest with ourselves, we all have a tendency to be lazy listeners. We switch on the TV, we select an MP3 track, we ask a friend how they are – and then we get distracted. The sounds carry on, but our mind is often elsewhere – although, if challenged, we'll hotly claim that we have been 'listening'.

Effective listening requires mental discipline. It also means being able to respond intelligently to what's being said. So how do we acquire the discipline needed to focus accurately on what's being said, filtering out the distractions around us? A simple checklist for good listening behaviour helps:

Adopt a positive attitude to the subject

Perhaps on the surface the subject doesn't appear particularly interesting to you. You cannot, however, afford to lose concentration. If you listen passively, letting the information wash over you, you'll lose marks. Listen **actively**; don't make negative assumptions about the interest or complexity of what you're going to hear; and keep alert. You may be surprised by the turn the talk takes.

Be ready to react

Active listening means being ready to react to what's being said with your own response, be it a plea for more evidence, a clarification of a difficult point, or a development of a good point already made. Jotting down points you might want to raise later is always useful. (But keep listening!)

Adopt a positive attitude to the speaker

Ignore distractions such as appearance, personality, weak delivery, accent, or mannerisms. It's the message not the messenger that counts. And don't lose concentration or patience because they adopt an opinion that doesn't coincide with yours.

Avoid external distractions

The view from the window, whispering behind you, the heat in the room and pre-lunch stomach rumbling are all very human distractions which can disturb concentration long enough for you to miss a key point.

Concentrate on central ideas

Don't let interesting stories or examples blind you to the reason for their inclusion in the talk. They are there to illustrate a point; they are not usually the point in themselves. Are there clues in the opening statements that indicate what the central ideas of the upcoming sections might be? Note them down. Listen for ideas, not individual words.

Be alert to the nonverbal

The emotional tone of the speaker may be saying as much, or more, about underlying feelings as the surface content of their words. Emotions are less easy to control than words. Skilled listening involves listening for messages which the speaker's voice, rather than words, may be unconsciously signalling. As in group discussion, body language can also give important hints as to the speaker's attitude and involvement. (We'll have more to say about body language in the discussion section.)

Make notes that matter

Trying to jot down everything that's said is not only impossible, it's distracting you from what IS being said. Make notes brief, concentrating on key ideas and keywords or phrases. And write them so they are readable afterwards! Write down, too, points you may want to raise yourself in response to what you have been listening to.

Classroom challenge

Practice in listening effectively

Watch and then listen to the TED talk 'Cameron Russell: Looks aren't everything. Believe me, I'm a model' at www.brightredbooks.net. Make notes as you listen.

Once you've listened, try to answer these questions in as much detail as you can and using your own words as far as possible:

1. Sum up Russell's overall view of modelling as a career. To back up your answer, what evidence would you point to?
2. How persuasive did Russell seem to be as a speaker? You could consider:
- her tone of voice,
- her gestures/mannerisms, and
- her attitude to others.

TALKING EFFECTIVELY IN DISCUSSION

WHAT MAKES A GOOD DISCUSSION?

So far, we've looked at developing basic listening skills. But those skills are not an end in themselves. We need to go a step further. How best can we put these listening skills to work for us? The most profitable result of good listening is being able to participate fully in a discussion.

As we touched on before, through active listening you can do a whole variety of things: you can ask for clarifications; you can ask for more evidence; you can develop a point of the speaker; you can challenge the argument; you can evaluate the speaker's contribution. However, all these talking activities first require sound listening skills, hence the preparatory exercises you have been doing.

In a group discussion, a number of participants exchange information and opinions on a given topic, problem or issue. In this exchange of views, agreement may or may not be achieved. But, for the discussion to succeed, each member has an obligation to make a significant contribution in helping add depth to the deliberations. Listening is not enough; participation is required by all. Each member must approach the group with an open mind, genuinely prepared to listen as well as to argue their point of view.

It's an activity in which your knowledge of the techniques of **persuasion** – which you learn about when studying persuasive writing – can again be made to work for your success. As you speak, think about how you might introduce, for example, **repetition** or **attitude markers** or **rhetorical questions**. Which others could you employ? Check out the list of persuasive writing techniques on page 158. You might be surprised at the extent their use will add to your authority – and boost your self-confidence.

In a good group discussion, you'll probably hear views that you strongly disagree with, but you must respect your opponent's point of view and their right to hold it. If, that is, you expect your own opinions to be given the same courtesy.

DON'T FORGET

A successful group discussion should leave **all** participants feeling they have contributed meaningfully to a full and balanced exploration of a subject. If you feel unhappy with your contribution, what will you need to do next time to improve matters? Listen more carefully? Participate more fully?

WHAT ARE THE ORAL SKILLS REQUIRED?

You now know quite a lot about listening skills. But what about the oral skills you'll need for a discussion? Let's look at how best to put forward your case.

Be concise

Other people are waiting to take part; make your case fully (with detailed information) but avoid being too long-winded. Don't hog the discussion!

Be clear

Clear expression is a sign of clear thinking. Avoid over-complicated sentences which will lose the attention of your fellow participants. Present ideas in a logical order which is easy to follow. Good sentence structure will help you here.

Be natural

Remember you're talking **to** people, not at them. Anything which sounds rehearsed sounds stilted, false and generally unconvincing. Cultivate a natural-sounding delivery in straightforward language. If you have an accent, be proud of it. It's part of you.

Be positive

Present persuasively the benefits/advantages of your viewpoint rather than insisting on the shortcomings/disadvantages of your opponent's. When you need to disagree, do so politely in unaggressive language.

Be persuasive

Be careful not to sound threatening in your approach to the topic. Use language with which others can agree. Remember, you're seeking support for your views. Win them over with your reasonable-sounding, considered stance. Use some of the persuasive techniques you learnt about when writing persuasive essays on page 158.

Be reactive

Don't be shy about picking up a point made by someone else and asking them to explain it further. Seeking clarification is an excellent way of moving on a discussion. Challenging (politely) a point of view is also an excellent way of demonstrating you've been an able listener. React, too, to the level of formality of the discussion. Sometimes, practice discussions might be fairly informal affairs; at other times, you'll need to adopt a more formal tone for more serious assessment discussions.

DON'T FORGET

A good discussion will often find you getting emotionally involved. But don't lose your temper over views that you disagree with, or with the people putting them forward. Keep your language calm to win and then retain the support of neutral members of the group. Nobody likes Mr Angry!

Classroom challenge

Think about and discuss with a partner how successful or otherwise you find the following extracts from a group discussion.

- How appropriate and/or persuasive would you rate these comments?
- Where you feel the participants have gone wrong, what alternative ways of expression would you suggest?

Use the guidelines above to help you evaluate. Identify any persuasive techniques being used.

I hear what you are saying, but surely discussing colour is not necessarily a sign of being a racist?

Yes, he's a fool. Yes, he's unreliable. But look at his generous actions, look at his willingness to admit his mistakes. Who couldn't warm to this side of the man?

What I value about the film is its supremely life-enhancing view of humanity, which is uplifting not to say astutely penetrating in its attitude to life.

It's not that I'm against this war, it's just that it's, you know, difficult to be for something that's, well, like killing innocent folk where life is difficult, what with the famine ... and stuff, like ...

I understand your point, I sympathise with your feelings and while I agree to a certain extent, I can't fully go along with your claim that exams are a total waste of time. For a start, they ...

Listen! You've totally misunderstood what the book is about. How wrong can you be?!

TEACHING NOTES

Download the Teaching Notes for this challenge at www.brightredpublishing.co.uk/Shop/national-5-english-course-book

A GOOD DISCUSSION NEEDS MORE THAN ORAL SKILLS

IS MY BODY LANGUAGE HELPING MY CASE?

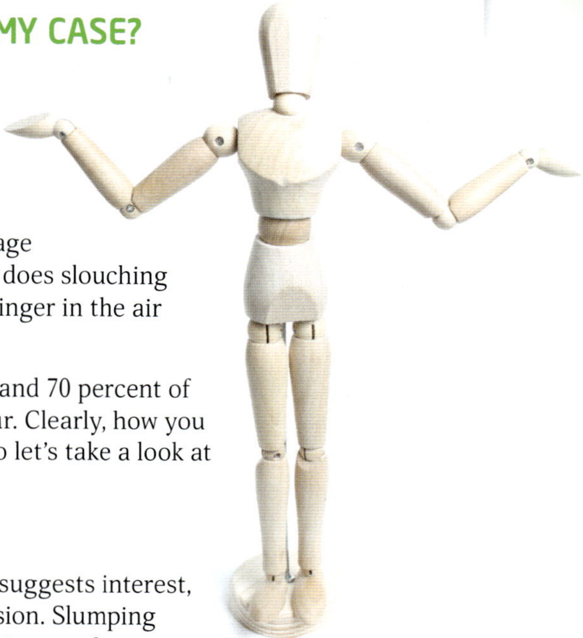

A successful group discussion is not just about **what** you say (although sound, detailed content is important); it's also about **how** you say it. You need to show yourself as being part of a group as well as part of a discussion. That means being as aware of your body language as of your oral input. For instance, what signals does slouching back in your chair send out? Or stabbing your finger in the air to make a point?

One researcher has suggested that between 60 and 70 percent of all meaning is derived from nonverbal behaviour. Clearly, how you sit and behave during the discussion matters, so let's take a look at what body language adds to group discussions.

Body posture

Find a comfortable position to sit in, one which suggests interest, and alert but relaxed engagement in the discussion. Slumping back in your chair might suggest boredom; leaning too far forward might suggest aggression.

Eye contact

Engage with the group as a whole. Fixing your attention on any one member might suggest lack of confidence; looking around the group reassures members that you're addressing them all and that you value everyone's opinion.

Hand gestures

Many people find it natural to express themselves with hand movements as well as words. This is not a problem here unless the gestures hint at aggression, for example, finger pointing or table thumping. Or if they become distracting and irritating to the group.

DON'T FORGET

Be an active listener as well as an active talker. Follow what others are saying. Show by your facial expression that you're taking in what's being said, whether as a supporter or critic. It helps speakers to gauge how well or badly they are getting through to their listeners.

A successful discussion requires the full cooperation of the group. Everyone must be prepared to talk, listen, show their involvement, respect the opinion of others and keep the flow of discussion moving to ensure that, at its completion, the discussion has enriched everyone's knowledge and understanding of the topic.

Here are two challenges which will help you evaluate the importance of body language in a group discussion.

DON'T FORGET

Note-taking while others are speaking suggests serious engagement with what's being said. It is also helpful to you should you want to seek clarification later, support or disagree with particular points, or use the information for an essay of your own.

Classroom challenge

Challenge 1

Study with a partner these participants in a group discussion and suggest what their body language, facial expression and hand gestures signal. How well or badly do you consider them to be performing in the discussion? Give your reasons.

Classroom challenge

Challenge 2

Form yourselves into groups of four or five. Consider this:

You have been stranded on a desert island. What three items would you want to have with you? Take a few minutes to make notes before starting (so you can back up your items with sensible reasoning). When you finish, check out these areas of your discussion and award your group a grade.

	REALLY WELL	SATISFACTORY	COULD HAVE BEEN MUCH BETTER
Avoided awkward pauses			
Balanced group participation			
Kept on task			
Group harmony			
Body language			
Active listening/responding			

TEACHING NOTES

Download the Teaching Notes for these challenges at www.brightredpublishing.co.uk/Shop/national-5-english-course-book

HOW TO GET THE BEST OUT OF YOUR GROUP

One way is to allocate roles to the various group members. So that once each person knows their role, they can intervene appropriately. What might these roles be?

The chairperson

The chairperson or leader will:

- introduce the topic and suggest what form the discussion will take,
- invite each member of the group to participate in turn,
- listen carefully to ensure the group remains on task/topic,
- ensure a balanced discussion, encouraging quieter members to talk and discouraging any one member from dominating the discussion, and
- listen carefully to intervene if conflict between members threatens.

The reporter

The reporter or recorder will:

- listen carefully for the main points in each contribution,
- make notes of the key points made during the discussion,

- summarise the outcome, outlining any divisions of opinion which emerged, and
- report back to the class on the findings of the group.

The individual member

Each individual group member will:

- provide personal, relevant and substantial ideas/opinions/experiences,
- listen carefully and take account of what others have to say,
- show support, raise questions or doubts, or seek clarification on contributions,
- make notes on points which might be raised later as a result of the contribution of others, and
- avoid interrupting the contributions of others until they are complete.

DON'T FORGET

Over the course of the term, it's a good idea to rotate the roles of chairperson and reporter around all members of the group so that everyone gets the benefit of developing these important life skills.

DON'T FORGET

Criticise an idea by all means, but don't attack the person putting it forward. Use **reason** not **emotion** to show what you think the shortcomings of the idea or argument are.

Team-building Talk

A good group discussion will often arouse strong feelings in the participants. Open conflict, however, is the enemy of progress. Good group discussion manners require you to choose your language carefully and think of the feelings of others when formulating your comments. That doesn't mean you avoid making your point strongly; you just do it in a way that doesn't upset the atmosphere in the group. This means the debate doesn't hit a brick wall of hostility.

Homework helper

Here are some dos and don'ts of discussion language. In which category would you place each one? Pair up what you think is the 'good' comment with the 'bad' one.

'Don't say!' or 'Do say!':

1. I think I see what you're getting at, but perhaps a few more details might help?

2. This is doing my head in. Just what are we on about here?

3. Am I the only one who's a bit lost here? Maybe we need to get back to the original question.

4. Since we only have a few minutes left, maybe we should move on to the next point.

5. I'm bored. Haven't we done this point to death?

6. Christine, you're bit quiet there. Would you agree with Mike on that point?

7. You've gone on long enough! Give other folk a chance.

8. Time's running on. Maybe someone else would like to come in here?

9. For heaven's sake, Christine, you must have something to say.

10. And what's that supposed to mean, eh? Ever heard of facts and figures?

TEACHING NOTES

Download the Teaching Notes for these challenges at www.brightredpublishing.co.uk/Shop/national-5-english-course-book

Everything we've said here is about creating an atmosphere in which profitable discussion can flourish. Respecting these simple guidelines can create an environment where everyone is included, where everyone is respected and where everyone's opinion is valued. In this way, discussion progresses, knowledge is enriched and understanding increases.

A good discussion, a commentator once remarked, should generate more light than heat. Be careful to ensure your discussions do just that: create helpful enlightenment, not pointless hot air.

Classroom challenge

Imagine you're taking on the role of chairperson in a group discussion on the topic of cloning. (Or choose another subject you're familiar with.)

1. How will you introduce the topic? (For example, general background; your personal feelings towards the topic; a quotation by an authority on the subject; etc.?)
2. What words and phrases will you use to draw in your various group members?
3. What sort of language will you use to diffuse any conflicts which may arise. What will you say to move the discussion on?

4. What sort of language will you use to move the group back onto task should it lose its way?

Now share some of your examples with a partner or the class. Ask them to assess their appropriateness and effectiveness. Make a list of the expressions your partner/class found appropriate or effective in each case. These could come in very handy should your mind go blank in discussion!

TEACHING NOTES

Download the Teaching Notes for these challenges at www.brightredpublishing.co.uk/Shop/national-5-english-course-book

Classroom challenge

What is your discussion personality?

There's nothing like a group discussion for defining personality. What kind of personality do **you** project in a group discussion? For a very brief overview of personality types, watch the video '6 types of student you will meet in a group discussion' at www.brightredbooks.net. Do you recognise yourself?

You might feel this is an oversimplification of behaviour, but it's thought-provoking. To what extent do you agree with what's being said about the personalities of group participants?

Classroom challenge

How will you say that?

As you sit listening to others' contributions in your group discussion, you'll benefit from working out in your own mind what form of words your intervention is going to take. Our private thoughts often need to be polished up a little before we actually articulate them in the discussion.

Here are a few fairly common ones; try turning a private thought into an appropriate public comment.

PRIVATE THOUGHT	PUBLIC COMMENT
What on earth is Mark going on about? It's all his opinion. There's no evidence to back this up.	
If they go on about this point much longer, I'm going to nod off.	
He's hogging the discussion. Claire knows a lot more about this than him. Why doesn't she say something?	
I don't have anything to say here, but I need to say something!	
I'm lost. I thought this was supposed to be about solar energy?	

TEACHING NOTES

Download the Teaching Notes for these challenges at www.brightredpublishing.co.uk/Shop/national-5-english-course-book

TALKING EFFECTIVELY: GOING SOLO

The skills we have been focusing on in this unit will make you a much more effective listener and a considerably more persuasive participant in a group discussion. And there's an added bonus still.

With these skills successfully mastered, your capabilities for giving a solo presentation will also have been strengthened significantly. How? By listening to expert communicators such as Cameron Russell you've been exposed to some of the techniques for engaging an audience with your topic. And by intervening in group discussions you're learning how best to put across your point of view to win approval. A solo presentation is merely an extension of these skills. Like a group discussion, it's yet another useful way to demonstrate your talking – and listening – skills.

GETTING ORGANISED: MAKING USE OF YOUR RESEARCH

Now, if you've already written a persuasive essay, it might be profitable to make the research you've done for this work for you again – as the basis for a persuasive talk. Let's think about how we might go about this.

Listen to the best

Once you hear how experienced talkers go about holding an audience's attention, you'll be better placed to adapt their persuasive techniques to your own subject.

Tony Shapshak is just one of the expert speakers you can enjoy at the TED website. Watch his talk 'You don't need an app for that' via the link at www.brightredbooks.net

Here, Shapshak makes an ingenious case for persuading the audience that Africa is a centre of innovation. Notice how he uses rhetorical questions and humour to great effect. What else can we learn here? While you're listening, note down the persuasive techniques you hear at work. Could you adapt them for your own presentation?

DON'T FORGET

Remember, good listening is the basis of good talking! Check out some other TED speakers who may be presenting on topics you're interested in.

Revisit persuasive techniques

On page 153, we looked at some of the basic techniques for persuading readers to adopt your point of views in a written text. These are techniques which will work equally well in a presentation. Indeed, some of the examples detailed there originated in successful political presentations.

Decide on a structure

A good presentation requires as much, if not more, attention to structure as a good essay. Listeners don't have a text to refer to, so they need to feel reassured that you're taking them on a journey which they can follow easily.

Reassurance comes with the construction of a helpful introduction which shows you to be an informed commentator. Early on, too, it's a good idea to build in some 'signposting' to your structure. This may take many forms: an initial question, the answers to which form the basis of the rest of the presentation; the number of areas to be covered mentioned early on – and adhered to; or a past contrasted to a present. The nature of your subject will probably dictate the talk's structure – but always make sure there is one! Indicate it early on. And don't forget a satisfying conclusion which sums up your key points.

Remember that a presentation is not an essay

Although a persuasive essay and a presentation have much in common, they're not the same thing. An essay is meant to be read; a presentation is meant to be listened to. Listeners don't have a text in front of them, so they can't go back to read something they haven't quite followed.

A presentation must be easy to follow. That means sentence structure must be considered even more fully than in an essay. Keep sentences fairly short (which makes life easier for the listener) and keep them easy to articulate (which makes life easier for you). Stumbling over long-winded sentences is a sure-fire way to lose your audience. Repetition and parallel structures are particularly useful in presentations since the listeners are being prepared for what's to come. Similarly useful are devices which steer listeners from one topic to another ... 'Turning now to the financial benefits, it is easy to see ...' / 'But what of the poor pedestrians?' / 'Let's consider for a moment how this will affect education.'

Control body language

The best presentation in the world can be undermined by body language that irritates or distracts. Go back and check what we said on page 231 about body language in group discussions. Much of that advice is equally valid in a solo presentation.

Monitor voice production

You don't need to have the voice of Liam Neeson to succeed in a presentation. But you **do** need to be able to vary your tone regularly to avoid droning on in a monotone, a certain way to lose your audience, no matter how gripping the topic. Think, too, about slowing down from time to time to emphasise certain points, then pick up speed again. Vary the pace as you would vary sentence structure in an essay – it'll keep your audience engaged.

Keep to your purpose

In a presentation, never lose sight of your purpose. By all means, inform, stimulate and entertain, but keep your key intention well to the fore as you present your material. Make sure you've built in a variety of the persuasive techniques. Don't overuse any particular one.

Listen to questions

A good presentation usually elicits comments afterwards. Listen carefully to the comments and questions. Respond to them respectfully in the way you would respond to points raised in a group discussion. (Shy audiences may need some prompting to ask questions, so think about some ways to get the post-presentation interaction going.)

Practise at home

The bathroom mirror is a great audience! As is the family dog! Don't do the first run-through of your presentation at the assessment. Try it out several times on anyone who'll listen. Get the feel of it in your mouth. Change any words you stumble over. Shorten that sentence if it's difficult to say.

Classroom challenge

Making the most of your research

1. If you've already written a persuasive essay, go back and examine what you would need to do to turn it into a persuasive talk. How will your opening need to change? How will sentence structure need to be revised for the listener? Will any quotations need shortening or paraphrasing? Which persuasive techniques would improve your talk? Which personal pronouns will you be using?
2. If you haven't already written a persuasive essay, try sketching out a presentation on the topic: 'Cars should be banned from city centres'.

This topic doesn't necessarily require intensive research, so it can be put together quite quickly. Or, choose a similarly accessible subject of your own. See how you get on making persuasive techniques work for you.

GLOSSARY OF CRITICAL TERMS

At this stage of your studies, you need to be able to use the professional vocabulary of criticism to maximise the impact of your comments in spoken and written work. The following list is by no means definitive, but it gives you some of the more common terms to add to your critical vocabulary.

Alliteration	The repetition of a particular consonant – or consonant sound – at the beginning of a group of words to create a certain sound effect. 'Cold clay clads his coffin.' Here the harsh sound of the letter 'c' matches the grimness of the description. 'Soft sighing of the southern seas.' Here the soft 's' sounds mimics the gentleness of the water's sound.
Anecdote	A brief story, often encountered in RUAE passages, to illustrate a point.
Anti-climax	Often encountered when the final item in a list is the least important or oddly out of place. In RUAE work, the effect is usually to add humour.
Aside	A remark in a play that is intended to be heard only by the audience and not by other characters on scene.
Assonance	The repetition of a certain group of similar-sounding vowels in words close to each other, again used to create a certain aural effect – 'And murmuring of innumerable bees.' Assonance is to vowels what alliteration is to consonants.
Characterisation	The building up and establishing of convincing character portrayals through means such as dialogue, actions, the reaction of others to the character in question.
Connotation	The associations we carry about in our minds – often unthinkingly – about certain words. For example, we associate 'dove' with peace or 'rose' with love. Alternatively, verbs like 'cling' suggest an insecure, dependent frame of mind, while 'skip' suggests a light-hearted mood. Referring to connotations is often very useful for dealing with word choice or imagery questions in RUAE.
Context	In RUAE work you may be asked to suggest how the context helps you understand the meaning of a word. The context is the surrounding sentence or paragraph in which the word appears.
Denotation	Usually discussed in association with connotation. It is the dictionary definition of a word or term, free of the associations we have with connotations.
Ellipsis	In mid-sentence, these three dots can be used to suggest an interruption, hesitation or indecision. Used at the end of the sentence, they can suggest anticipation or suspense – 'The door opened and a hand appeared ...'
Enjambment	In poetry, this is the running on of one line into another or into several others, at times to give either a conversational feel to the content or sometimes to suggest a speeding up for an effect of urgency. It can also make the reader wait for a key point to be made when the sentence finally stops. '... for my purpose holds To sail beyond the sunset, and the baths Of all the western stars, until I die.'
Figurative language	This is language which uses figures of speech such as similes, metaphors, personification to create pictures ('figures') in our minds to make descriptions more vivid and graphic. Will often turn up in RUAE work and literature study. Useful, too, in persuasive writing
Foreshadow	Useful term for your critical essays or context work. A fairly minor event or incident can be said to 'foreshadow' a much more important one later in the text. It prepares the reader for a more significant event so that the later one is not wholly unexpected. For example, a mildly aggressive action can suggest a more violent one to come.
Genre	This is the type or category literature may fall into: poetry, drama, prose. Genre also categorises the type of writing you may select for your Folio: discursive or creative being the main genres here.

Hyperbole	This is the technical literary name for exaggeration. It is often used to create a certain effect (often humorous) or to emphasise something – 'The list goes on for miles.' 'He never fails to get lost.' 'I've seen more fat on a chip.' Hyperbole often turns up in tone questions in RUAE. Can also be useful in persuasive writing.
Image/imagery	A device used to create a picture ('image') in the mind which exploits the connotations (see above) of a word to give it greater impact on the reader. Frequently at the core of questions in RUAE work. Understanding of the working of imagery is also very necessary for commenting on literature and in your own creative writing where you wish to make a point with graphic vividness.
Irony	Often saying the opposite of what you mean – 'The concert lasts four hours? With no interval? Wonderful!' Used frequently in questions of tone in RUAE to criticise or mock something or somebody in a humorous or bitter way to make a critical point. Useful, too, in persuasive writing.
Literal/literally	Used when you want a word or phrase to mean exactly what it says, as opposed to being 'metaphorical' in its use, where the meaning is more figurative. For example, 'My teacher went through the roof' is metaphorical, suggesting simply the anger of your teacher. If the phrase were used literally, it would suggest that your teacher did structural damage to the building.
Litotes	This is the opposite of hyperbole (see above) whereby something is understated rather than exaggerated, often for humorous effect. 'Hamish is not the sharpest knife in the drawer' suggests that the intelligence of Hamish is somewhat limited.
Metaphor	This is a literary device whereby two items are compared. They are not, as in a simile, *like* each other; one *becomes* the other – 'You're an angel.' 'He was rocked by a tsunami of self-pity.'
Octave	Stanza of eight lines.
Onomatopoeia	Here, the sound of the word mimics and thereby gives a clue to its meaning. 'Clink', 'fizz', 'rip', 'honk', 'boom', 'purr' are all words which suggest their meaning in their sound. 'Bubbles gargled delicately' is an example of this used for effective aural effect by Seamus Heaney, suggesting a sound picture of the noise of bubbles emerging gently from mud at the bottom of a pond.
Oxymoron	The placing side by side of two words which appear to contradict each other, to startle and create a vivid impact on the reader – 'A deafening silence.' 'A wise fool.'
Pairing	The putting together of two people in a play/scene, often to bring out some comparison, contrast or tension.
Paradox	This is a form of extended oxymoron in which seemingly contradictory ideas are placed side by side – 'The child is father of the man.' Its aim, like that of the oxymoron, is to arrest the reader's attention by its startling and, at first glance, puzzling nature.
Parallel structure	These are patterns of either phrases or words which give a pleasing predictability and rhythm to the sentence. The effect is to add emphasis to what is being said – 'It is <u>by logic we prove</u>, but <u>by intuition we discover</u>. (da Vinci) The ants were everywhere: <u>climbing over</u> jam pots, <u>swarming under</u> the sink, <u>scrambling into</u> cupboards, <u>diving into</u> the bin.' The likeness of pattern here ('ing' form of verb + preposition) makes for a more memorable phrase and creates a greater impact than a less patterned structure would.
Paraphrase	To express the meaning of a word or phrase in different words.
Parenthesis	A parenthesis can be found between two dashes, two brackets or two commas. It is a phrase which adds interesting additional, but not essential, information to what is being discussed. It is often targeted by examiners in sentence structure questions in RUAE.
Personification	Personification is when an inanimate object is given living qualities – 'The sun caressed her back.' 'Hunger stalked the land.'
Quatrain	A stanza of four lines.
Repetition	This may take the form of repeated words or phrases to underline/intensify the idea the writer is seeking to emphasise at a particular point – 'A good cyclist needs ... A good cyclist hopes that ... But a good cyclist knows above all that ...' Note that these repetitions in the closing stages of a text might be building to a climax. Sentence structure questions in RUAE work may focus on this device.

Rhetorical question	These are questions expecting no direct answer, rather the reader's support for the writer's views – 'Who wants to see a child suffer in this way?' Here the reader is expected to share the writer's horror at the ill treatment of children.
Rhyme	The pairing of words with the same sound, used usually at the ends of lines in poetry: 'On either side the river lie Long fields of barley and of rye.' In more modern poetry, poets may attempt what is called a half-rhyme: 'When have I last looked on The round green eyes and the long wavering bodies Of the dark leopards of the moon? All the wild witches, those most noble ladies.' Here the words 'on'/'moon' and 'bodies'/'ladies' are related but not identical in sound, thus targeting aural cohesion but avoiding undue attention to rhyming words.
Rhythm	The pulse felt within a line of poetry, created through alternating unstressed and stressed syllables – 'On either side the river lie...' or, alternatively, stressed and unstressed – 'Willows whiten, aspens quiver'.
Sarcasm	Frequently expressed by the uttering the opposite of what is meant – 'My good friend, the traffic warden'. Be alert for this in tone questions in RUAE work. You can also use it to good effect in your own persuasive writing.
Sestet	Stanza of six lines.
Simile	One of the most common devices found in figurative language. It is a comparison between two items using 'like' or 'as' – 'As idle as a painted ship upon a painted ocean'. Used to bring the comparison vividly alive in the mind's eye.
Soliloquy	A speech in a play in which the speaker utters his/her most private thoughts, disregarding or oblivious to any hearers present.
Stanza	This is a means of referring to formal units in a poem, often when the units are of unequal length, for example, a Petrarchan sonnet has two stanzas: an octet followed by a sestet.
Style	This is a reference to how a writer creates his effects in his work by, say, imagery, word choice, tone, anecdote, sentence structure or any other features which help mark out the distinctive signature of that particular author or passage.
Symbolism	This is an item or action which stands for more than itself in a novel or poem. A dove might symbolise peace; a rose might symbolise love. A character might be seen to be pulling the petals off a flower, suggesting some later act of violence of a more serious nature.
Synonym	An alternative word for the same thing. Vital for success in understanding questions in RUAE.
Theme	A central idea that binds together characters or situations in a novel or short story. It is what the text is *about*. For instance, the theme of the dangers of false appearance is everywhere you look in *Macbeth*. The Macbeths exploit it, as do the witches. Other people such as Duncan become its victim, as, ultimately, do the Macbeths themselves.
Tone	This is the unspoken attitude of writers to their subject. In RUAE work, you are expected to tease this out by looking for internal clues such as hyperbole, emotive language, colloquial language.
Word choice	In RUAE, this is one of the more common questions you will encounter. You need to select words from the text which appear to you to identify an effect or tone the writer is attempting to convey. For instance, does he refer to a woman as 'slim' or 'scrawny'? The word chosen will indicate his attitude to the woman in question, that is, elegant and trim or underweight to the point of being unattractive.